MILITANT *Islamist* Ideology

MILITANT *Islamist* Ideology

UNDERSTANDING THE GLOBAL THREAT

YOUSSEF H. ABOUL-ENEIN

NAVAL INSTITUTE PRESS
Annapolis, Maryland

Naval Institute Press
291 Wood Road
Annapolis, MD 21402

First Naval Institute paperback edition published in 2013.
ISBN 978-1-59114-070-2

The Library of Congress has cataloged the hardcover edition as follows:
Aboul-Enein, Youssef H.
  Militant Islamist ideology : understanding the global threat / Youssef H. Aboul-Enein.
    p. cm.
  Includes bibliographical references and index.
  ISBN 978-1-59114-001-6 (acid-free paper) 1. Jihad. 2. Islamic fundamentalism. 3.
Terrorism—Religious aspects—Islam. 4. Qaida (Organization) I. Title.
  BP182.A21357 2010
  320.5'57—dc22

                                                        2010004369

Printed in the United States of America on acid-free paper

19 18 17 16 15 14 13   7 6 5 4 3 2 1
First printing

*Disclaimer: The statements of fact, opinion, or analysis expressed in this book are
those of the author and do not reflect the official policy or position of the Department of
Defense or the U.S. government. Review of the material does not imply Department of
Defense or U.S. government endorsement of factual accuracy or opinion.*

To Arlington Cemetery Section 60,
to the Soldiers, Sailors, Airmen, and Marines, and
to our families
who enable us to defend the United States

CONTENTS

FOREWORD

It is better to debate a question without settling it than to settle a question
without debating it.

JOSEPH JOUBERT (FRENCH ESSAYIST AND MORALIST, 1754–1824)

In this fascinating book, Commander Aboul-Enein takes readers into an exploration that, in his view, delineates between Islam, a faith that gives comfort to
over one billion people; Islamists, the millions who desire to see an Islamic
character to their local governments and wish to attain this through a political process; and finally Militant Islamists, the adversaries who wish to impose a narrow
form of Islam through violence upon a diverse Muslim community.

For years I have been an advocate for sailors and officers putting pen to paper,
bringing to life their ideas in various publications. I have publicly stated that the
people who want to do this country harm are doing so; they are thinkers and
writers, and often highly effective strategic communicators. We as senior leaders
can do no better service than to encourage the imagination and creativity of our
officers as well as our enlisted personnel to read, think, write, and publish. Those
willing to courageously put their ideas in print will ultimately bring us all closer
to providing policy options that will advance America's national interest.

I believe this book will provoke the kind of thought and reflection needed to
define new ways of defending the interests of the United States around the globe
and undermining al-Qaida ideologically. This is a book that will clearly stimulate
debate and contribute directly to the national discussion of an important challenge ahead.

Commander Aboul-Enein is a scholar, naval officer, writer, thinker, leader, listener, and teacher who has contributed greatly to increasing our understanding of Islam from the national level to the individual soldier, sailor, airman, and marine. This is a culmination of Commander Aboul-Enein's essays, lectures, and myriad answers to questions posed to him by members of the United States Armed Forces and Federal Government of all ranks. It is a book intended to help us all understand one of the most complicated forces shaping our world in this unfolding and dangerous 21st century.

Adm. James G. Stavridis, USN
Miami, Florida
October 10, 2008

ACKNOWLEDGMENTS

There are many individuals who made this work possible. First and foremost are the officers, enlisted, and civilian personnel within the U.S. armed forces and Department of Defense who attended my lectures on this topic and whose questions led to further inquiry, discovery, and refinement of the subject of this volume. I am grateful to have been given the opportunity to engage with thousands of soldiers, sailors, airman, and marines over the years, traveling from Camp Pendleton, California, to Fort Benning, Georgia, and all bases in between, lecturing on Islam, Islamist groups, and violent Militant Islamists. Specifically my appreciation goes to Mr. Gary Greco and Ms. Jacky Hardy, who offered many mornings of stimulating debate, argumentation, and support for my efforts to reduce my lectures to a book. Mr. Tom Cutler of the Naval Institute Press must be recognized: he hounded me on an annual basis after our first association and friendship in 2002 to write this book. I am a letter writer, and over the years I have written hundreds of letters to officers, who include Lt. Gen. Richard Natonski, USMC; Capt. David Tomlinson, MSC, USN; Capt. David Davis, MSC, USN (Ret.); Capt. Rick Cocrane, MSC, USN (Ret.); Capt. David Gibson, MSC, USN; Capt. William Frank, MSC, USN (Ret.); Capt. Eugene Smallwood, MSC, USN; Cdr. Robert Anderson, USN (Ret.); Lt. Cdr. Andrew Bertrand, MSC, USN; Lt. Cdr. Marrie Read, MSC, USN; and PS1 (AW/SW) David Tranberg, USN. In addition, I wish to acknowledge the support of my two brothers, Lt. Cdr. Faisal Aboul-Enein, USPHS, and 1st Lt. Basil Aboul-Enein, USAF; I am very proud that all three of us are in the uniformed service of the United States. Penning these letters offered a mental escape and further refined my thoughts on how to define the threat. In addition, the John T. Hughes Library and Library of Congress Near East Reading

Room both provided not only valuable research material but quiet places to write. I am indebted also to retired shipmate CTIC David Ely, USN (Ret.) for his valuable assistance. Christopher Robinson brought life to my hand-drawn maps for this book. Military families are an integral part of America's national security, and they support husbands and wives on the tip of the spear, battling in the field or in the arena of ideas, to improve our safety and challenge our adversaries.

I am also indebted to enlisted personnel, noncommissioned officers, officers, college professors, and policy makers who enabled me to have experiences in my Navy career, helped to manage difficult military seniors, and gave me the privilege of advising at the highest levels of the Defense Department. A successful military career requires many diverse mentors. In addition, this work could not have been possible without the support of my spouse, Cheryl Anne, who discussed the concepts of this book with me for long hours, or of my children, Maryam and Omar, who endured far too many days while I was traveling, in watch centers, involved in Defense Department–level bilateral discussions, or deployed—only to have me return home thinking about this book. Finally, I must acknowledge my childhood education and exposure to the globe that my parents provided me, along with a love of the Arabic language, eloquence in English, and immersion in the history of the Middle East. Also shaping me as a youth were my grandparents, in particular my late maternal grandmother, who steeped me in her Ottoman heritage and taught me many things about the intricacies of the Middle East.

LIST OF ACRONYMS

AAM	American designation for al-Qaida in Iraq leader Abu Ayyub al-Masri
AKP	Justice and Development Party (Turkey)
AQI	Al-Qaida in Iraq
AQIM	Al-Qaida in the Land of the Islamic Maghreb
EIJ	Egyptian Islamic Jihad
FIS	Algeria's Front Islamique du Salut (Islamic Salvation Front)
Frente POLISARIO	Frente Popular para la Liberación de Saguia el-Hamra y de Río de Oro
GIA	Groupe Islamique Armeé (Armed Islamic Group)
GICM	Groupe Islamique Combattant Marocain (Islamic Combat Group of Morocco)
GSPC	Groupe Salafiste pour la Prédication et le Combat (Islamic Group for Propagation and Combat)
HAMAS	Harakat al-Muqawamah al-Filisteeniyah
HDS	Houmat Daawa Salafia
IG	Egyptian Gamaa al-Islamiyah (Islamic Group)
IAI	Islamic Army of Iraq
ISI	Islamic State of Iraq, or Pakistan's Interservices Intelligence agency
JaM	Jaysh al-Mahdi (Mahdi Army of Shiite cleric Muqtada al-Sadr)
KSM	American designation for Khalid Sheikh Muhammad, mastermind of 9-11

LIFG	Libyan Islamic Fighting Group
MaK	Maktab al-Khidmat lil Mujahideen
MB	Egyptian Muslim Brotherhood
NDP	National Democratic Party (Egypt)
NIF	Sudanese National Islamic Front
OPEC	Organization of the Petroleum Exporting Countries
PFLP	Popular Front for the Liberation of Palestine
PJD	Peace and Justice Party (Morocco)
PLO	Palestine Liberation Organization
RCC	Egypt's Revolution Command Council
TTP	Tehrik e-Taliban Pakistan
YMMA	Young Men Muslim Association
YSP	Yemeni Socialist Party

INTRODUCTION

I think that you're making a very important point. And that is that the language we use matters. And what we need to understand is, is that there are extremist organizations—whether Muslim or any other faith in the past—that will use faith as a justification for violence. We cannot paint with a broad brush a faith as a consequence of the violence that is done in that faith's name.

And so you will, I think, see our administration be very clear in distinguishing between organizations like al-Qaida—that espouse violence, espouse terror and act on it—and people who may disagree with my administration and certain actions, or may have a particular viewpoint in terms of how their countries should develop. We can have legitimate disagreements but still be respectful. I cannot respect terrorist organizations that would kill innocent civilians and we will hunt them down.

President Barack Obama, January 29, 2009
first presidential interview on al-Arabiyah TV

Since the writing of these pages, seven years have passed since the attacks of September 11, yet the U.S. armed forces still lack a common definition of the threat posed by Militant Islamist groups like al-Qaida and their affiliates. There have been unfortunate incidents wherein Islam, Islamists, and Militant Islamists have become conflated in the thinking and consciousness of American fighting men and women, and regrettably this occurs at all ranks. This confusion leads to an undermining of our national security objectives and our relations with allies, and it feeds into al-Qaida's objectives of portraying themselves as the defenders against injustices committed upon Muslims. This book was designed to propose a common framework and definition of the threat for the use of all ranks within the U.S. military. It will seek to define the differences between "Islam," "Islamist," and "Militant Islamist," with the objective of focusing scarce resources and effort on the true threat posed by Militant Islamist groups, disaggregating them from Islamists and Islam. This definition is my own; it is not endorsed by the U.S. government. Finally, winning this long war will require a higher level of nuanced understanding that will enable U.S. military personnel to comprehend that:

- The threat ideologically stems from Militant Islamist Ideology, not Islam and not entirely from Islamist groups.
- There are differences and divisions inherent within Militant Islamists.
- Islamists and Militant Islamists compete in the world of ideas and method-ologies.
- The diversity inherent in a community of 1.5 billion Muslims cannot accom-modate the narrow views of Militant Islamists.
- There are correlations between Militant Islamist ideologues and the actions of violent Militant Islamist groups.
- Militant Islamists operate with the friction of diverse Islamic practices, nation-alism, and tribalism.
- There are different Salafi movements, not all Salafis are Militant Islamists, and many Salafis fall in the category of "Islamist."

The idea for this volume of explaining the nature of the threat came from a book entitled *Soviet Military Power,* published annually during the last decade of the Cold War. *Soviet Military Power* offered an unclassified common reference for all U.S. military personnel; it was developed to explain annual developments of the Soviet threat to all U.S. military personnel, from E-1 to O-10. The document was signed annually by the secretary of defense. Although this conflict against Militant Islamist Ideology is very different from the Cold War, there are concepts and tools utilized during those years that need to be examined, reformed, updated, and pieces of it evaluated for potential application in this conflict. Without a real-istic, sound, and doctrine-based definition of the threat, we shall be stuck between two extremes in American national policy discourse—that is, between those who argue that all Islam is evil and those who insist that all Islam is peaceful. These extremes are not effective in deriving effective policy, addressing nuances, or cap-turing the distortions that Militant Islamist Ideology has wrought upon Islam, distortions that are just beginning to outrage many Muslims. We cannot afford to call this phenomenon "Islamism" or "Islamo-fascism" and somehow consider it the new fascism or communism. It is imperative to begin thinking about this problem in new ways, distinguishing between "Islam," "Islamist," and "Militant Islamist," thereby providing Muslims and non-Muslims a common reference to the ideology of the Militant Islamist that al-Qaida represents. Militant Islamists alienate not only the United States but even Islamist political groups like the Muslim Brotherhood and Hamas. It is time for a more nuanced definition of the threat.

The risks of not engaging in the ideological aspect of this conflict are too high to ignore. For the adversary places much emphasis on the war of perception. The United States must draft a long-range strategic document that identifies violent Islamist extremism as an ideology and include means of countering it, incorporating the constructive interpretations of Islam that argue against the destructive interpretations of the fringe that threatens global peace and stability. Finally, it must take into account the language, concepts, and interpretations of Islamist militants that justify violence against Muslim and non-Muslim alike.

We once viewed every communist incursion as a threat to the United States, whether or not it involved actual centers of interest—a misperception that drove the United States to involve itself in Vietnam. Militant Islamist Ideology has not reached the maturation, level of organization, or cohesiveness in ideology that would give rise to a "Domino Theory." Unlike communism, against which free enterprise and democracy were used as ideological counterweights, Militant Islamist Ideology can be opposed among the Muslim masses only by Islamic counter-argumentation. We cannot contain Militant Islamist Ideology but only work to marginalize, de-popularize, and erode its influence and mass appeal, by identifying it as different from Islam or even from Islamist political groups. Militant Islamist Ideology, this book will argue, is in fact an isolated strain within Salafi Islam, a "return to fundamentals" movement. Michael Dobbs, in his *One Minute to Midnight,* on the Cuban missile crisis, wrote, "History does not always flow in predictable directions. Sometimes it can be hijacked by fanatics of various descriptions, by men with long beards, by ideologues living in caves, by assassins with rifles."[1] It is only through ideological deconstruction that we can take back Islamic history from al-Qaida and its sympathizers. In the end, we cannot hope to have a strategy without defining the threat. After all, a strategy is written against a defined challenger, and we have yet to define clearly the challenge to America's national security in the twenty-first century.

one

Precise Definitions of the Threat

In the absence of clearly-defined goals, we become strangely loyal to performing daily trivia until ultimately we become enslaved by it.

ROBERT HEINLEIN, SCIENCE FICTION AUTHOR (1907–1988)

I t is important to begin by defining the differences between "Islam," "Islamist," and "Militant Islamist." Disaggregating these three terms will begin the process of understanding the nuances needed to pursue this long-term campaign. The *Washington Times* has reported the existence of a "Red Team" charged with challenging conventional thinking, arguing that terms like "Islamist" are needed in discussing twenty-first-century terrorism.[1] Although one can disagree with elements of the article, it does highlight the continuing debate over what to call the ideology of our adversary, who preys upon many who have only a sense of history, not a true knowledge of history. These are the defined terms:

Militant Islamist: a group or individual advocating Islamist ideological goals, principally by violent means. Militant Islamists call for the strictest possible interpretation of both the Qur'an (Muslim book of divine revelation) and the *hadith* (the Prophet Muhammad's actions and deeds). This narrow interpretation opposes the beliefs of Muslims and non-Muslims alike; Militant Islamists stand against Western democracies, Middle Eastern institutions of government, and Islamist political parties that participate nonviolently in elections. Although Militant Islamists call for the establishment of an Islamic state, they are characterized by a lack of any socioeconomic agenda and impose their narrow views by force upon

1

other Muslims as well as non-Muslims. Examples of Militant Islamists include al-Qaida and its affiliates.

Islamists: a group or individual advocating Islam as a political as well as a religious system. Chief Islamist objectives include implementing *sharia* (Islamic) law as the basis of all statutory issues and living as did the earliest adherents to Islam. Many Islamists also assert that implementation of sharia law requires the elimination of all non-Islamic influences in social, political, economic, and military spheres of life. Islamists principally achieve those objectives within the political and electoral frameworks of the countries in which they operate. An example is the Egyptian Muslim Brotherhood.

Islam: the religious faith of Muslims, involving (as defined in *Merriam-Webster's*) belief in Allah as the sole deity and in Muhammad as his prophet. There are 1.5 billion Muslims in the world of various subdivisions, from the main sects of the Sunni and Shiites to doctrinal groups within Sunni and Shiite Islam, as well as Sufi orders.

It is the Militant Islamists who are our adversary. They represent an immediate threat to the national security of the United States. They must not be confused with Islamists, who, although desiring the establishment of an Islamic state that might bear animosity toward the United States, wish to achieve changes within the political frameworks of their respective countries and abhor the violent methodologies espoused by Militant Islamists. The objective of the United States in fighting Militant Islamists must be to:

- Isolate, through all instruments of national power and in collaboration with allies, partners of convenience, and tribes, those who fit the definition of Militant Islamist
- Foster divisions within Militant Islamist groups over leadership, resources, strategy, vision, and influence
- Make comprehensible the damage that Militant Islamists are doing to Islamist politics and the wider Islamic world
- Promote Muslims who treat Islam as a source of values that guide conduct rather than a system that offers solutions to all problems.

Clarity of thought, history, and language is required to begin separating Islamist Militant Ideology from Islamists and Islam. Therefore, it is important to address the foundations of Islam, since the time of Prophet Muhammad (570–632). Militant Islamists wish to suppress the debate among Islamists and the wider Muslim world over matters of faith, government, morals, and much more. While the agenda of the Islamist political groups represents unacceptable outcomes for the United States in the long run, this should not blind us to the potential of Islamist groups as an alternative to Militant Islamist Ideology (like al-Qaida) or prevent careful assessments of the nature of Islamist movements that eventually attain power by democratic processes.

There are also Islamists who do not fit into a neat category, such as the Palestinian Islamist group Hamas. On one hand, Hamas provides social services, won 44 percent of the electorate in 2006, and is the government of the Palestinian territories. On the other hand, it has failed to compromise effectively with other Palestinian rejectionist and secular groups to form a governing coalition, and it has failed to provide social services for a wider Palestinian populace. In addition, it has conducted suicide operations directed against Israeli civilians—though it has not widened its campaign beyond targeting Israel. Further, al-Qaida senior leaders have viciously attacked Hamas for participating in electoral politics. The question for Americans is whether Hamas is an Islamist or Militant Islamist group.

Clearer examples of Islamist parties include the Turkish Justice and Development Party (AKP). Currently in government, it must work within Turkey's political process, where it can be challenged by Kemalists. The AKP promotes Turkey's inclusion in the European Union but has secularists worried about its attempts to alter the constitution. The Moroccan Peace and Justice Party (PJD) is much more conservative than the Turkish AKP, and before the 2003 Casablanca bombings it issued vicious and incendiary diatribes against Morocco's westernization, though stopping short of criticizing the monarch. The PJD has not engaged in violence, and its views on civil liberties are vague, yet in 2007 it won forty-six out of 325 seats in parliament. Similarly, the Egyptian Muslim Brotherhood won eighty-eight of 425 seats of parliament. While its long-term objectives may run counter to American interests, there are nuanced positive elements that should not be overlooked, such as its dedication to serve in parliament, which has had the effect of forcing legislators of the more entrenched ruling National Democratic Party (NDP) actually to show up for votes, in order to keep a legislative eye on the Muslim Brotherhood voting bloc.

It is, then, in the interest of the United States to assess each Islamist party individually, looking for constructive and nonconstructive elements within their

platforms. One important criterion is level of respect for the principles of the democratic process. Do its public statements reflect contempt for democracy? Does
it show an aversion to *hizbiyah* (party politics)? Does it argue that the only *hizb*
(party) is Hezbollah (the Party of God)—in effect, a code for a wish to impose a
singular religio-political vision? (This was held by the former "supreme guide" of
the Muslim Brotherhood, Mustafa Mahshur.) These are counterproductive views;
however, not all Islamist practice them. An example of nuanced, long-term problems
posed by Islamists is that of Saudi-run al-Arabiyah TV attacking al-Qaida ideologically while Iqra TV, also Saudi-run, features clerics who incite the killing of
Americans and propagate hatred.

We can only make ourselves aware of these complexities and attempt to
address them through gradual and long-term diplomacy. Abd al-Hamid al-Ansari,
a former dean of Islamic law at Qatar University, believes that propaganda of hate
and extremist rhetoric are the first step toward *ghilu* (a Quranic term meaning
excessiveness or extremism in matters of faith) and then toward terrorism.[2] He
lays out the stages of evolution using such Arabic terms as *taasub* (fanaticism),
tataturf (extremism), *unf* (violence), and finally *irhab* (terrorism). We need to
immerse ourselves in this language as we search for ways to distinguish between
Islam, Islamist groups, and Militant Islamists and to understand the differences
between the three, how people move between them, and how they compete with
one another (particularly the Islamist and Militant Islamists), and where they appear to complement one another.

In keeping with its egalitarian principles and tradition of tolerance, the United
States will oppose any attempt to impose a singular form of Islamic interpretation
upon the world's 1.5 billion diverse Muslims. We will stand with Muslims who
uphold the Qur'an's ideal that "no human being can limit divine mercy in any way
or regulate its entitlement" (2:105, 3:74, 35:2, 38:9, 39:38, 40:7, 43:32).

The earliest coherent attempt at defining the threat was that by Professor
Michael Palmer of East Carolina University, who discusses the need for a precise
definition of what this volume terms "Militant Islamists." His three definitions, in
Last Crusade: Americanism and the Islamic Reformation, are:

- *Islamism:* the ideal of reestablishing the caliphate and its global dominion
- *Islamist:* one who believes in that ideal
- *Jihadist:* one who believes in the ideal and is willing to kill (perhaps even
  himself or herself) to achieve it.[3]

Palmer's book rightly places emphasis on Qutb and Azzam (see the glossary and later chapters), but he does not place their writings in the wider context of Islam, the Islamist political movements, or Militant Islamist groups. This distinction is commendable, but it is not precise enough. Whether to give Militant Islamists the label of "Jihadist" has already been debated within Washington, and there seems to be a general sense that "Jihadist" is a badge of honor for Militant Islamists. But the imprecision of such descriptions has the potential of lumping together Islamist groups and Militant Islamists by describing them as adherents of Islamism. Disaggregating "Islam" from "Islamist" and both from "Militant Islamist Ideology" can remedy this problem.[4]

One of the benefits of reading Arabic books is that they identify ideological and militant philosophical divisions under which Zarqawi had to operate. One Arabic author, the Egyptian Gamal Rahim, is a prolific writer, historian, and journalist covering the Militant Islamist movement for Arab readers. His biography of former al-Qaida in Iraq leader Abu Musab al-Zarqawi has an excellent chapter that discusses the divisions within radical Salafism, what he calls *al-Tayyar al-Islami* (Islamist trend). Gamal Rahim classifies its subgroupings as:

- *Ikhwani* (Muslim Brotherhood): Those wanting to attain an Islamist state through participation in government and parliaments, as well as through grassroots means, such as social services and proselytizing. Today their slogan is reform, not revolution.
- *Salafi Ilmi* (Practical Salafists): These are Salafists who wish to attain an Islamic state exclusively through *dawa* (proselytizing) but do not see any use in participating with corrupt regimes. They feel that the perfection of Islamic society in neighborhoods and hamlets speaks for itself. They want an Islamist fundamentalist regime and to impose a single brand of Islam, but they wish to do it through financing mosques and schools and by evangelizing.
- *Salafi Jihadi* (Salafi Jihadists): These are Militant Islamists who, like al-Qaida, desire the attainment of an Islamic state through violent means. In addition, they utilize their brand of Islam not for any moral purpose but to instill fear.[5]

These are the types of nuances that Arab watchers of Militant Islamists discern in the constant changes inherent in this movement. It is constructive to view al-Qaida and Militant Islamist movements not as monolithic but as subject to disagreements, disputes, and divisions. Identifying these divisions and properly describing them will be paramount.

Two extremes have developed in America's national security discourse over what to do about the threat from Militant Islamists. Neither extreme is constructive for developing credible policy options. The first extreme is to label all Islam as the problem, to deduce from a narrow reading of Islamic texts that Islam is inherently violent and that our struggle is a bipolar one between Islam and the West. This negates the reality that Muslims are needed to fight Militant Islamists. It also causes many Arab and Asian governments with Muslim majorities who cooperate with the United States on many levels against terrorism to be less willing to aid in the achievement of counterterrorism policy objectives. More importantly, it deprives us of the means to understand the nuances and disagreements between Militant Islamists, Salafis, Islamists, and the wider Muslim world over al-Qaida methodology and ideology. Another extreme, espoused by a few leading members of the Muslim community, argues that Islam is a peaceful and nonviolent religion. Islam, like the other monotheistic faiths, over the course of its history has had its share of violence, and to paint Islam simply as a religion of peace ignores the reality that Militant Islamists have exploited Islam, through misuse of religious impulses, to induce individuals to take direct violent action against Muslims and non-Muslims alike. It is in our interest to isolate Militant Islamist Ideology from Islamists and from Islam and then to focus on eroding the influence of Militant Islamists.

Former president George W. Bush said in October 2005, "Some call this evil Islamic radicalism; others, militant Jihadism; still others, Islamo-fascism. Whatever it's called, this ideology is very different from the religion of Islam." In that speech he referred to the threat as "Islamic radicalism."[6] The Defense Department, in its 2006 annual report to Congress, *Measuring Stability in Iraq,* in accordance with the 2006 Defense Department Appropriations Act (section 9010), referred to the threat as "extremist Islamist ideology."[7] This shows the urgent need of a uniform identification of the threat (Militant Islamist Ideology is the term proposed in this book) and of a clear distinction of it from Islamist political groups and Islam. President Bush understood that this ideology is different from the religion of Islam and went on to explain how it misuses Islam to justify terrorism and their politicized agenda.

two

A Hidden Center of Gravity

Militant Islamists Cloaking Themselves in Islam

Islam is a vibrant faith. Millions of our fellow citizens are Muslim. We respect
the faith. We honor its traditions. Our enemy does not. Our enemy doesn't
follow the great traditions of Islam. They've hijacked a great religion.

PRESIDENT GEORGE W. BUSH, WASHINGTON, D.C., OCTOBER 11, 2002

One of the main centers of gravity for Militant Islamists is the cloaking of
their actions and ultimate goals in Islam. Militant Islamist Ideology is
composed of fragmented pieces of Islam. These fragments do not stand
alone, and they are recombined out of context to make up the bulwark of Militant Islamist Ideology, which is not the religion of Islam. Militant Islamists use
Islam to attain naked power and control. The fragmentation of Islam by Militant
Islamists to rationalize violent action must be attacked by restoring the context
that militants remove. Their objective is not to reform or revive but to create a
new world through the imposition of a singular view of Islam. Militant Islamist
Ideology seeks to establish a totalitarian state steeped in the language, symbols,
and narrowly selective aspects of Islam. It is important to explain how Islam has
been hijacked by Militant Islamists as a means of promoting violence. They have
reduced Islam to a simple common denominator, a lifestyle of perpetual warfare.

Militant Islamists compel belief in their ideology through intimidation and violence; in this regard they are similar to fascists, communists, and even Saddam
Hussein's Baathists. American leaders are more comfortable attacking a political
ideology than concepts like "Islamist" or "Militant Islamist," because they contain
the word "Islam." Yet although we may disagree with the Islamist political groups'

goals of establishing an Islamic state, we must concede that they do so through proselytizing and political action within the frameworks of their governments. Militant Islamists, in contrast, use elements of Islam to create a distinct militant ideology and reinforce their views through violence and intimidation.

This is like a hypothetical Christian cult that attempts to evangelize at the point of a gun, take over a state county in the United States, and then attempt to convert neighboring counties forcibly. The United States would not stand for such actions and would send in federal and state authorities to challenge not its ideas but its violent actions to impose those ideas. In addition, Americans are free to question any ideology, religious or otherwise, that incites violence and deprives people of basic freedoms and rights. In antebellum America, slavery was justified by the story of Cain and Abel in Genesis. Cain was to wander the earth marked, and this mark came to be misinterpreted by slaveholders and their sympathizers to mean skin color—a narrow and militant reading of the Bible was used to deprive human beings of their natural rights. Americans spoke out against the misuse of scripture, arguing that the mark could be a physical mark, a mark upon the soul, or the guilt Cain felt for slaying Abel. They also questioned whether the actual sin was the murder or the jealousy and envy of Cain.

If Christians questioned the interpretation of other Christians, then Muslims must be led to question the misuse of Islam by Militant Islamists. Only by defining "Islam," "Islamist," and "Militant Islamists" are these nuances made clear. We criticize the Chinese government's handling of Tibet and the forcing of communist Chinese ideology on the people of Tibet; a Muslim or non-Muslim should be able to express the same outrage when Militant Islamists impose their ideology through violence. The Nixon administration capitalized upon the nuanced differences between communists in China and the Soviet Union, orchestrating Nixon's visit to China and driving a further wedge between Moscow and Beijing. There are differences between Islamist and Militant Islamist Ideology, and these views have a hard time fitting into the wider Islamic world; our challenge is to begin thinking in those terms. It is vital to our national security to dispense with the notion that by attacking Militant Islamist Ideology we are attacking Islam. Whether abroad or in the United States, Militant Islamists seek to impose their ideology, composed of mere fragments of Islam, through violence.

An example of the misuse of an Islamic concept by Militant Islamists is the notion that Muslims are to prohibit vice and promote virtue. This can simply mean if you see someone doing something harmful to themselves or others, you are duty-bound to speak out against this behavior. The ultimate intent is the establishment of a just society. Militant Islamists use the concept to enforce morality, intimidate, and engage in violence against those deemed to be propagating vice. Their ultimate objective is not moral salvation but societal control, block by block and neighborhood by neighborhood. Militant Islamist Ideology, like the writing of Sayyid Qutb, is linked to such actions as the murder of Anwar Sadat and 9/11. Abu Musab al-Suri, considered the twenty-first-century strategic thinker for al-Qaida, follows a narrow range of Islamist Militant ideologues, drawn from Ibn Taymiyyah, Ibn Qayim, Qutb, and Azzam. Abu Musab al-Suri directly and indirectly caused the 1995 Paris subway bombing, the Madrid bombing, and the London bombing.

The common strain is this narrow view of Militant Islamist theorists, who discount whole swaths of the Qur'an and reduce 1,400 years of Islamic thought into sound bites. In addition, the methodology of Militant Islamists differs from Islamist political groups, and the wider Islamic community is diverse and in disagreement over the actions of Militant Islamists and the agendas of Islamist political groups. Since 2007 many clerics and former Militant Islamists have been outspoken about the damage al-Qaida is doing to Islam.

It is regrettable that in today's mainstream Islam, the Prophet's life is effectively considered to have begun at the age of forty, when he received the first of what would be twenty-three years of divine revelations from Angel Gabriel, revelations that would form the foundations of the Qur'an. To understand truly how extraordinary Muhammad was, it is necessary to explore his pre-Prophetic life. One can select portions of Muhammad's life, misinterpret its historical context, and even judge him by twenty-first-century standards instead of sixth- and seventh-century Arabian standards. But the main focus of this volume is to highlight aspects of Muhammad's life that Islamist militants simply dismiss, as it would interfere with their politicized agenda as well as with their acquisition of influence and power.

Amplifying positive aspects of Islamic history and marginalizing destructive Militant Islamist interpretations is the task at hand. Today Militant Islamists have been so proficient in the use of the media that the meaning and contributions of Islamic civilization have become lost not just in mainstream Western discourse but tragically in the Muslim world itself. We should not be reluctant to recognize and salute the positive interpretations of Islam, which was integral to bringing Europe out of the Dark Ages. It was Muslims who drove the main effort to preserve and even advance the classical texts of the Romans and ancient Greeks when such material was being neglected and destroyed in Western Europe.

The Muslims of ninth-century Baghdad (the zenith of the Islamic civilization) and twelfth-century Spain made a gift of the Greek and Roman classics to the Renaissance. These Muslims collaborated with Jews and other non-Muslims in the search for knowledge. Just as there is a popular fixation with word "Jihad" today, the fixation of ninth-century Muslim scientists and discoverers was *ilm* (knowledge), a word that appears more than *jihad* in the Qur'an. These are narrow and singular words in the Qur'an that stimulate movements, one that is positive and one that is negative. The pattern of Militant Islamists is to ignore this history, to view these enlightened Muslims as Hellenized and therefore corrupted by Western influences. This is also a view taken by a majority of Islamists; however, they do not usually propagate their ideas through violent means but through proselytizing.

In addition, Militant Islamists deemphasize aspects of Islamic history and heritage that do not support their worldview. Examples include the importance of Christians in early Islam and the details about Muhammad's relations with Jewish tribes in Arabia. Militant Islamists teach a selective and narrow view of Islamic texts, starting from Ibn Taymiyyah in the fourteenth century to Sayyid Qutb, who was executed in 1966. It is important to highlight these works and study them even more aggressively than our adversaries, for even within Qutbism and the works of Ibn Taymiyyah and Abdul-Wahab (the founder of Wahhabism) there are writings that contradict al-Qaida ideology. An example relates to Muhammad's admonition to his army that "it is better they come back with Muslims amongst them which is dearer to me, than bringing me back their women and children [as captives] and killing their men."[1] Aside from the Militant Islamist selective obsession with Ibn Taymiyyah, there is a complete suppression in their ideology of the works of Ibn Rushd (Averroes), who postulated three levels of Quranic interpretation—the judicial, theological, and philosophic—to demonstrate its complexities.

The Arabic version of the Qur'an as codified by Uthman cannot be altered without grave sin. However, the issue is not with the Qur'an itself as much as with the commentaries and translations, which can vary widely; there are no restrictions on what constitutes an acceptable commentary. In Zahid al Hussaini's book *Commentators of the Holy Qur'an,* published in 1970, there are 625 commentators of the Qur'an, beginning with Prophet Muhammad's scribes and ending with the likes of Qutb. Islamists and Militant Islamists zero in on certain commentators that fit their worldview; this is by no means true Islamic scholarship. One must read various commentators on a topic of interest and consider their work as opinion, not orthodoxy.

Militant Islamists offer a narrow and pseudo-intellectual reading of the Qur'an, and their use of its verses is driven by an agenda. Bin Laden studied the Qur'an through the lenses of Saudi Wahhabism, then Qutbism, and finally North Indian Deobandism (a form of Salafist Islam). The Qur'an needs to be patiently studied by American military leaders hoping for an understanding of the Middle East.[2]

three

What Is *Not* Being Taught in Politicized Madrassas

Beginning to Understand Militant Islamist Ideology

A fool's brain digests philosophy into folly, science into superstition, and art into pedantry.

GEORGE BERNARD SHAW (1856–1950), *MAN AND SUPERMAN* (1903)

Militant Islamist Ideology can be fought only by using *Islamic* argumentation and exposing Militant Islamist views as narrow and doing a disservice to the legacy of Islam. In addition, one cannot understand Militant Islamist Ideology without comparing it to the wider Islamist movement and within this context the wider Islamic world. The assertion that Militant Islamists have "hijacked a great religion" can be understood only from the vantage point of what they pass off as orthodoxy and what they choose to emphasize in their indoctrination of militant fighters and suicide operatives.

Prophet Muhammad lived sixty-three years, from about 570 to 632; his Prophethood lasted only the last twenty-three years of his life. He began to receive what he believed to be divine revelation from Angel Gabriel at age forty. Muhammad was born into the most important tribe (the Quraysh) of the Hijaz, which stretched along the Red Sea coast from modern Jordan to Yemen. The Quraysh oversaw the city tribal confederacy of Mecca, the most important city in the Hijaz. Muhammad would be orphaned as a child and would learn the caravan trade from his paternal grandfather and uncle.

Muhammad was deeply interested in theological debates, and his exposure to more advanced societies in Byzantium led him to question why Meccan society was structured the way it was. Being an orphan, Muhammad was interested in

12

the plight of those without tribal protection. Had Muhammad died at the age of forty, he would be known as a good arbiter; he was so reliable that he was given the title of *al-Amin* (the trusted one). In Muhammad's time, the Kaaba was being renovated. It had been a revered structure even before his time, and upon completion of the renovations a blood feud threatened to break out over which tribe would have the honor of placing the Black Stone (a sacred relic) into its corner. Muhammad suggested that a large blanket or carpet be brought out and the Black Stone placed at its center; each tribal representative would grab the edge of the carpet, and a person without tribal protection would place the Black Stone. This averted the feud. Muhammad would speak out against practices deemed unjust, such as female infanticide, calling such practices *jahiliyah* (ignorant). Both Qutb and Mawdudi would redefine *jahiliyah* in the twentieth century, giving it a political connotation by condemning entire swaths of Muslim society as *jahiliyah*.

Before his prophecy in 609, Muhammad returned from the Levant with his uncle, and was drafted into a tribal war. He was troubled that the war had to do with a simple dispute that in Byzantine cities could be resolved through rudimentary courts. Muhammad asked why Meccan tribes could not avert their differences through arbitration. Issues of social justice of interest to Muhammad included the protection of slaves, widows, and orphans. He wondered why Meccans had abandoned codes of chivalry and virtue, known as *muruwah,* in favor of exploiting the weak.

Christians and Jews would shape Muhammad's understanding of monotheism; Mecca was a mixture of ideas, since pilgrims from several religious traditions paid homage to the Kaaba. The Kaaba is considered by Muslims to be the first house dedicated to the worship of a single God, to have been built by Adam, the first man and prophet, and rebuilt by Prophet Abraham. The Old Testament and Qur'an discuss Abraham's constant tests of faith. Among his tests was to leave his Egyptian mistress Hagar and his son Ishmael in a desolate location and to trust in God. Abandoned, Hagar traversed the hillocks of Safa and Marwa looking for a caravan to rescue her and her son. All the while Ishmael cried from thirst, kicking his feet; up from under his feet the Well of Zamzam bubbled. When Abraham returned, he was commanded by God to rebuild the Kaaba, the house dedicated by Adam to the worship of God alone.

This story predated Muhammad's arrival and was likely influenced by Jews and Christians living in Arabia. Mecca, and Arabia in general, were to be havens for Christians wanting to continue the debate on the nature of Christ unmolested by church authorities who compelled adherence to the Nicene Creed. Those wanting to debate the nature of Christ in Alexandria or Antioch in Muhammad's time were deemed heretical, and many fled to the deserts of Arabia to continue this discussion.[1] Muhammad likely was influenced by what were known as Diophysite and Monophysite Christians, referred to in Arabic as *hanifs* (hermits). Among the Christians who made an impression on Muhammad was Zeid, who would come into Mecca decrying the defilement of the house that Abraham had built to God with idols and totems.

The Kaaba before the arrival of Muhammad contained icons of Mary, Jewish relics, Zoroastrian items, and pagan totems.[2] In the year of Muhammad's birth 570, a Yemeni Christian leader attempted to destroy the Kaaba, because it competed with a cathedral he built in Yemen, with a massive force that included elephants. The Meccans could only hide in the hills, but the force, led by a general named Abraha, was afflicted with smallpox, and the structure was spared. Muhammad's birth is called the "Year of the Elephant," as many Meccans had never seen this animal of war. Their defeat was taken to be a symbol of divine protection of the Kaaba. The story of the war elephants is recounted in the Qur'an. When Muhammad joined his uncle to learn caravaneering, he would be exposed to, and take an interest in, Christian theology.[3]

Christians would play a pivotal role in the evolution of early Islam. When Muhammad began to receive revelations, he thought he was possessed. His wife Khadija sent him to see her cousin Waraqa ibn Naufal, a Monophysite Christian, who calmed him and explained that he would be the awaited Prophet of God sent to the Arabs. Waraqa warned that Muhammad's trials had just begun. Another monk who interacted with Muhammad was Bahira of Busra, who lived along the Meccan trade routes to Syria.

As Muhammad began preaching, the Meccans began to block his message and then conducted a genocidal campaign against Muslims in Mecca. When Muhammad eventually fled to Yathrib (what would become Medina), he asked a group of Muslims to seek asylum in Christian Abyssinia (Somalia and Ethiopia). These Muslims would be granted asylum by the Axum king known in Islam as Najashi (Abyssinian emperors were given the title Negus, in which the Arabic term derives) in 615. The story does not end there, for a Meccan emissary Amr ibn al-A'as arrived on the shores of Abyssinia to negotiate the return of runaway slaves. The Meccan demanded that these Meccans return with him. Ibn al-A'as asked the Christian monarch to inquire of these Muslims their attitudes on Christ. After interviewing the Muslims and studying the documents, Najashi concluded that these were not slaves but religious objectors whose monotheism was little different from that of Christians who had not accepted the Nicene Creed. When Muhammad, now leader of Medina, learned of Najashi's death, he mourned him as a just Christian king. Here is an example of how Militant Islamist suppresses and marginalizes aspects of Islamic history that do not support their agenda of political change through violent action, using religious impulses derived from Islam.

It is said that Jafar ibn Abi Talib, cousin of Muhammad and brother of Ali ibn Abi Talib (who would become Caliph Ali, revered by the Shiites), narrated this verse (Maryam, verses 29 to 32) from the Qur'an to King Najashi:

> Mary pointed to the child [Jesus] as her only answer [to charges of fornication]. Her people asked, "how can we inquire of an infant in the cradle?" At this Jesus spoke, "I am the servant of God to whom He has given the Book and whom He has blessed and commissioned with prophethood. . . . [M]y mother is innocent. . . . Peace be upon me on the day I was born, on the day I shall die, and on the day I shall be resurrected."[4]

MUHAMMAD ENDURES THE DOUBT OF TAIF
WITH THE AID OF A CHRISTIAN

Muhammad would endure his greatest trial in the city of Taif, east of Mecca. Barely escaping with his life after preaching in Taif, he asked God whether he was strong enough for this mission. A young boy tending a vineyard approached Muhammad, giving him water and grapes. Learning Muhammad's identity, the boy exclaimed that Muhammad's mission to protect those without tribal protection—like himself, a slave—was important and not to be discouraged. The boy gave Muhammad the strength to continue, and this young boy was a Christian. Of Muhammad's eleven (by some account thirteen) wives, two were Jewish and one was Coptic Christian, Mariya al-Qibtiya (died 637), who never converted to Islam.

Such stories as that of Mariya, taken directly from Islamic history, humanize Christians and are suppressed by Militant Islamist groups who wish to demonize Christians and all others who do not espouse their beliefs. Another problem in twenty-first-century Islam is the view that Prophet Muhammad is *ma'soum* (infallible). This has evolved to actual infallibility among Shiite Muslims and for Sunni Muslims to his having been the perfect man; some Muslims argue that he never was a pagan. What is more accurate was that Muhammad was steeped in the culture and theology swirling around in Mecca. He dabbled in paganism, but his interest in theologic questions led him to a path toward monotheism. This view is supported by chapter 93, verses 6–8, of the Qur'an: "Did He not find you [Muhammad] orphaned and He gave you a home? He found you astray, and guided you; He found you poor, and made you rich." Note the words "He found you astray, and guided you," meaning that God found Muhammad and mankind in the path of paganism and guided them toward monotheism.

HOW MUHAMMAD BECAME LEADER OF MEDINA:
A MUSLIM OR BROADER *UMMAH*?

The Meccan genocide involved not only killing weaker Muslims but oppressing all Muslims. Meccans forbade Muslims from marrying or trading with Meccans. This would lead indirectly to the death of Muhammad's first wife and love, Khadija, as well as of his protector, his uncle Abi Talib. Emissaries from the city confederacy of Yathrib approached Muhammad offering him asylum in return for his services in arbitrating between the various tribal factions of Yathrib. For decades, the city of Yathrib (320 kilometers north of Mecca) had suffered from internecine civil war, and now it was desperate for peace. Muhammad accepted the task and performed his *hijrah* (migration) to Yathrib/Medina in 622, fleeing Meccan persecution and a plot to murder him in his bed.

Muhammad would indeed solve the problems of the Yathrib confederacy, ending decades of fighting among different tribes, including three Jewish tribes. So desperate for peace were the leaders of Yathrib that they offered Muhammad the leadership of the city to retain him as "Grand Arbiter." The tribal chiefs were more interested in his arbitration skills than his prophecy. As the majority of the inhabitants of Yathrib were non-Muslim, Muhammad had to determine how to govern this city tribal confederation. He drew up what would be called the Pact of Medina, which in essence listed the different tribes and committed the signatories to become one and the same *ummah* (community). The pact bound together the *Ansar* (tribes both Muslim and a majority non-Muslim, linked to Yathrib), the *muhajiroun* (those who emigrated with Muhammad from Mecca to Medina and were typically the earliest converts to Islam), and the *yahud* (the three Jewish tribes) into a federation of tribes with equal rights and responsibilities. It was a revolutionary concept in Arabia. In this historical context *ummah* means not the community of Muslim believers but all those Muslims and non-Muslims bound to Muhammad through the pact.

Militant Islamists reduce Muhammad to warlord and do not emphasize the complex and extraordinary character of this individual, who was not only a military commander but a prophet, husband, merchant, arbiter, father, and negotiator. Another tactic of Militant Islamists is the use of terms and labels of the period to give their movement the appearance of legitimacy among Muslims. For instance, Militant Islamist groups call themselves Ansar al-Sunnah. Although *Ansar al-Sunnah* literally means "Supporters of the Path of Islam," the word *Ansar,* as we have seen, has a historical meaning harking back to the supporters of Muhammad in Medina. Another example is *al-Tawhid wal-Jihad,* literally "monotheism and Jihad." However the term *tawhid* connotes an important theological concept in Islam, that of God not sharing adulation and worship with any other being. Evangelization of this concept is supposed to be performed by *dawa* (proselytize), but Militant Islamists argue it must be done by force. This gives Militant Islamist groups a missionary justification to their violence, but it only does a disservice to the reputation of Islam, as one of the clerics bin Laden respects, Salman al-Awdah, wrote in an open letter to the al-Qaida leader in 2007.[5]

Although *dawa* and Jihad have been mentioned together in Islamic texts, interpretations combining the two have ranged from the struggle to evangelize to giving offensive warfare the veneer of religious legitimacy. This pattern of linking the spreading of faith to warfare is not new; it is a regrettable reality of the history of ethical monotheistic faiths, including Christianity. What is not helpful in the twenty-first century is linking the two as the same side of one coin, asserting that *dawa* and Jihad are part of the same strategy.[6] It is important to expose how Militant Islamists exploit *dawa,* as they exploit fragments of other Islamic concepts, texts, and history, and to state clearly that the way people like Ayman al-Zawahiri or Usama bin Laden call people to Islam does damage to the faith. They cannot be, and are not, acceptable ambassadors of the Muslim faith. *Dawa* is exploited by Militant Islamists not only to give them legitimacy but to aid in recruiting and collecting donations. The Saudi government understands this and has taken measures to restrict and clamp down on free forms of donations in the cities' mosques, as it subjects the good intentions of Muslims to give alms to fraud that ranges from outright theft of funds to the collection of money for nefarious causes.[7]

The two concepts *dawa* and Jihad must be strategically delinked. Those engaging in *dawa* run the spectrum from Islamist political groups to wider Islam, but those linking offensive Jihad to *dawa* or engaging and supporting offensive Jihad are the Militant Islamist adversary. Linking *dawa* and offensive Jihad blinds us to Salafists and Islamists who agree with al-Qaida's agenda in concept but disagree with, even abhor, the methodology of the group. This schism can be seen in Iraq's Anbar Awakening and in London's Muslim community. We cannot afford to miss such nuances and schisms as a means of undermining them.

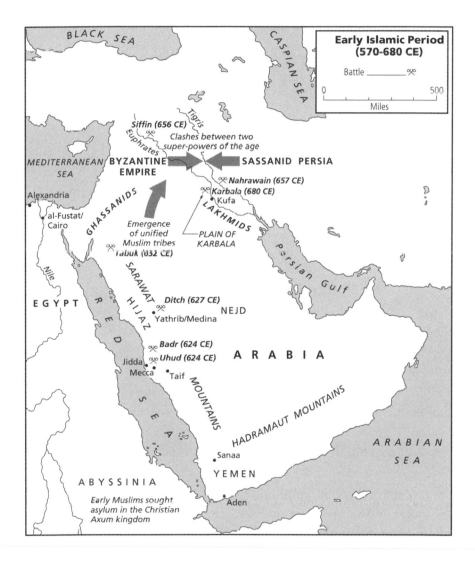

BLACK SEA

CASPIAN SEA

**Early Islamic Period
(570-680 CE)**

Battle ⚔

0   500

Miles

MEDITERRANEAN
SEA

Siffin (656 CE)

Tigris

Euphrates

Clashes between two
super-powers of the age

**BYZANTINE
EMPIRE**

SASSANID PERSIA

Alexandria

GHASSANIDS

al-Fustat/
Cairo

Nahrawain (657 CE)

Karbala (680 CE)

Kufa

LAKHMIDS

*Emergence
of unified
Muslim tribes*

*PLAIN OF
KARBALA*

Tabuk (632 CE)

Nile

EGYPT

SARAWAT

HIJAZ

NEJD

Ditch (627 CE)

Yathrib/Medina

R
E
D

S
E
A

Badr (624 CE)

Uhud (624 CE)

Jidda

Mecca

Taif

A R A B I A

MOUNTAINS

Persian Gulf

HADRAMAUT MOUNTAINS

**ARABIAN
SEA**

Sanaa

YEMEN

ABYSSINIA

*Early Muslims sought
asylum in the Christian
Axum kingdom*

Aden

four

The Qur'an

How Do Militant Islamists Abuse Verses?

Many American military leaders and others immersed in the issues of the Middle East have expressed frustration when attempting to read the Qur'an. This frustration can be alleviated by first reading a general history of early Islam and a biography of Muhammad. Even Muslim Arabs have to be taught how to read the Qur'an. To gain a context of the times in which the revelations of Muhammad were received, Karen Armstrong's books on Islam and Muhammad are a good start. Then, before reading the actual Qur'an, connect with verses that have a Judeo-Christian link; Michael Sell's *Approaching the Quran* focuses on religious traditions common to Judaism, Christianity, and Islam.[1] Sell highlights the chapter on Mary, mother of Christ, and her tribulations in bringing Christ into the world amid accusations of fornication. Christ is mentioned more than Muhammad in the Qur'an, and he is revered as a prophet by Muslims.

The first verses of the Qur'an were revealed to Muhammad on the twenty-seventh day of Ramadan in 609. Today, the twenty-seventh day of Ramadan is celebrated as *laylat ul-qadr,* "the Night of Power," the most sanctified of all days in the holy month of Ramadan. Regrettably, Militant Islamists seize upon this special night to undertake savage attacks and suicide missions, perversely believing their dastardly deeds will be specially rewarded if undertaken on that day. They also mean to demonstrate their callous disregard for anything sacred by conducting attacks on that day. After all, their objective is to strike fear among the populace, and what better way than to desecrate the holiest night of Islam?

Muhammad would receive revelations from Gabriel for twenty-three years, until 632, with Muhammad's farewell pilgrimage representing the final verses of the Qur'an. The book contains 6,236 *ayahs* (verses), 114 *suras* (chapters), and thirty *ju'z* (sections); the Qur'an's longest chapter contains 286 verses, and the shortest has three verses. The Qur'an is less than three hundred pages long, shorter than the New Testament. Notwithstanding the obsession of some with Jihad, the Qur'an's overarching themes actually revolve around humankind's relationship with God, other human beings (whether through Jihad or toleration), the environment and God's creation, and the universe.

The book also contains personal laws on inheritance and divorce. Within the concept of God in the Qur'an is an emphasis upon God as one and absolute; the sovereign creator, revealed through creation; sender of messengers; the writer, recorder, and predestiner of the deeds of humankind; the giver of life and death and the raiser of the soul; the most just and merciful of judges; and guide to humankind.

Other ways of classifying passages of the Qur'an are laws, the previous prophets, and final judgment. On the topic of prophets, the Qur'an reserves the most mention for Moses (Musa), who appears 136 times, then Jesus (Isa), mentions of whom are concentrated in chapters 3, 5, and 19, with the greatest attention being paid to the circumstances of his birth. Muhammad is mentioned only four times, and only in the third person. The prophets and monotheistic personalities mentioned in the Qur'an are not only Muhammad (and, as we have seen, Jesus) but Adam and Eve, Cain and Abel, Idris, Noah, Hud, Salih, Abraham, Ishmael, Lot, Joseph, Job, Jonah, Moses, Khidr, Elijah, Saul, David, Solomon, and Mary (known in the Qur'an as Maryam).

The Qur'an's complex themes are compressed into rhythmic form, what is considered by many Muslims to be perfect Arabic oration. The literal meaning of the word *Qur'an* is "the Reciter"; the book is meant to be read out loud. Its rhythmic form also aids in memorization. Those learning Arabic will recognize the three-letter root word of *Qur'an*, which is *Qa'ra aa*, or *q-r-a* in the tri-letter system used to learn basic Arabic.

THE QUR'AN AS MUHAMMAD'S ONLY MIRACLE

The Qur'an has several names, such as *mushaf* (the preserved book), *al-furqan* (to discern), *al-huda* (the guide), and *al-hikma* (the wisdom), or simply *al-kitab* (the Book). Muslims believe that Muhammad's only miracle was the Qur'an and that it was given to him by God, as Arabs preserved their history orally and had a passion for poetry and good oratory. Muslims believe that Moses was given his staff (which turned into a serpent, in the book of Exodus) to impress the court of the pharaoh, which was obsessed with sleight-of-hand and magic illusions, and that Christ's miracles of giving sight to the blind and healing the sick were designed to impress the people of the time, who had a reputation as master healers. Each prophet is given a miracle that fits the time, people, and place in which his message is revealed, according to Muslim understanding of prophetic miracles.

It is important to understand that Muhammad delineated between revelation and his own personal, inner thoughts. Muhammad describes the process of receiving revelation as physically painful, remarking, "Never once did I receive revelation, without thinking that my soul had been torn from me." This could be the result of deep inner reflection to find solutions for the troubled social structure of Meccan and Arabian society; some have also compared these described sensations to seizures. What is known is that Muhammad could not have written the Qur'an, because he was illiterate. Whenever Muhammad received revelations, those around him would memorize the words, or a scribe, if one was nearby, would transmit his words on bone, leather, flat stones, parchment, papyrus, or palm fronds. Quranic recitation is admired, as if it were opera, but it is also considered a connection to God. Many Muslims believe, when they read the Qur'an or hear it, that it is God speaking directly to them; I have witnessed listeners moved to tears. Muslims believe that no piece of human-inspired literature can match the literary excellence of the Qur'an in either content or form. Direct quotations of the Qur'an abound in the literature of the languages of all Muslim nations.

The Qur'an in the Pantheon of Divine Revelations

The Qur'an confirms previous monotheistic revelations like the Christian Bible and the Jewish Torah; however, Muslims believe that the Qur'an was sent as corrective revelations to them. The Qur'an is considered the final message from God until the Second Coming of Christ. In Islamic epistemology, Jesus and his book were sent to correct the Jewish scripture, which had become corrupted by innovations, translations, and additions that had altered God's words and replaced them with man's words. The Qur'an does the same for the Christian Bible, which, Muslim scholars believe, was revealed to Jesus but was then altered through translation from Hebrew to Aramaic, to Greek, to Latin, and so forth. Muhammad is considered the final prophet sent by God until the Second Coming, one final chance for mankind to get the Message of God right.

The Qur'an was never collected in book form until the reign of the third caliph, Uthman, around 650, twenty-three years after Muhammad's death. Abu

Bakr, the first caliph, noticed that those who had memorized the Qur'an were the first to die in battle and worried that at that rate the Qur'an would soon be lost. Abu Bakr ordered Zayd ibn Thabit, one of Muhammad's four scribes, to begin the process of compiling the Qur'an. Among the other scribes of Prophet Muhammad were Mua'wiya ibn Abu Sufyan, Ubey ibn Kaab, and Ali ibn Abi Talib (the Prophet's cousin). Zayd located a trunk containing the scraps of what would be the Qur'an; he then interviewed and cross-referenced sources who had heard Muhammad. The task was completed under the reign of Caliph Uthman. The Uthmani version of the Qur'an is the one in common usage today in both Shiite and Sunni Islam. Uthman ordered all other versions to be destroyed—an unpopular decision but made in the name of Muslim unity. Some scholars suggest that after the discovery of scraps of the Qur'an Uthman may have exorcised verses unkind to his family lineage; Uthman was an early convert to Islam in Mecca and married two of Muhammad's daughters, but he came from a subclan of Muhammad's tribe that viciously persecuted the Prophet. It is said that Uthman had in his hand perhaps the earliest version of the Qur'an in book form when Muhammad ibn Abu Bakr (son of the first caliph) assassinated him in 656.

The book is organized generally from longer verses to shorter verses, and there is no chronology. In addition, verses are identified as to whether they were revealed to Prophet Muhammad in Mecca (the first ten years of his Prophecy) or in Medina (the last thirteen years of his Prophecy). They are known as "Meccan" or "Medinan" verses, respectively. The "sword verses" were exclusively revealed to Muhammad in Medina. The Meccan verses of the Qur'an contain verses on belief, *tawhid* (absolute monotheism), the necessity of prophethood, and methods of reasoning and calling people to Islam. The Medinan verses address legal rules, social and economic teachings, and issues of war.

Generally a chapter is designated Meccan or Medinan depending on where Muhammad first received the revelation. So if verses to a chapter were revealed in Mecca but the chapter was completed in Medina, the chapter would be Meccan. Some scholars debate this designation and argue that the location of the audience in which the verses were publicly introduced determines if the verses are Meccan or Medinan. Others classify the verses based on the phase of Muhammad's prophecy, whether he was in Mecca or Medina.

The Qur'an was to influence the Arabic language, adding diacritic and syntactical marks that aid in the pronunciation and writing of the language. As converts who did not speak Arabic grew in number, these marks were added as aids to the proper utterance of the Qur'an. From there the formal rules of Arabic grammar would evolve. Before the arrival of Islam, the Arabic letters had no dots or syntactical and diacritic marks; one had to infer what a letter was from the words and sentences. Today it is impossible even for Arabs to learn the language without these marks; the process of adding them began in 661 and ended in 786. The Qur'an, although internal evidence indicates it was revealed in Arabic (16:30, al-Nahl), does contain words from Greek, such as *qista (qistas),* meaning "scale" (17:35, al-Isra); Turkish, such as *ghassaq,* meaning "cold" or "extreme cold"; and Persian, such as *sijjil,* meaning "baked clay" (15:74, al-Hijr).

Logically one would reason that compilation, as a human process, is subject to the human error. For instance, there is a minority debate about which verses are divine and which are Muhammad's thoughts. The persecution of Muhammad (by persons named specifically, like Abu Lahab) and the exoneration of the Prophet's wife Aisha from rumors of adultery are examples, some argue, of Muhammad's thoughts interjected in the revelation. Would God, creator of the universe, trouble himself with such matters? Nonetheless, the majority of Muslims consider the process of compiling the Qur'an to be divinely inspired, similar to the Christian views of the compilation and translation of the Bible.

One can find in the Qur'an justifications for peace and war, forgiveness and punishment. Islamists and Militant Islamists quote from the *hudud* verses that sanction lashing and capital punishment but cut off these verses in midsentence or ignore subsequent verses about repentance. In essence, Islamists and Militant Islamists focus on punishment and ignore the teaching that if individuals repent they are to be forgiven and that their reward is with God. Other misuses of the Qur'an deal with the rights of women; while it does sanction the beating of women who neglect their duty, it also says that women are a garment to men and men a garment to women, that they complement one another. In addition, Muhammad's example of treating his wives suggests a healthier and more constructive relationship than what is practiced by the Taliban, Islamists, and Wahhabis in Saudi Arabia. The *hadith* (actions and sayings of Muhammad) are rife with examples of Muhammad helping with chores, mending his own clothes, taking seriously the counsel of his wives. This astonished Arab males around Muhammad, so much that it is reputed that Omar questioned Muhammad on the progressive way he treated his wives.[2] On the issue of adultery, the Qur'an warns that four witnesses to the act must be present, a standard of proof so high that convictions and punishment for adultery should be rare; yet in Iran, among the Taliban, and in some

Arab countries executions for adultery happen. Worse, the penalty for fornication (sexual relations among nonmarried persons), as opposed to adultery, is lashing, yet in fact someone who is unmarried today is punished by execution.

The Qur'an, according to Islamic doctrine is untranslatable; English versions, for instance, are considered by Muslims to be not translations but interpretations. Why is this important in the realm of Militant Islamist theory? To change the actual Arabic is considered sacrilegious, but interpretation and translation are different matters. That is why there are militant interpretations of aspects of the Qur'an and why in the English language there are several versions. The Saudi English translation (with English and Arabic on facing pages) of the Qur'an, for instance, contains a preface extolling the virtues of violent Jihad; its English side adds commentaries about the infidel, adding in parenthesis such glosses as "(such as Jews and Christians)," or under the word *quwa,* "(literally 'strength')," or in the context of a war verse, the phrase "(such as missiles and tanks)."[3] For Muslims who do not speak Arabic, these English versions represent the only version of the Qur'an they understand. Although I would categorize the Saudis as simply Islamist, such translations only encourage Militant Islamist Ideology.

Another authority Militant Islamists and Islamists use to justify their narrow Islamic justifications is select Quranic commentary. They typically accept only such commentaries as Sayyid Qutb's fifteen-volume *In the Shade of the Qur'an* and others by Ibn Taymiyyah and Ibn Jawziyyah. They neglect hundreds of the six hundred or more commentators on the Qur'an, starting with Prophet Muhammad's scribes, who have differing views on the interpretation of verses. It is important to read various commentators on a subject of interest and to consider that commentary as opinion and not orthodoxy.

Muslims consider the Qur'an to be the sacred word of God, its utterance, the book itself as something to be revered, in the sense of John 1:1: "In the beginning was the Word, and the Word was with God, and the Word was God." This is important, as incidents of desecrating the Qur'an, such as letting the Qur'an fall to the ground during a search, or more blatant instances, allow our adversary to capitalize on outrage and to score points in the arena of public opinion. Although such behavior is not representative of the American serviceman or -woman, al-Qaida and Militant Islamists are very proficient at taking isolated incidents to aid in recruiting and fund-raising and to incite hatred. Desecration of the Qur'an, however, would be considered an offense not only by Militant Islamists but by Islamists and wider muslim community as well. The Militant Islamist, however, is likely to incite violence; the Islamist political groups would use the incident to call for the removal of American cultural and political influences from the Islamic world. Aside from damage to America's image, such actions place American lives in danger, as they poison the atmosphere of the battle space. Such desecrations should be quickly acknowledged, with unconditional apologies and reassurances to the public that the accused do not represent the United States or its military, that they have been ejected from the country and referred to their service's judge advocate general for punishment.

A May 2008 incident where a U.S. Army sniper used the Qur'an for target practice on an Iraqi police training center's firing range represents an excellent case for how American military leaders should handle such a situation. Maj. Gen. Jeffrey Hammond, commander of U.S. forces in Baghdad, took the following immediate steps, which in my opinion formed the basis by which American officials and Iraqi tribal leaders fighting al-Qaida can at least alleviate the emotionalism of such an event:

- Major General Hammond elected to hold an apology ceremony, not a press conference, and he issued this statement, flanked by Iraqi Sunni leaders of the Radwaniyah District, where the incident had happened: "I come before you here seeking your forgiveness, in the most humble manner I look in your eyes today, and I say please forgive me and my soldiers."
- An American official kissed a new copy of the Qur'an and ceremoniously presented it to the tribal leaders.
- Major General Hammond also read a letter from the shooter: "I sincerely hope that my actions have not diminished the partnership that our two nations have developed together. . . . My actions were shortsighted, very reckless and irresponsible, but in my heart [the actions] were not malicious."
- The soldier was relieved of duty and reassigned.
- Major General Hammond said, "The actions of one soldier were nothing more than criminal behavior. . . . I've come to this land to protect you, to support you—not to harm you—and the behavior of this soldier was nothing short of wrong and unacceptable."[4]

This, of course, did not please everyone, but one must think of it as a means of providing a narrative, America's story, in the region. Ignoring desecrations or promoting the individual sustains the Islamist and Militant Islamist fervor. Major

General Hammond's decision to hold an apology ceremony restored somewhat the loss of face by Sunni tribal leaders who had cooperated with U.S. forces in Iraq, a key constituency in undermining al-Qaida in Iraq.

THE ORIGINS OF THE QURANIC WAR VERSES

Half a Mullah is a danger to your faith, half a doctor is a danger to your life.

A person who is not a proper doctor can kill, and a person who is not a proper mullah can ruin the faith of Muslims.

AFGHAN PROVERB, QUOTED BY FORMER AFGHAN LEADER BURHANNUDDIN RABANI TO *NEWSWEEK* REPORTER BABAK DEHGHANPISHEH, JANUARY 28, 2002

Militant Islamist clerics, leaders, and bloggers quote incessantly from a set of seventy verses known as the "war," or "sword" verses. The Qur'an comprises 6,236 verses, which primarily deal with humankind's relationship to God, other human beings, and their environment. In effect, Militant Islamists ignore 98 percent of the book in their sermons, speeches, and diatribes.

In addition, the historical context of these verses is completely left out. When Muhammad was selected to be leader and Grand Arbiter of Medina, Meccan leaders, led by Abu Sufyan, realized that Muhammad, a man they had tried to kill, stood between them and the caravan routes to the Levant, Egypt, and Iraq. It was of paramount importance to them that this threat be terminated, and the Meccans began harassing Muslims and Muhammad's allies on the outskirts of Medina. As the Meccans amassed a large army to crush Muhammad's society in its infancy, the Prophet appealed to God for guidance. He did not have the religious sanction to wage war, and every month the Levantine caravans arrived in Mecca to feed the Meccan war machine. It is in this context that the first of what would be several dozen sword verses were revealed to Muhammad. Historically, a reference in the Qur'an to "the infidel" means the Meccans. This history is completely ignored by Militant Islamists today, as it leads to questions and intellectual inquiry. In the Qur'an these war verses are accompanied by warnings not to transgress limits if the enemy ceases fighting. Finally, Militant Islamist clerics do not mention that of the seventy war verses, fifty-nine are defensive and only eleven are offensive.

They use these eleven verses over and over again, when in fact 140 verses deal with devotional matters, like prayer, fasting, and the pilgrimage, alone. Seventy more verses address personal laws, like marriage, divorce, and inheritance.

Another seventy deal with commercial transactions. Finally, thirty verses concern crime and punishment:

- *Qisas:* meaning retaliation, and following the biblical principle of "an eye for an eye."
- *Diyya:* compensation paid to the heirs of a victim. In Arabic the word means both blood money and ransom.
- *Hudud:* fixed punishments.
- *Tazir:* punishment, usually corporal, administered at the discretion of the judge.

This breakdown offers a general idea of the Qur'an beyond the seventy war verses. Imagine focusing on certain verses while ignoring others like the seventy verses on commercial transactions or the thirty on crime and punishment. It is looking at the Qur'an through a narrow lens, when it must be taken in its totality. Our adversary "markets" the narrow, violent verses of the Qur'an with logos, images, and slogans combining crossed swords, Kalashnikovs, and the Qur'an. Suicide bombers are shown holding an assault rifle with one hand and the Qur'an in another. All this is part of a media saturation that undermines the complexity of the Qur'an. Notably, the Qur'an (5:52) warns of such abuses as narrowly reading the Qur'an: "Beware of them, lest they seduce you away from part of that which God has sent down to you."

NASKH (ABROGATION): MILITANT ISLAMIST ABUSE OF THIS CONCEPT

Another ideological tactic to emphasize these war verses and de-emphasize tolerant verses uses the concept of *naskh* (abrogation). Militant Islamists argue that the war verses are more recent than the earlier revealed Meccan verses and that therefore they supersede the tolerant Meccan verses. They argue for the complete negation of tolerant verses. This idea is not in the mainstream, as the verse in the Qur'an that sanctions the practice argues that you must understand the older verses to comprehend the newer revelations—that you cannot ignore the older verses. The verse declares, "None of our revelations do we abrogate or cause to be forgotten, but we substitute something better or similar; knowest thou not that Allah hath power over all things" (Qur'an 2:106). In addition, many Muslims are uncomfortable with the concept of abrogation as practiced by Militant Islamists, as it calls into question the divine nature of the Qur'an. Saudi Islamic scholar Abdul-Hamid Abu Sulayman writes that sword verses are being used to cancel out 140 verses of tolerance and moderation.[5] He is critical of the Militant Islamist method of outright negation of major portions of the Qur'an.

The scholarly approach to reading the Qur'an is to take it holistically and not narrowly, not reading the text to justify actions. Dr. Imam al-Sherief (also known as Dr. Fadl), a mentor to al-Qaida deputy Ayman al-Zawahiri, has issued a scathing critique of al-Qaida and Zawahiri, arguing the danger of committing an act and then making the Qur'an justify it. He argues that a good Muslim should consult the Qur'an first before acting. The majority of Islamic scholars, both Shiite and Sunni, would agree that the application of *naskh* is more complex than Militant Islamists portray it and use it. For instance, *naskh* can be partial or total, implicit or explicit. Linguistically, *naskh* can mean "obliteration," "transfer," "suspension," "replacement," even "reincarnation." All of these senses attracted Islamic scholars of the previous centuries.

Here is a sampling of verses suppressed by Militant Islamists using their perverted application of *naskh:*

- "There shall be no compulsion in matters of religion" (2:256).
- "We have honored the sons of Adam, provided them transport on land and sea, sustained them with good things, and conferred on them special favors above a great part of our creation" (17:70).
- "Humankind! We created you from a male and female, and made you into peoples and tribes that you may know each other. Truly the most honored of you before God is the most pious of you" (49:13).
- "And let not the hatred of others make you swerve to wrong and depart from justice. Be just: that is closer to piety" (5:8).
- "God commands you to return trusts to their owners, and if you judge between people, you shall judge with justice" (4:58).
- "So give [full] measure and [full] weight and do not deny the people their goods, and work no corruption in the land, after it has been set right" (7:85).
- "Whoever kills a soul for other than slaying a soul or corruption upon the earth it is as if he has killed the whole of humanity, and whoever saves a life, it is as if has revived the whole of humanity" (5:32).

The verses that run counter to the Militant Islamists' almost exclusive emphasis on sword verses are many. Among the items lost in Islamic public discourse is

Muhammad's establishing as ransom for prisoners the task of teaching ten Muslims to read and write.[6]

HOW THE QUR'AN FITS WITHIN SHARIA

The basic building blocks of the sharia (Islamic law) are the Qur'an, then the *hadith,* and finally a corpus of commentaries on both the Qur'an and *hadith*. There is no strictly static set of laws. Sharia is more a system of law, a consensus of the unified spirit, based on the Qur'an, *hadith* (sayings and doings of Muhammad and his companions), *Ijma* (consensus), *Qiyas* (reasoning by analogy), and centuries of debate, interpretation, and precedent. Sharia, its study, and more importantly its interpretation differ among Muslims. Islam is one faith but with varying interpretations, doctrines, and social outlooks. The forty-eighth verse of the chapter al-Ma'ida in the Qur'an says: "If God so willed, He would have made you a single people, but His plan to test you in what He hath given you. . . . The goal of you all is to God, it is He that will show you the truth of the matters in which ye dispute." This undermines the wish of the Taliban, bin Laden, and Jihadists to impose upon Muslims a single, neo-fundamentalist belief.

Using this verse from the Qur'an one can begin to understand that Jihadist doctrines have no room for the diversity that even this holiest of books outlines. Islam is first and foremost a religion, but it is a religion from which a political system can be inferred. Verse 13 of al-Hujayrat says, "O mankind! We created you from a single pair male and female, and made you into nations and tribes that you may know one another." This verse advocates equality among human beings. The issue of egalitarianism was also the subject of Prophet Muhammad's final address to his community, in which he said: "O people! Your God is one, and you all are from Adam, and Adam is from dust, there is no preference between an Arab over *Ajami* [Westerners], or an *Ajamai* over an Arab, or a red over a white [-skinned person], or a white over a red [-skinned person], [their preference] is only distinguished in piety, as God is my witness."

Al-Qaida's very structure denies this equality; it has a hierarchy in which Egyptians reign supreme, followed by Saudis and Yemenis, with African and South Asian members on the bottom. In addition, the Taliban under Mullah Omar failed to implement a just society and were unwilling to engage in compromise, as called for in verse 10 of al-Hujayrat: "The believers are but a single brotherhood, so make peace and reconcile between your two brothers and fear God, that ye may receive mercy." Another required concept of governance in Islamic societies is that of *Shura* (consultation). This was a means of preserving rights and giving the community a voice in affairs. Prophet Muhammad, when he was governor of Medina, took the issue of consultation seriously, as it was the only way in which to govern a city in which non-Muslims were a majority in the early stages of his rule.

Another important element in the governance of an Islamic society is striving toward human happiness. The Taliban made no effort to satisfy this goal, calling on Afghans' trust in God and focus on the hereafter instead of truly attempting to solve their economic problems. The Qur'an is clear that human happiness is not limited to the afterlife but is a balance between the happiness in this life and the next. Verse 77 of the Qisas chapter states, "But seek with the [wealth] which God has bestowed on thee, the home of the hereafter, nor forget thy portion in this world." This is perhaps the closest link to Thomas Jefferson's "life, liberty, and the pursuit of happiness" found in Islamic law. This verse urges a balance; suicide bombers obsess about the hereafter, violating this precept of the Qur'an.

The Qur'an contains no specific commandments on how Muslims should govern themselves, nor does it uphold a certain type of authority *(sultah)* in government. It does not endorse one type of political or economic system, leaving these issues to the public interest *(maslahah),* as long as basic morality was not contravened. Prophet Muhammad later in life said, "You are better suited to decide upon worldly affairs." Some inviolable issues in establishing a government in an Islamic society are *Adalah* (justice), *Musawah* (equity), and *Shura* (consultation).

The respected Tunisian cleric Abdul-Aziz Thalabi (d. 1944) postulated that Islam came to bring humankind together and for that reason recognizes the "People of the Book" (Jews and Christians) and urges that Muslims not proselytize among them except with pure intentions (Qur'an, Ankabut chapter, verse 46). Thalabi reviewed the Qur'an and found that the words for tolerance and forgiveness appear in thirty-six of the Qur'an's 114 chapters and 125 of its verses. He was troubled by the conversion of the Qur'an into a book that encourages radicalism and encouraged clerics to object to this misuse, saying that such interpretations represent *Afkar Daiyiiqah,* or narrow-mindedness.

CONTEXTUAL READING OF THE QUR'AN

It is important to mention here a constructive method of memorizing the Qur'an used by schools preparing students for entry into al-Azhar University. The Qur'an is divided into thirty *ju'z* (segments). In elementary school eighteen *ju'z* are memorized, seven in secondary school, and five in high school, completing the memorization of all 6,236 verses. During this process students are given courses in *tafsir* (exegesis), *hadith,* and *tajweed* (oration). Of course, such topics as English as a second language, math, science, and history are included in a constructive twelve-year course of study leading to graduation from high school. Memorizing the Qur'an is a basic requirement to enter al-Azhar, whose schools include not only a seminary but medical, law, engineering, and social studies colleges. Compare this course of Quranic memorization with the experience of the so-called American Taliban, John Walker Lindh, whose impatience to be a good Muslim (and influence from Militant Islamists) led him toward the narrow path of deriving self-confidence through the Militant Islamist lifestyle. By the time Lindh arrived in Yemen for language training, he was unreceptive to any Islamic view except for the narrow doctrine he had received at a mosque in San Francisco. Militant Islamist Ideology's arrogant certainty as to what Islam is supposed to be murders faith and inquiry.

Another component of Quranic study is *asbab al-nuzul,* which is necessary for anyone wanting to acquire more than a superficial knowledge of the Qur'an: the context in which a particular verse was revealed to Muhammad at a particular time. Another concept is *tafsir* (exegesis), exploration of the grammatical, lexicographical, theological, and historical reasons for the revelation of each verse in the Qur'an. It is manifest that years are needed for proper Quranic study, something Militant Islamists do not generally accomplish. Those who do possess this training do not pass it on to people about to become suicide bombers.

The chapter *al-Anfal* (The Spoils) was revealed to Prophet Muhammad after the Battle of Badr, Islam's first battle, to address and deter disagreements over the spoils of war. Another example involves the verses allowing men to take four wives, in the chapter *al-Nisa'a* (Women), which also includes an injunction that all wives are to be treated equally and that a Muslim who cannot treat them equally needs to limit himself to one wife. These verses were revealed to Muhammad after the Battle of Uhud, which left many Muslim orphans and widows.

Regrettably, since the late twentieth century, there seems to have been a fixation on a narrow definition of the single word *jihad*. This fixation has stimulated the counterproductive actions of Militant Islamist groups like al-Qaida. This fixation upon single words in the Qur'an is not new, for in ninth-century Baghdad and twelfth-century Spain the Greek and Roman classics were preserved by Muslims because of their focus upon the Quranic word *ilm* (knowledge). This word stimulated Muslim scholars to seek out knowledge from diverse sources, interacting and translating classical works with Jews, Zoroastrians, and, Christians. It produced an intellectual ferment that advanced human understanding of mathematics, science, philosophy, and medicine.

five

The Term *Jihad*

Various Interpretations

J*ihad* in a broad, Islamic view, means to struggle or exert effort. Jihad can be as simple as struggling to get up in the early morning to say your dawn prayers or struggling to learn and improve yourself spiritually or intellectually. It also can mean struggling in the path of God, which does not necessarily mean engaging in warfare but might be making time to teach Islam to children or providing financial support for an Islamic project. Jihad means to struggle to fulfill your obligations to God, both moral and spiritual, on a daily basis. Islamists narrow this definition, insisting that Jihad means to expend every effort fighting against the disbelievers, but even Islamists delineate who can fight and when; unlike Militant Islamists, they generally set rules and limits for engaging in fighting in the name of God. Islamists generally believe that the Jihad (in their definition) is a communal obligation and that if enough members of the community fulfill this responsibility, the rest of the community is absolved. It makes Jihad obligatory upon all Muslims only if the enemy has entered Muslim lands and if the imam calls for Jihad. Jihad is obligatory only upon individuals meeting certain conditions, according to Islamists—such as being sane, adult, male, and free from physical infirmities, and having the funds needed to participate.[1] Some Islamists also prescribe a protocol of warfare in which a noble Muslim warrior should be free of arrogance and conceit. The etiquette also includes warnings not to kill non-combatant women and children.[2] Compare these Islamist and Islamic rulings with Militant Islamist practice. In addition, the condition that a Muslim warrior must be male was not always followed in Muhammad's time; females played a vital role in early Islamic battles. Females not only tended to the wounded but engaged in combat and plundered as the Islamic army moved forward. In al-Bukhari, vol-

34

ume 6, *hadith* numbers 344–416, five women fought alongside Muhammad in the Battle of Uhud, and one, Umm Ahmara, dies engaging a Meccan with a sword. In the *hadith* collection of the Books of Muslim, volume 3, *hadith* number 1,442: "Muhammad asked a woman where she got this dagger. She replied at Uhud and used it to kill a Meccan. Muhammad was satisfied with her answer."

Compare these Islamist rules to Militant Islamists, who use women, children, and the mentally infirm as suicide bombers, who reduce Jihad to fighting or supporting the fighting through financial means, and who make Jihad incumbent upon all Muslims, with no distinction between communal and individual responsibility. In addition, Militant Islamists have reduced Jihad (as fighting) to a way of life, and some have made the twisted argument that since one can alter one's prayers in times of Jihad, Jihad supersedes prayers in significance. This concept refers to a ruling altering prayer times during times of Jihad. It actually falls in the category of altering prayers when traveling and is designed to make fulfilling the prayer obligation easier; stretching the idea to make Jihad a more important practice than prayer is a radical departure from the norms of *fiqh* (Islamic jurisprudence). Take the notion of Jihad and compare the narrow Militant Islamist view with that of the Islamists and finally the wider Islamic view, and you begin to understand the nuances of a reductionist Militant Islamist Ideology that takes fragments of Islam to justify its actions and impose control through violence—an abuse of Islam that it is up to Muslims to isolate and expose.

Militant Islamists and Islamists are even narrow in their historical understanding of early Islamic conquests, crediting all successes to faith and not delving into the tactics and strategy that made Muslim armies successful. When you acknowledge the importance of faith and set that aside, you discover that Muslim armies that conquered the Levant and Persia were multitasked. Before they reached adulthood, Arab tribalism demanded that every male be able to wield a bow, a javelin, a spear, and a sword and to ride a horse. Muslim formations would face a Persian formation and empty their quivers of arrows, advance, throw their javelins en masse, advance again, approach with short spears, and then close with the sword. By the time Muslim infantry reached them, the Persian lines would decimated. All the while, Muslim cavalry would attack and retreat on the flanks, attempting to loosen the Persian center, enticing the flanks to give chase.[3]

David Levering Lewis, in his 2008 *God's Crucible,* writes, "Arab warfare was a lethal choreography of stunning speed and maneuver—*al-farr wal karr*—furious attack and withdrawal in which initiative and improvisation was encouraged."[4] The mechanics of Muslim military successes are lost to Arabs today. Early Muslim women following these mobile forces would collect weapons and booty, administer the coup de grâce to enemy wounded left on the battlefield, care for the Muslim wounded, and feed the army. The first opinions and commentary on Jihad, known as *Ahkam al-Jihad,* appeared in the eighth and ninth centuries; this writing outlines the rules of Islamic warfare. These Islamic rules were developed, two centuries after Prophet Muhammad's death, from the study of the seventy war verses in the Qur'an, coupled with Prophet Muhammad's example, in particular his wars with the Meccans between 622 and 632. The expansion of the Islamic empire led to new complexities and a redefinition of warfare and its conduct. However, al-Qaida does not rely on these early treatises but limits itself to selective opinions on Jihad as warfare in order to weave a perverse narrative.

The Battle of al-Khandaq (the Ditch) is an example of the manipulation of Islamic history to condemn Jews. Muhammad participated or planned thirty-seven battles, most of them with the Meccans. He had defeated the Meccans at the Battle of Badr and fought them to a draw at Uhud. Now Abu Sufyan was determined to destroy Muhammad once and for all; he amassed the largest army ever fielded by the Meccans, with allies from all corners of Arabia. This time he would not meet Muhammad in the field of battle but would march straight for Medina. Muhammad, learning of this, prepared for what he thought might be his last battle; there was concern among the Muslims and Muhammad's non-Muslim allies. A Persian convert to Islam recommended that Muhammad construct a ditch around Medina, arguing that the Meccans were a mobile force and that their alliances were based on the possibility of plunder. If you construct a ditch, he suggested, they will be forced to lay a siege they are not prepared for, the alliances will break apart, and you will be victorious. This is exactly what happened in what became known as the Battle of the Ditch (627).

Among the allies of Muhammad who had in 622 signed the Compact of Medina and now guarded a section of the defensive trench was the Jewish tribe of the Banu Qurayza. Looking at the massive force arrayed against them, they switched sides during battle, in the name of self-preservation. Usually Militant Islamists stop there, condemning all Jews as betrayers of prophets—as have militant Christians at least since the Inquisition. But the story of the Battle of the Ditch does not end there. After the battle, Muhammad recused himself from arbitrating the actions of the Banu Qurayza; the leader of the Jewish tribe and Muhammad would settle upon an arbiter. They chose Saad ibn Mua'dh, who levied the seventh-century punishment for breaking a compact in a time of war—execution of all males of certain ages and enslavement of the women and children. Militant Islamists do not discuss these details with people they want to transform into suicide bombers in Israel, as they lead to questions: Did Muhammad punish the Banu Qurayza because of their faith or because they broke the compact? Such questions are inconvenient in brainwashing.

In the century after Prophet Muhammad's death in 632, the Islamic empire spread from Arabia to the Atlantic shores of Spain, southern France, and northern China. The common wisdom in the Middle East and even in the United States is that faith led to this success. This is a simplistic view, one that hides the complexity of tribe, theological disagreements, the military exhaustion of Byzantium and Persia, as well as the adeptness of the early Muslims in keeping what they conquered through negotiation, intermarriage, and much more.[5]

six

Muhammad and the Succession Crisis

Religion is a candle inside a multicolored lantern. Everyone looks through a particular color, but the candle is always there.

GENERAL MUHAMMAD NEGUIB (1901–1984), FIRST PRESIDENT OF EGYPT

Prophet Muhammad left no clear guidance on a successor upon his death in 632. He also left no real instructions how Muslims were to govern themselves after his death. His main mission was to leave behind a social order through prophecy, not governance. Muhammad, according to Qur'an 33:40, is considered to be *khatim al-anbiyah* (seal of the prophets), meaning he was the last prophet who will be sent by God until the Second Coming of Christ. Some scholars postulate that Muhammad's mission as prophet was so consuming that God left him no surviving male heirs and that he did not designate a successor because he was a Messenger of God—and only God can only select his messengers.

The first three caliphs after Muhammad's death were Abu Bakr, Omar, and Uthman. During this time a fringe group of Muslims called the Kharijites emerged who developed new religio-political theories. They included a doctrine that since Ali had not directly succeeded Muhammad, God had been cheated of his divine will, and thus the Muslim majority were apostates, worthy of death by Jihad. The Kharijites, Islam's first Militant Islamists, were eventually suppressed by Ali at the Battle of Nahrawain in modern-day southern Iraq. The Kharijites would reverse the significance of Jihad, making its higher form death in the name of God, versus Muhammad's teaching—that is, to do what is morally right in the eyes of God. Among the labels given al-Qaida by Saudi clerics is "Kharijite."

THE FIRST AND SECOND CALIPHS (ABU-BAKR AND OMAR)

The Prophet Muhammad lingered on his deathbed, by some accounts, for three months. As he lay dying, as we have seen, factions began to form to determine who would be Muhammad's successor and preserve the infant Islamic state. From a sociopolitical perspective, the Prophet in only twenty-three years had been able to convert or strike alliances with the bulk of tribes in western and central Arabia. His society went from being a quasi-city-state in Medina to a conglomerate of tribes never before unified in the history of Arabia. The factions included:

- The *Ansar* (the helpers): Those from Medina (formerly Yathrib) who argued they were the first Muslim society and granted Muhammad asylum, freedom from persecution, and accepted his leadership over their agricultural enclave.

- The *Muhajiroon* (the émigrés): Those Meccans who converted to Islam in Mecca, suffered persecution with Muhammad, and fled with him to Medina, leaving behind all personal possessions. They were represented by Abu Bakr, Omar, and Abu Ubaydah. They argued they were Muhammad's companions, advisers, and supporters when he was undergoing the most severe of persecutions in Mecca. Surely one of them, they presumed, would succeed Muhammad.

- The *Quraysh* (Muhammad's tribe): This was Muhammad's clan, and it argued that its members having always been leaders of Mecca, should continue its leadership role. The problem was that the leader of the Quraysh, Abu Sufyan, was a late convert to Islam and formerly one of the chief persecutors of Muhammad in Mecca. His succession was considered unacceptable. This is the reason those Muslims today who believe leadership should extend to Prophet Muhammad's family tend to limit the line to the Bani Hashim clan, excluding the other Quraysh clans.

These three factions set the stage for a political struggle that would determine the survival of Islam. Among the most important figures to emerge was Omar ibn al-Khattab, who would become the second caliph. He would negotiate, cajole, strategize, intimidate, and argue for the succession of Abu Bakr. When Prophet Muhammad had wanted to send a military expedition to Tabuk to address the problem of the Byzantine Empire's assertion of its authority in what it had always been considered the backwater of Arabia, Omar stalled, arguing successfully that Muslim forces were needed in Arabia, to keep order upon his, Muhammad's, death. When the *Ansar* held a strategy session to plan a peaceful coup to put forth their candidate, Omar found out about the meeting and barged into it, asserting the right of all Muslims to be present, on what would be called *Yawm al-Saqifa* (The Day of the Portico). Perhaps the biggest challenge to Omar was from the Prophet's cousin and son-in-law Ali ibn Abi Talib and his supporters, who argued that in a watering stop called Ghadir Khumm, between Mecca and Medina, the Prophet was reputed to have pointed to Ali and said, "If you follow me, follow Ali." The widely accepted version of what Muhammad said was: "Whomsoever's *mawla* I am, this Ali is also his *mawla*. O Allah, befriend whosoever befriends him and be the enemy of whosoever is hostile to him." Aside from disagreements over authenticity, there is disagreement over the meaning of *mawla;* definitions range from "lord" to "cousin," to "friend." Omar countered that if Muhammad had said this, he would have affirmed it in Mecca or Medina and ratified it when asked as he lay dying. In addition, when Muhammad was too ill to lead the prayers, he had designated Abu Bakr to serve as imam (prayer leader), Omar argued this was the clearest sign he wanted Abu Bakr to succeed. Finally, the ill Muhammad had been tended by two of his wives—Aisha, daughter of Abu Bakr, and Hafsa, daughter of Omar, who controlled access to Muhammad in his last days. Shiite Muslims use this incident to assert that the line of succession should descend from Muhammad's family and that this was frustrated by Omar and the Muhajiroon. Omar is reviled in Shiite Islam, which is a narrow view of the man who did so much to preserve the infant Islamic society and understood the realities of tribal politics.

When Muhammad died in 632, Abu Bakr succeeded him and began consolidating Islamic influence in all of Arabia. He, along with Omar, had to contend with tribes who had made their alliance with Muhammad and now felt that upon his death that they could leave the Muslim alliance. Place yourself in the minds of these tribal elders, some of whom must have felt that Muhammad's charisma and blessing from God had kept the alliance successful and now wondered if this success would continue now that he had died. Additionally, other tribes in the interior of Arabia were declaring that they possessed prophets, in order to attract the kind of prestige and power enjoyed by Mecca and Medina. These are the issues that led to the *Ridda* (Apostasy) Wars. The details of Muhammad's succession are important, as it reveals the human and realistic side of the early Islamic caliphate. It also portrays the early caliphs as real people, with real challenges and problems, a perspective that in turn reveals them as extraordinary leaders in the context of seventh-century Arabia. Unfortunately, the actual political and historical details of Prophet Muhammad's succession are not taught in schools in the Middle East. They can only be found in seminary studies, and even then only a serious school of Islamic studies would cover and debate such historical details, however important.

The events of Ghadir Khumm are clouded in history. Among Shiite Muslims it is a certainty that Muhammad designated Ali his successor at the oasis of Ghadir Khumm and that Omar and Abu Bakr conspired to deprive him of his rights. The majority Sunni Muslims do not claim this certainty but only that the majority, through negotiation and politicking, settled upon Abu Bakr, Omar, Uthman, and then Ali. Another version of Ghadir Khumm is that Muhammad said pointing to Ali, "Be a friend to whoever he befriends, an enemy to whomever he takes as an enemy." This is still vague. Yet another version of the story is that Ali asserted his rights under Ghadir Khumm in his battle with Mua'wiyah over the succession. Ali had called upon those who witnessed the event two decades after Muhammad's death, and twelve were certified in Kufa.[1] If this is the case, it shows Ali's tacit acceptance of the first three caliphs and that he only asserted his right when the consensus made him caliph and Mua'wiyah refused to recognize him as such.

CALIPH UTHMAN AND ALI:
THE CONTROVERSY AND FIRST MUSLIM CIVIL WAR

Abu Bakr, Omar, and Uthman would rule as caliphs from 632 to 656. Under Abu Bakr and Omar, the Muslim empire encompassed the conquest of the Levant, Egypt, and modern day Iraq. It was an extraordinary expansion, which was achieved through military prowess, faith, and the collaboration of Christians like the Lakhmids in the Levant, as well as Copts in Egypt, who were chafing under the rule of Christian Byzantium.

The early Muslim conquests of Byzantine Syria and assanid Persia were due partly to discontented Arab tribal allies of both powers. These allies—the tribal confederation of the Ghassanids, allied to Byzantium, and that of the Lakhmids, allied to Persia—guarded the northern approaches from marauding Arab tribes, both confederations. In 581, Emperor Maurice dropped his annual subsidies to the Ghassanids and by 584 had arrested a Ghassanid chief, Mundhiri, some say for heretical Christian beliefs.[2] The Sassanid Persians had entered into a quarrel with the Lakhmid tribal confederacy. These two powers would alienate confederacies that had kept a lid on the pre-Islamic and divided tribes of Arabia. With the arrival of Muhammad and the unification of Arabian tribes under Islam, this Byzantine strategy of defense in depth using the Ghassanid tribal confederacy would be undermined. The arrogant Byzantine Christian officials failed to see that the Ghassanids were made up of clans (like the Bali, Quddah, and Hadas, to name a few) and that these clans had ties with the Arabs of Arabia. As an example, the mother of Amr ibn al-A'as, one of the three generals who conquered the Levant and went on to conquer Egypt, was from the Bali clan. As another instance, the Muslims captured Palmyra with the support of Christian Arab tribes under the command of a Ghassanid prince.[3] Another added pressure that worked to the advantage of the Muslims was a decade of warfare between the powers of Christian Byzantium and the Sassanid Persians; they exhausted one another in what is today Turkey, Syria, and Iraq.

Uthman's rule would see the expansion into modern-day Libya and a push into Persia. His rule saw the compilation of the Qur'an, but it would also be characterized by rampant nepotism, but also by his assumption of such titles as Shadow of God on earth, which outraged a segment of Muslims. He would be murdered in 656, in Islam's first political murder. His alleged murderer was Muhammad ibn Abu Bakr, son of the first caliph Abu Bakr and half-brother of Muhammad's wife Aisha.

Ali would be selected as caliph in Medina in 656, but under the cloud of the murder of his predecessor Uthman ibn Affan. Among those challenging Ali for the caliphate was Aisha bint Abu Bakr, Muhammad's wife, who put forth Talhah as a successor. A second challenger to Ali was Mua'wiyah ibn Abu Sufyan, the governor of the Levant, who demanded that the blood of his uncle, Uthman, be avenged. Ali did not exercise good political judgment, and although Uthman's killers were known, he did not aggressively pursue them. To make matters worse, Ali appointed Uthman's alleged killer, Muhammad ibn Abu Bakr, governor of Egypt.[4] This was a huge political miscalculation on the part of Ali. This also demonstrates why it is important to study the "Rightly Guided caliphs" (Abu Bakr, Omar, Uthman, and Ali) as persons, leaders, and decision makers, not semidivine, mythological figures.

ALI VERSUS AISHA

Both Sunnis and Shiites agree that Ali was not directly involved in Uthman's death, but the image of him not dealing aggressively with Uthman's assassin, let alone appointing him a governor, would produce two major civil wars. The first was between Ali and Aisha, and her allies Talhah and Zubair; it culminated in Aisha's defeat in the Battle of the Camel in 656, on the outskirts of Basra, in southern Iraq. Aisha was not only Prophet Muhammad's wife and daughter of the first caliph, Abu Bakr, but also was a significant repository of Prophet Muhammad's sayings and deeds, known collectively as the *hadith*. It is estimated that 378 *hadiths* are attributable to her.[5] But this does not answer why Aisha bore such animosity to Ali, a man who not only was Muhammad's cousin but had been raised by him. One story was when Muhammad and his companions were returning from Mecca to Medina, after performing his final pilgrimage, they stopped in an oasis to water the camels. When Aisha dismounted her *howdah* (a small shelter mounted atop a camel to shield women from the sun and the gaze of others) to relieve herself, she lost her onyx necklace, a wedding gift. The caravan left without her, and in the desert this was a death sentence. She was rescued by Safwan ibn Muattal, and as they rode together into camp, rumors began insinuating the infidelity of Aisha. This pressure on the reputation of Aisha did not let up, her parents did not come to her defense, and Muhammad did not aggressively deal with this issue, but rather became depressed by the rumors. Muhammad went to Ali for his advice, and Ali is reputed to have advised Muhammad to divorce Aisha. It was a recommendation that Aisha never forgave, and it was not until a verse from the Qur'an exonerated Aisha that the matter was laid to rest. Chastising her parents for pushing her to thank the Prophet and for not defending her, she said, "Why should I thank the Prophet, when all thanks goes to God!"[6] She also expressed surprise that God, creator of the universe, would take an interest in her.[7]

ALI VERSUS MUA'WIYAH

Ali's second major challenger, Mua'wiyah, not only demanded that his uncle be avenged but refused to recognize Ali as caliph and then declared himself caliph from Damascus. Ali had transferred the seat of Islamic government from Medina to Kufa. Mua'wiyah understood that Damascus was a more central and longer-established location for the seat of the growing Islamic empire. There were wider geopolitical issues at stake, even ultimate control of the Islamic empire. But as the saying goes, "All politics is local"; the dispute between Ali and Mua'wiyah was reduced to Mua'wiyah's calling for the vengeance of Caliph Uthman and Ali's refusal to undertake it until Mua'wiyah recognized his authority as caliph. Battles were fought in southern Iraq, culminating in the Battle of Siffin in the spring of 657.

This would be a titanic struggle involving 170,000 men on both sides. When it was apparent that Mua'wiyah's forces were wavering, pages of the Qur'an were placed on their lances and swords on the recommendation of Amr ibn al-A'as, causing Ali's army to stop fighting lest the sacred words of God be defiled. Mua'wiyah used this break in fighting to ask for arbitration, to which the Kharijites, who were allied with Ali, objected that their enemies were apostates and deserved nothing less than extermination. In addition, the Kharijites rightly smelled a ruse. Ali, however, rightly assessed that he had to negotiate as he would have to govern all Muslims in the end. The Kharijites refused, leading Ali to break away from the negotiations to suppress the Kharijites in the Battle of Nahrawain, in July.

Another way of looking at this civil war between Muslims over succession is that aside from seeking justice for the murder of Uthman, the Kharijites elevated the significance of Muslim divisions to the extent that your decision to follow Mua'wiyah or Ali determined the fate of your salvation—a fanatical view that took salvation out of the hands of God and tied it to the fate of two men. In addition it made a political dispute between Shiat Uthman (the Party of Uthman) and the Shiat Ali (Party of Ali) a cosmic and existential issue. The term "Shiite" is derived from the Arabic for "Party of Ali." The schism began during this civil war between Ali and his son Hussein versus Mua'wiyah and his son Yazid, starting in 656 and ending with the ambush of Ali's son and Prophet Muhammad's grandson Hussein in the plains of Karbala in 680.

ALI'S ASSASSINATION AND AFTERMATH

In 661, a brother of a Kharijite killed by Ali's forces in the Battle of Nahrawain in 657, named Ibn Muljam, murdered Ali in Kufa as he was praying in a mosque. Ali's assassin struck Ali with a poison-tipped sword. Another version of the story is that Ibn Muljam's betrothed, Qatam, who had lost her father and brother at Nahrawain, asked for Ali's life as her dowry. Ali survived the sword blow, but a few days later the poison set in and killed him. One Shiite version of events is that Ali gave instructions that his body be placed on a white camel and that the camel be left to roam—where it stopped was where Ali was to be buried. Ali's burial site evolved into the Imam Ali mosque, today centerpiece of the city of Najaf in Iraq. There is also a story that Ali's body was taken to northern Afghanistan and was buried in the famous Blue Mosque at Mazar-e-Sherif. However most Muslims, and particularly Shiite Muslims, believe he was buried in Najaf.

The story does not end there, for upon the death of Ali, Mua'wiyah would rise to be the prominent leader of the Muslim community, his only challenger being Ali's son Hussein. He declared Amr ibn al-A'as governor of Egypt, and Ibn al-A'as marched with six thousand mounted infantry to assert his own right and remove Ali's choice as successor, the assassin of Uthman, Muhammad ibn Abu Bakr. Many abandoned Muhammad ibn Abu Bakr, and he was finally killed resisting arrest by al-A'as's forces. Legend has it Muhammad ibn Abu Bakr was buried not in a white sheet of cloth but a donkey's carcass.[8]

HUSSEIN VERSUS MUA'WIYAH, AND MUA'WIYAH'S SON YAZID

Ali's older son, Hussein, would perform the *qisas* (beheading) of his father's murderer Ibn Muljam, and the matter ended there. However the matter of succession over the caliphate continued, as Mua'wiyah asserted his right to the caliphate, and Ali's younger son, Hussein, continued the challenge. Mua'wiya bought off Ali's older son Hassan and sent assassins to Mecca to murder Hussein. The power base of Hussein centered around Mecca and Medina, and upon Mua'wiyah's death his son Yazid declared himself caliph. The fight continued between Hussein (Ali's son and Muhammad's grandson from his mother Fatima) and Yazid (son of Mua'wiyah and grandson of Abu Sufyan). Yazid sent a message to Hussein asking him to come to Kufa to negotiate their differences under flag of truce. Hussein was ambushed in the plains of Karbala and murdered, his head severed and presented to Yazid. He had been was the Prophet Muhammad's grandson, and this outrage would lead to the schism in Islam. Karbala, in southern Iraq, is to Shiites as Golgotha (Calvary), the site of Christ's crucifixion, is to Christians. Yazid would become the unchallenged leader of the Muslims, and his caliphate would evolve into the Umayyad dynasty, which lasted from 680 to 750.

WHY DOES THIS HISTORY MATTER IN THE WAR
AGAINST MILITANT ISLAMISTS?

It is important to note that these events occurred in southern Iraq. These conflicts are called the Wars of the First *Fitna* (dissent, or division). There can be no more serious accusation among Muslims than that one is causing *fitna* among believers. These *fitna* wars were traumatic not only for their Muslim-on-Muslim fighting but because they exposed Muslims as fighting for earthly causes—political, tribal, regional, and factional—and not in the defense of Islam. Some Arab governments level the charge of *fitna* against al-Qaida. Critics of Militant Islamists accuse them of only succeeding in dividing the Muslim community through their declarations of apostasy, blurring the lines between Salafism and Militant Islamist Ideology, and sullying the reputation of Islam as a whole.

Blows to al-Qaida by the Muslim Brotherhood include:

- The 2005 elections in Egypt, which brought the Muslim Brotherhood, albeit as independents, into parliament
- The 2005 Amman hotel bombings, which led to public criticism of al-Qaida by the Muslim Brotherhood
- Tariq al-Hashimi entering the Iraqi political system with his Islamic Party, representing the interests of the Sunnis within the context of Iraq's government.

This has split the Muslim Brotherhood, as there is deep hostility toward the U.S. presence in Iraq, support for *muqawama* (resistance) and for the Muslim Brotherhood concept of *wasatiyah* (moderation), and recognition of the need for grassroots representation of the *Ahl-al-Sunnah* (formal term for Sunni Muslims). The trend has been to be critical of al-Hashimi, and some make the argument that no Muslim Brotherhood speaks for the global branches of the organization. This may be true; however, there is no question but that the Egyptian Muslim Brotherhood's taking a position on Iraq's Islamic Party would set the tone for its acceptability or rejection in the public sphere among Sunnis.

Three other blows to al-Qaida by the Muslim Brotherhood have been:

- The 2006 election of Hamas
- The Muslim Brotherhood and Islamists siding with the popular wave of adulation for Hezbollah's 2006 war with Israel, while Militant Islamists and al-Qaida still consider Hezbollah apostate Shiites
- Blogs and statements by al-Qaida that the TV network al-Jazeera is part of a Muslim Brotherhood conspiracy, giving it epithets like "al-Khanzeera" (the pig station).

The above examples have opened a wedge between Militant Islamists and Islamists, between violent versus merely politicized Muslims. Al-Qaida realizes that the Muslim Brotherhood enjoys more credibility as a contender for the leadership of the Muslim community within regions of interest to al-Qaida; its members, like Sheikh Yussuf al-Qaradawi, are considered in the region to be respected interlocutors and authorities on how to be a better Muslim. Al-Qaida craves this kind of popular appeal, but one is Islamist, the other Militant Islamist, with too many adversaries. The Muslim Brotherhood enjoys appeal because its members view themselves as part of society and seek through *dawa* (proselytizing and social programs) to change society gradually from the ground up. Al-Qaida views society as *jahiliya* and alien, sees itself as swimming in an ocean of apostasy, and holds that only violence can change the social condition. An Islamist will participate in a governing council or elections, using the concept of *wasatiyah* (moderation). Al-Qaida and Militant Islamists view elections and *wasatiyah* as drawing energy away from violent action, and working with the regime as an anathema. Perhaps one of the most surprising developments has been the Egyptian Muslim Brotherhood's adopting new slogans in preparation for the 2009 parliamentary elections, setting aside their infamous slogan "Islam Is the Solution" and adding "For combating corruption," "Struggle against *ghilu*" (a Quranic term meaning "excessiveness in matters of faith"), and "For the popular good."[9]

However, the United States must be under no illusions that the agenda of the Muslim Brotherhood includes limiting the rights of women, setting up a society based on its interpretation of Islam, and that different regional offices of the Muslim Brotherhood have been shaped by different internal forces. For example, the Syrian Muslim Brotherhood tends to be less accommodating than the Egyptian. Another challenge for the twenty-first century is the penetration of Iranian influence into the Jordanian and Egyptian Muslim Brotherhoods.[10] Iran has already fully drawn in the Sunni group Hamas (formerly the Palestinian Muslim Brotherhood) into its sphere of influence. Should it succeed in exerting influence over the Sunni Jordanian and Egyptian Muslim Brotherhoods, this would negatively change the political identity of these nations in new and unknown ways.

In Lebanon, conditions are ripe for groups inspired by al-Qaida to act as alternatives in addressing perceived or real Sunni vulnerabilities. That is why the weak Lebanese Council of Muftis needs to be bolstered. It is led by the top Sunni cleric of the republic, Muhammad Rasheed Qabani, who called in March 2008 for the reopening of the Lebanese Parliament and the election of a president.[11] These statements by a cluster of clergy are anathema to al-Qaida. The perceived victory of the Lebanese Shiite group Hezbollah against the Israeli Defense Forces in 2006 added pressure on al-Qaida and Sunni Militant Islamist groups to make their presence felt along Israel's border. Sunni Militant Islamists must share with Hezbollah the mantle of avenger of Palestinian victimization. Within these pressures, Hezbollah and Hamas wish to distance al-Qaida from the Palestinian cause and will work to undermine, overtly and covertly, al-Qaida affiliates in Gaza as well as Lebanon.

These are the nuances within the Islamist movement that we must be cognizant of, just as there are schisms and nuances among our real adversary, the Militant Islamists. We need to know our adversaries in such nuanced detail in order to make effective military and political decisions.

seven

Islamic Government

A Highly Debatable Concept among Muslims

Democracy can shield the Islamic community from autocrats.

TUNISIAN ISLAMIST RACHID GHANNOUCHI

As previously mentioned, when Prophet Muhammad died in 632, he did not clearly designate a successor or leave guidance on how Muslims were to govern themselves. A central problem of the Middle East is an attempt to find a solution to the problem of re-creating an Islamic government created fourteen centuries ago. Muhammad's governorship of Medina and then Arabia represented the only time in which a city-state confederacy on the Arabian Peninsula was governed by a single man who was divinely inspired. Muhammad, through divine revelation, applied religious orthodoxy to the city-state of Medina. Upon his death, the link to the divine was cut and his followers debated what form Islamic society and governance would take, with little or no guidance from the Qur'an or the Prophet's *hadith*. Segments of Muslim society fail to realize that Islamic governance in the truest sense of the word died with Prophet Muhammad in 632, and that all alleged experiments with Islamic government—including the caliphate, the Iranian model of a supreme jurisprudent, or the abysmal model of the Taliban—are mere interpretations of what subsections of Muslims consider the utopian ideal of Prophet Muhammad's society. The Qur'an prescribes government by consultation (chapter 42, verse 38). However, the mechanism by which this consultation is exercised is left entirely to Muslims. There is an entire chapter (42) of the Qur'an entitled *al-Shura* (consultation) referring to God's command to conduct affairs in consultation with others.

As we have seen, companion of Prophet Muhammad, Omar ibn al-Khattab, led the debate as to the form of what a Muslim government should be, and after vigorous debate, cajoling, and threats of tribalism, settled on the caliphate of Abu Bakr. Keeping the Muslim society intact after Muhammad's death was what concerned Omar. What the debates over governance revealed was a realistic struggle to incorporate the morals of Islam with the reality of brutal tribal politics of seventh-century Arabia. Muhammad's society in Medina was one that cannot possibly be re-created today. The question and is subject to interpretations even from the likes of bin Laden, Zawahiri, and one of their founding ideologues, Sayyid Qutb (1906–1966). Qutb argued that sovereignty belongs to God alone and that legislatures, parliaments, and democracy are a means of robbing the divine from his sovereignty. He was really arguing for social chaos. The basic fact is that once in power, Militant Islamists will introduce the human element of interpreting God's laws. That will place the so-called Qutbist issues of God's sovereignty back into the hands of a person or persons who will render judgment and impose a form of Islam that may not be conducive to the welfare of all Muslims. Qutbist political theory can be deconstructed using the simple Quranic logic that while sovereignty belongs to God, it has been delegated in the form of human agency. In essence, the Qur'an is appealing to the Western notion of sovereignty in principle (de jure) and sovereignty in fact (de facto). De facto sovereignty is inescapable, whether in a democracy or so-called caliphate.

The reason for the failure of Islamist politics is simple. To impose an Islamic state in the twenty-first century begs the questions: Whose Islam will reign supreme? Whose Islam will be imposed upon other Muslims? The Taliban failed because their Deobandi-Wahhabi school of Islam was not inclusive of all Muslims within Afghan society. In Algeria, the Islamic Salvation Front failed because its Salafi-Hanbali militant ideology excluded the Maliki Sunni and Sufi traditions of Algeria. In Egypt, when President Sadat amended the constitution to make Islam the source of legislation for the country, a conflict arose in the courts over whose interpretation of Islam to use in rulings. The majority of Muslims do not want the restrictive government imposed by the Taliban or to have one Islamic discipline forced upon them. Within Islam's 1.5 billion followers, the different disciplines include Shiite-Akhbari, Shiite-Usuli, Sunni-Maliki, Sunni-Hanafi, Sunni-Hanbali, Sufi-Qadari, and Sufi-Naqshabandi—and the list goes on. The United States need not shy away from declaring the enemy an Islamist political actor who imposes his brand of Islam on Muslim and non-Muslim alike through violence as a Militant Islamist.

Fouad Ajami, in his *A Foreigner's Gift,* details his discussions with Shiite cleric Sheikh Humam Hamoudi, of the Supreme Council for Islamic Revolution in Iraq. Hamoudi says: "A turbaned man should not be head of state, for religion would then be made to bear the burden of executive decisions." This appears to be the view of Grand Ayatollah al-Sistani, and on more than one occasion Shiite Iraqi clerical leaders have declared that they do not want a government on the model of Iran's Islamic Republic.[1]

The U.S. military must immerse itself in the language of the adversary. Seven years have passed since the national tragedy of September 11, and our nation in that time has identified ideology as the center of gravity for Islamist militant movements. On January 10, 2007, President Bush called Iraq "the decisive ideological struggle of our time."[2] Yet there is no single document or definition that outlines with precision the nature of, and what is to be done about, the threat of Militant Islamist Ideology. It is an ideology that demonizes not only non-Muslims but also Muslims who do not share in its orthodoxy or worldview. The United States could benefit from instruments like those that defined the Cold War. Documents such as "NSC 68," drafted by Paul Nitze, or the late George Kennan's "Long Telegram" defined the nature of the Soviet ideological threat. Although ideologically different, the modalities that helped mobilize America's national power during the early years of the Cold War could serve as well against Militant Islamist movements. The United States is desperately in need of a clearly enunciated description of the threats posed by Militant Islamist Ideology. We are in need of moral and linguistic clarity. Free democracies and stable nation-states should not be intimidated by the language, heinous actions, and personalities of Militant Islamists. Instead, we should strive to deconstruct this ideology and counter it using the very religion they have sought to pervert. Militant Islamist methodology and goals are a failure. The examples of this failure abound:

■   The fall of the Taliban emirate within weeks of the launch of Operation Enduring Freedom.

■   The short-lived experiment in Somalia with the Council of Islamic Court Group, lasting under a year in 2006, snuffed out by Somalis with the aid of African neighbors.

- Sudan's experimentation with Islamist politics in the early nineties, which has led to inter-Islamic violence between the Arab-Sudanese in the north and African-Darfurians in the west.
- The failure of Algeria's Islamist politics, which led the army to concern itself with the changing character of Islam in the country.
- Murder and threats of Muslim intellectuals, silencing innovation, scholarship and inquiry.
- Al-Qaida naming the United States, the West, multinational corporations, Arab regimes, and the Shiites as enemies. (They have so many adversaries they cannot realistically build a grassroots presence of the caliber of Hamas or Hezbollah.)
- The entry of Mahfouz Nahnah of the Algerian Islamic Salvation Front into an agreement with the Algerian regime.
- The entry of Iraq's Sunni Hizb Islami Party into Iraq's provisional government, working with the coalition to represent Iraqi Sunnis.

eight

The 1925 Caliphate Debates

T he abolishment of the caliphate by Kemal Ataturk needs to be discussed with some precision. Ataturk deposed and exiled the last Ottoman sultan, Mehmet VI, in 1922, declared the Turkish Republic in 1923, and in 1924 constitutionally abolished the Ottoman sultanate and caliphate. Since then, Islamist militants have made the reestablishment of this form of governance a significant part of their totalitarian platform. Therefore, it is important to revive Islamic counterargument on the very nature of the caliphate as a means of challenging those who wish to impose a single form of Islam upon a diverse Islamic community, as well as to isolate the international community, as was seen by the Taliban in Afghanistan, the Council of Islamic Courts in Somalia, and other failed experiments of Islamist radicals attempting to establish an emirate or caliphate. This chapter will introduce readers to the little-known debate about the book *al-Islam wa Usul al-Hukm* (Islam and the Fundamentals of Government), published in 1925 by the Egyptian Sheikh Ali Abdul-Razak (1887–1966) and considered to be the finest example of Islamizing secularism. Abdul-Razak was ostracized for his views by Egypt's Higher Ulema Council. Sadly, in the twenty-first century writing such a book would earn death threats and accusations of apostasy.

With the abolishment of the caliphate Muslim intellectuals and leading theological scholars began a debate as to the origins and essence of this political institution, beyond the inviolable characteristics of government in an Islamic society: *Adalah* (justice), *Musawah* (equity), and *Shura* (consultation). Razak argued that the Qur'an and *sunnah* (Prophet's sayings and deeds) declare that Islam is not both a state and religion but a religion first and foremost, a religion that provides a moral philosophical rudder to the state. He stated that nowhere in the Qur'an or the Prophet's sayings is a form of government ordained; he held that the caliphate is not ordained in Islam but is a political tradition, expedientially created after the death of Prophet Muhammad in 632. Razak, an Islamic judge, argued that Prophet Muhammad's main mission as ordained in the Qur'an was to be a messenger, that his message was a religious and not a political one.

Razak's defense of his book reveals volumes about what ails constructive discourse in Islam today. Razak argued that he did not dispute the foundations of Islam—not its *ibadat* (orthodoxy), not its fundamental creed of the centrality and oneness of God, not the affirmation that Muhammad is the Messenger of God. His disagreement was simply over the role of Islam in government. Razak classified his clerical colleagues into two groups. The first were those who saw Islam and the practices of Islamic law as emulating the *salaf al-saliheen* (pious founders). The second group took a holistic approach to Islam, an overarching view of its law, history, philosophy, and heritage. This second group, of which Razak was part, used terms like *tawasul* (molding Islamic law to fit the times and circumstances) and *maslahah* (the public good). They employed analytical methods of "synthesis" and "anti-synthesis" to bring Islam into modernity. It is vital to reexplore today Razak's work and the debates that followed, to begin to dispute the central notion of Islamist militants that a caliphate is mandatory, for religious reasons, in Islamic polity.

Among those who opposed Razak in print was Sheikh Rashid Rida (1865–1935), whose *al-Khilafa wal Imamah al-Uzmah* (The Caliphate and the Great Imamate) called for the abrogation of the Ottoman caliphate and its replacement with an Arab monarch. Sheikh Muhammad al-Khidr Hussein (1875–1957) also responded to Razak, with *Naqd al-Kitab al-Islam wa Usul al-Hukm* (A Refutation of Islam and the Essence of Governance), in 1926, a point-by-point refutation of Razak's work. Finally, Sheikh Muhammad al-Mutai (1854–1935) came out with another detailed rebuttal, *Haqiqah al-Islam wa Usul al-Hukm* (The Truth of Islam and the Essence of Governance). Those who attacked Razak were not as scholarly as he; their central thesis was the pseudo-intellectual view that if you deny the Islamic state, you are a secularist. For them there was no middle ground and no such thing as a secular state with an Islamic character.

Among the external political pressures that weighed against Razak when he published *al-Islam wa Usul al-Hukm* was the fact that Egypt was just then experimenting with a constitutional monarchy, the first in the Arab world. Egypt's quasi-independence had been granted in 1922, when the country was declared a monarchy, and Sultan Ahmed Fouad had become King Fouad I of Egypt and the Sudan. Three years later, Egypt would have three major political parties: the Wafd (or delegation), the Union Party (a pro-monarchist group), and the Free Constitutionalists, a subsidiary of the Union Party. The emotionalism of the abolition of the caliphate and initial momentum in finding a replacement blinded many to the important discussion on the essence and origins of the political tradition of the caliphate. Other external pressures included the application of carving up the mod ern Middle East from the remnants of the Ottoman Empire, with the enforcement of the Treaty of San Remo (1920). This saw the insertion into Syria of French forces to enforce France's assertion of its mandate. These tensions inflamed passions in the Middle East, where there was optimism about a chance for Arab nationalism and the establishment of an independent Arab state.

THE 1925 PAN-ISLAMIC CONFERENCE ON THE CALIPHATE

The abolishment of the political institution of the caliphate led several leaders to vie for the title. They included King Fouad of Egypt, Sherief Hussein ibn Ali of Mecca, and the deposed Ottoman sultan, Mehmed VI, who publicly insisted that his titles were still in force despite his exile. Adding to this complexity was the 1925 takeover of Mecca and Medina by the Wahhabi forces of Abdul-Aziz ibn Saud. Many questions arose not only on the essence of the caliphate and whether it was political tradition or ordained in the faith, but if one believes in the necessity of the caliphate, who was to assume the title?

Hussein ibn Ali was a Hashemite, a descendent of Prophet Muhammad, an Arab, whose sons Abdullah and Faisal led the Arab Revolt and became kings of Transjordan and Iraq, respectively. As soon as he learned of Kemal Ataturk's abolishing the Ottoman caliphate, Hussein ibn Ali declared himself the new caliph. This move was opposed by King Fouad I of Egypt, who saw in the caliphate a chance to not only speak on behalf of the wider Muslim world but to utilize pan-Islamism to regain additional powers within the framework of his constitutional monarchy. In 1925, King Abdul-Aziz ibn Saud's forces, led by his son Faisal (who would the third king of Saudi Arabia), defeated the Hashemite forces and took over the Hijaz region, including Mecca and Medina. Hussein ibn Ali fled to Transjordan, and in 1926 Ibn Saud declared himself king of Hijaz and the sultan of Nejd (the region of central Arabia).

These complex issues, affecting the evolution of what would be the modern Arab states of Iraq, Jordan, and Saudi Arabia, would necessitate a pan-Islamic conference, called and led by King Fouad of Egypt. His clerics produced the journal *al-Khilafa al-Islamiyah* (the Islamic caliphate), which called for one of the Arab rulers to assume the title. Fouad calculated that by providing the momentum for the meeting he could shape and control events and so posture himself for the title of caliph. Within Egypt, the pro-constitutionalist Wafd Party was elected into power and named a prime minister in March 1925. This political party would be a check against the Egyptian monarchy. It is important to gain an appreciation for these external and internal nuances to understand why Razak knew his book would be condemned, prefacing his book with an affirmation of his belief in God before attacking fourteen centuries of Islamic political tradition embodied in the person of the caliph.

WHO WAS SHEIKH ALI ABDUL-RAZAK?

Abdul-Razak was born in al-Minia, a Nile Delta town, in 1887 in a privileged family. He entered the track for religious studies early, memorizing the entire Qur'an in childhood. Memorization of the holy text was a precursor for being able to analyze it and engage in a lifetime of *tafsir* (Quranic analysis and interpretation). Razak, like many of his colleagues about to enter seminary, memorized the Qur'an also as a means of perfecting oratory in the highly prized Arabic style of the Qur'an, considered the Arabic language in its most pristine form. At al-Azhar University, Islam's premier Sunni school of learning, his initial senior clerical mentors at al-Azhar were Sheikh Abu Khatwah, Sheikh Abu Alyan, and the reformist Grand Mufti Muhammad Abdu (1849–1905), who later rose to become Grand Mufti of Cairo until his death. Abdu and his disciples pondered the question of an Islamic state and the Western notions of theocracy, and they came to the conclusion that an Islamic state is one in which the moral philosophy of Islam is grafted upon institutions and mechanisms of governance chosen by Muslims. God's only concern, they felt, arose where the teachings of the Qur'an and the *sunnah* center upon justice, consultation, and making provision for the disadvantaged.

Razak was not immune from Egyptian politics as a seminarian; he first joined the pro-monarchist Union Party before becoming active in Egypt's Free Constitutionalist Party. In 1908 he elected to take a few classes to supplement his religious education at what would evolve into Cairo University; there he read Western literature and studied Western civilization. Upon graduating from al-Azhar University in 1912, he proceeded on a grant to study economic theory at Oxford University, but he did not complete a degree there, departing England in 1915 to accept a position as a minor judge in an Islamic court. For a decade he served as an Islamic judge, rising to become chief judge of the Mansura Islamic Court Circuit when he published *al-Islam wa Usul al-Hukm,* his counter-caliphate book. He also was a member of the Higher Ulema (Clerical) Council at al-Azhar, making him an established member of Egypt's clerical class. In late 1925, as a result of his book he was removed from the Higher Ulema Council and exiled. He became an active spokesman in London and North Africa for the Free Constitutionalist Party, returning to Egypt in 1945, when his brother became Grand Mufti of al-Azhar. In 1948, Razak served as Minister of Awqaf (Religious Endowments) for one year, under Prime Minister Abdel-Hadi Pasha. Razak authored four books, including his controversial *al-Islam wa Usul al-Hukm,* and was close to such reformers as the education minister, author, and constitutionalist Doctor Taha Hussein. Razak died in September 1966.

INSIDE RAZAK'S WORK: THE CALIPHATE AS POLITICAL TRADITION, NOT ISLAMIC ORTHODOXY

The central thesis of Razak is that Islam is a religion and not a state; it is a spiritual message, with no relation to government or politics. The Prophet Muhammad did not initially seek to establish a state or lead a form of governance but was the Messenger of God. As such, Prophet Muhammad's main function, as narrated in many sections of the Qur'an, was an evangelical one. Had the Prophet not been persecuted in Mecca, it is likely he would have remained there preaching. It was only his persecution that opened an opportunity for him to flee to Yathrib, a city-state that had endured decades of civil and tribal strife that Muhammad was seen able to resolve. He did so skillfully and thus was asked to remain in Yathrib as its leader; the city in his lifetime would be renamed Medinat al-Nabi (City of the Prophet), later shortened to Medina. Moral philosophy and consultation are the only themes in the Qur'an that suggest any political guidance; there is no opinion either in the Qur'an or wider *sunnah* on what type of government system Muslims should pursue. Instead Muslims are left to derive and evolve governments that fit their circumstances and heritage with an eye toward justice and morality, not regressing into the problems, oligarchy, or tribalism of pre-Islamic Arabia. Those who insist on calling upon the caliphate as the only means of governance are rendering an opinion based on *taqlid* (tradition) and not *ibadat* (orthodoxy).[1]

Razak then delves into the question of Prophet Muhammad's central mission from God: was it as messenger (Prophecy) or governor? If both, which role took precedence, which role drove all other roles Prophet Muhammad took in his twenty-three years of prophethood? These questions then beg other questions and imply theories. The Qur'an is laced with the sense that Muhammad was commanded by God to be *hafeezan* (preserver of the message of God), *wakeelan* (keeper of God's message), and *khabara* (bringer of God's message). Surat Qaf, verse 45, best articulates God's instructions to Muhammad: "We know best what they say; and thou art not one to overawe them by force. So admonish with the Qur'an such as fear My Warning!" One theory postulated by Razak was that the Prophet Muhammad's governance cannot be duplicated, as he was influenced directly by the divine. Therefore, Islamic government as practiced by the Prophet can never be re-created; all governance after it is an interpretation of so-called Islamic government. In addition, Razak postulated that the divinely inspired governance of Prophet Muhammad superseded the earthly governance of kings, sultans, potentates, and even caliphs—this because Prophet Muhammad's central objective of governance lay primarily in the spiritual aspects of human moral development. Therefore, according to Razak, its scope is wider than the relation between the governor and the governed, and Muhammad's mandate exceeds those of kings or rulers. Muhammad's mandate, as a prophet, stretches into the very soul of humankind.

Those critical of Abdul-Rakaz quote incessantly from verses in the Qur'an that, in modern English translation, read, "He who does not govern according to Islamic law is in a state of apostasy." (In Arabic, *"Wa mal lam yahkum bima anzal allaahu ulaaika fa humul kaafiroon,"* Qur'an, chapter al-Maida, verse 44). Variations of this verse appear several times in the Qur'an. However, when deconstructing the verse linguistically, *hukm* does mean "govern" and *hukumah* means "government" in current Arabic, but in seventh-century Arabic *hukm* meant to adjudicate, and the exegesis of this verse has much to do with incidences wherein Muhammad served as adjudicator and resisted attempts to influence the outcome of arbitration by one party or another. Muhammad served as adjudicator to non-Muslims, like the Jews, that were part of his Compact of Medina. In addition, *"anzal allaahu"* does not mean "according to Islamic law" but "according to God's commands." So the correct translation is: "He who does not adjudicate according to God's commands is in a state of apostasy." This verse has nothing to do with governance, but Militant Islamists and Islamists seize upon these verses exclusively, in order to justify a system of Islamic government.

In madrassas (Islamic schools) in the Muslim world, Arabic is taught as an archaic and revered language, with a focus on pronunciation to aid in rote memorization. As the majority of Muslims in the world are not Arabs, this means that students must learn an unfamiliar and complex grammar. Hence, in many countries, like Pakistan, Indonesia, and Afghanistan, little attention is given to exploring the actual implications and applications of Prophet Muhammad's words or to the differences in interpretation that affect translation. Further, even native speakers of Arabic are fluent in dialects that vary from seventh-century "classical" Arabic and do not easily read or comprehend older texts, which possess specialized, often archaic vocabulary, idioms, and references. While native speakers may memorize portions, or even all, of the Qur'an, interpretation and *hadith* scholarship require guidance and interpretive skills. For these, students must rely on instructors, whose expertise and ideological orientation vary.

All other slogans created after the death of Prophet Muhammad, such as *Amir al-Mumineen* (Commander of the Faithful), Shadow of God on Earth, and in Iran, *Velayat al-Faqih* (Supreme Jurisprudent), are attempts to associate with the Prophet Muhammad, when in essence there can be no succession to the Prophet of God in Islamic belief. This pattern began soon after the death of Prophet Muhammad, when his companion Abu Bakr became first caliph and took the title *khalifat al-nabi* (Successor to the Prophet); then came Omar ibn al-Khattab, who could not be called *khalifat Abu Bakr* (successor to Abu Bakr) and so assumed the title *amir al-mumineen,* Commander of the Faithful; then came Uthman, from the Abu Sufyan line (early persecutors of Muhammad). Although an early Muslim and husband of Muhammad's daughters, he felt that he needed a title to firm his political credibility and took "Shadow of God on Earth." These titles would grow in pomposity, depending on the security or insecurity of the reigning caliph.

Islam, like Christianity, started as a message; it only later evolved into a state structure, although Muhammad was technically ruler of the city-state of Medina. Muslims attempt to interpret Prophet Muhammad's total life as including his governance of Medina to organize society, raising the question of whether Medina was an Islamic state or social order. The time lines of the evolution of Christian and Islamic states differ, for the concept of an Islamic state occurred in Muhammad's lifetime, but in the Islamic case it is still subject to attempts to understand his legacy and incorporate it into the state. The problem with Islamists is that for them the attainment of a state is the ultimate objective; the state's central mission is not calling people to Islam as a means of moral and spiritual sustenance. After the death of Muhammad in 632, society assumed an Islamic character, in contrast to today, when Islamic doctrine and character are imposed upon states.

Classifying a state as having an Islamic character, versus Islam as the state religion, implies a more general, gradual, and wider means of giving people (Muslim and non-Muslim) not only the choice of faith but the choice of the variety of Islam they intend to observe. In essence, the Militant Islamists sacrifice spirituality for governance and material concerns. In Islam the concept of *niyah* (intent) is extremely important. Serious thinkers of Islamic theosophy always assess an action from its intention; only God, not bin Laden, knows what lies in the heart or soul of a person. This is also why the label of *kafir* (apostate) was never used against Razak by the sixty-two clerics sitting in judgment on his book. Militant Islamists use of *takfir* (condemnation of Muslims as apostates and non-Muslims as infidels) has been so frequent that it has diluted the Islamic view that only God can judge the intent and actions of his creations.

An intellectual supporter of Razak was Sheikh Muhammad al-Khidr Hussein, who was born in Tunisia in 1876 and attained the highest level of Islamic education from Zaytuna University, in Tunisia, and at al-Azhar University, in Egypt. He mixed Islam with a high sense of Arab nationalism; while preaching in Syria he was imprisoned by the Turkish governor, Djemal Pasha. Al-Khidr defended Razak with the argument the caliphate was evolving into an Islamic form of papacy and that an Islamist state is a constitutionalist state. He saw the corrupting influence that obsession with governance had on the main mission of clerics, which properly was tending to the spiritual concerns of the community. Al-Khidr was no friend of westernization but saw the concept of Islamic secularization as a means of preserving the integrity of the clergy from the complexity and immorality of governing a state. (Although he did not phrase it like this, al-Khidr was concerned with the corrupting influences of realpolitik, the realism required in the undertaking of Hobbesian decisions in governing a state.)

When closely studying the most important and central clerical source for Islamist militants, Taqi-al-Din ibn Taymiyyah (1263–1327), one finds that even he admitted that the governance—the imamate or caliphate—is not among Islam's pillars or among the foundations of *iman* (piety) or the pillars of *ihsan* (moral improvements).[2] Islamist militants read Ibn Taymiyyah's opinions narrowly and suppress sentences that do not fit their worldview. Sheikh al-Khidr's central thesis is that the *khilafa* (caliphate) is not among the types of *aqaid* (orthodoxy) but is instead a practical political expedient created by mankind and not the divine. The cleric and philosopher al-Ghazali (450–505) said that there is no place for *takfir* (declaring a Muslim an apostate), as even this action is an opinion, and even a wrong opinion must be debated. Abdul-Razak in his own defense argued that debates over the imamate, caliphate, and the nature of the Islamic state do not cross the boundary of *inkar* (denial of Islam's basic creeds), such as the denial of God or the mission of Prophet Muhammad as the Messenger of God. Therefore, he insisted, his opinions on the caliphate should be subjected to honest and rigorous debate without condemnation or the application of labels.

WHY KING FOUAD OF EGYPT COVETED THE TITLE OF CALIPH

Why Egypt's King Fouad I wanted to be named the new caliph of all Muslims gets at some of the historical issues involved. Aside from prestige, assuming the title of caliph would give King Fouad predominance in matters of religion, enabling him to control the different factions of Islam and balance Islamic-Christian relations in Egypt, and it would provide him a counterweight against the popularity of his arch nemesis the Egyptian nationalist Saad Zaghlul.

After World War I, Egypt was technically under Ottoman suzerainty yet had actually been controlled by the British since 1882. After the war it was determined to make Egypt independent but still a protectorate of Britain; this was achieved when Fouad I, a descendant of the Muhammad Ali dynasty that had ruled Egypt since 1803, was declared king of an independent Egypt in 1922. He was thus a British creation. In 1923 a constitutional monarchy was established that required King Fouad to balance a hostile parliament filled with nationalists, the clerical establishment in the great Islamic university of al-Azhar, and the Egyptian army. These four spheres were the only organized entities that posed a challenge to Fouad's rule.

King Fouad was the first Egyptian ruler to give the rector of al-Azhar ministerial status. He did this to encourage efforts to make him caliph and give him control over assignment and leadership of the religious institution. When the leader of al-Azhar became a member of the king's cabinet his school was no longer an independent body but an organ of government. This became apparent when King Fouad used mobs from al-Azhar to counter nationalist and pro-Zaghlul riots in Cairo.

The Caliphate Conference did not materialize in 1924, but it would spark an Islamic judge and lecturer at al-Azhar to write a book that would send shock waves through the debate over the role of religion in politics. It was then that

Sheikh Ali Abdul-Razak wrote *Al-Islam wa Usu al-Hukm* (Islam and the Basis of Rule). Abdul-Razak's views came at a time when the tide was pushing for moving the caliphate to Cairo and the aftereffects of World War I on the Middle East were spreading ideas in the Muslim street that colonialism was another iteration of the Crusades. (Usama bin Laden, ironically, has reinvented these concepts, railing against secularism and globalization as Crusader ideas.)

Another Islamic modernist was the Grand Mufti of Cairo, Muhammad Abduh, who, with Sheikh Khalid Muhammad Khalid, argued that clerical fatwas need to concentrate on the industrial age and address such issues as modern finance, the concept of life insurance, and the rapid pace of ideas coming from the West, like Darwinism, secularism, and modern science. Aside from being a senior religious cleric, Abduh led the drive to reform Egypt's education system, arguing for the need for more modern science, mathematics, and rational philosophy, balanced with Islamic studies. He along with Abdul-Razak were attacked by the clerical establishment of al-Azhar and suppressed. One can only dream of how Egypt, if not the Arab world, would look today if they had been allowed to pursue this line of debate. The Islamic center of al-Azhar was split into three camps by these debates and arguments: *Mujaddidoon* (Renewers), led by Abduh; *Taqlidoon* (Traditionalists/fundamentalists), the main al-Azhar establishment; and selective *Mujadiddoon,* led by Rashid Rida and adopted by Islamists and Militant Islamists.

This debate also renewed the call to open the gates of *ijtihaad* (analytical reasoning), an Islamic concept used at the time of Prophet Muhammad but done away with in the eleventh century in Sunni Islam. Rashid Rida and Muhammad Abduh had in common a charismatic and controversial cleric who arrived in Cairo in 1890 and addressed the issue of Islam needing *ijtihaad* to survive; he also renewed the doctrines of Ibn Taymiyyah and the Kharijites to declare all Muslim leaders who enabled the colonization of Muslim lands as apostates. The man was Sheikh Jamal al-Din al-Afghani, a fascinating figure, little understood in the West. Originally al-Afghani was Persian; he had learned as much as he could from Shiite centers of learning and then decided to travel and learn from Sunni traditions. This led him to the Sunni center of al-Azhar University, in Cairo, where he rose from student to one of the more popular lecturers on Islamic jurisprudence. His emphasis on the need to renew analytical reasoning in Islam stimulated clerics like Muhammad Abduh. Applying the label of apostasy on Muslims enabling the colonization of Islamic lands earned him the admiration of Rashid Rida and Hassan al-Banna, who form the basis of Jihadist rhetoric today.

Rashid Rida, representing the Islamists, and a future inspiration to Militant Islamists, used the label of apostasy to silence critical and vocal elements of the Islamic modernists. For instance, he wrote that the Wafd Party had no Islamic agenda and that the 1923 Egyptian constitution had not been written in an Islamic character. Rashid Rida, using his magazine *al-Manar* and pamphlets, was able to give a voice to al-Azhar clerics like Sheikh al-Jaweesh, who is often quoted because he argued that there was no nationalism in Islam and that Arabist movements in Egypt should be rejected. Al-Jaweesh went on to preach that Islam was under assault with the carving up of Muslim lands by European powers—the Italians colonizing and killing Libyans, the French fighting and killing Muslims in Morocco. He gave listeners, as early as 1920, an "Islam under siege!" mentality. This rhetoric spawned organizations ranging from Jamiat al-Islami (the Islamic Group) in 1912 to the Young Muslim Men's Association in 1927, and finally the Muslim Brotherhood in 1928. Reading Egyptian newspapers of the era shows that the debate did not look back at Islamic texts to ascertain the requirement for the caliphate but assumed the need for a caliph to unite all Muslims coming under assault, in many ways a reemergence of the title "Defender of the Faithful." While the clerics of al-Azhar in Egypt championed King Fouad I, clerics at al-Aqsa in Palestine claimed the caliphate should go to Hussein Bin Ali (Sherief of Mecca whose sons Faisal and Abdullah had led the Arab Revolt). Other contenders included the king of Afghanistan and a delegation representing the Iranian *Hawza* (Shiite clerical hierarchy). These competing interests and constituencies surfaced when the Caliphate Conference convened in Cairo in May 1926. It did not agree on a successor to the Ottoman sultan.

RECONCILING ISLAM AND THE STATE

Islam and the state need to be reconciled, using enlightenment and education to develop a political system that takes the best moral aspects and constructive interpretations of Islam. The system also must emphasize and be inclusive of the expression of all Islamic beliefs, and it must be stated in a constitution that a republic or a state is to have an Islamic character. The Taliban attempted to impose a version of Islam that was a Deobandi and Wahhabi mixture and ended up oppressing other Muslims. In Somalia, the Council of Islamic Courts lost power within less than a year because of lack of grassroots support.

A more subtle problem of reconciling Islam and the state is reflected in chapter 1, article 2 of the Egyptian constitution: "The principal source of legislation is

Sharia [Islamic law]"; the post-Baathist Iraqi constitution contains a similar construct. Maybe they should have be rewritten as: "The Islamic character of Egypt [or Iraq] is central to the state." This allows for more legal room; for declaring Islam or sharia the source of law begs the question of whose Islam and which interpretation of sharia. If you impose one form of Islam, Sunni over Shiite, you will have civil war. In a Sunni-dominant nation, if you impose one Sunni *madhab* or sects like Wahhabism in a predominately North African Sunni Maliki society, you will have civil war. In addition, many Arabs on the street blur the difference between *sharia* and *fiqh* (Islamic jurisprudence). *Fiqh* is jurisprudence, derived from the sharia and subject to speculation, interpretation, and evolution over time. Unlike sharia, *fiqh* can be debated and amended. This view, if popularized, could accommodate the Muslim and the Islamist and isolate the Militant Islamist who is uncompromising in his narrow interpretations of Islam.

Also, the question of whose Islam will be imposed does not address other religious minorities residing in the Middle East or tribal or ethnic differences. Central to the preservation of an Islamic state are representative governance, democracy, and the institutions of democratic governance. Bin Laden and other Islamist militants who seek to impose only one form of Islam will in the end destroy the faith, causing people to become disgusted with the very faith they claim to preserve; it is for Muslims to confront this doctrine of hatred that emphasizes destructive over constructive interpretations of Islam. It is for Muslims to challenge Jihadist clerics ideologically and support clerics willing to show how Jihadists, in their obsession over creating an Islamic state as an end, sacrifice the *maqasid al-shariah* (the very essence of Islamic law). This essence embraces five objectives: the protection of life, of religion (can be interpreted as freedom of religious practice), of property, of offspring (children), and of mind.[3] Bin Laden dispenses with these essences of Islamic law as well as such important practices as *tafsir* (Quranic exegesis), *asbab al-nuzul* (circumstances of Quranic revelation), and knowledge and authenticity of the *hadith* to craft a pseudo-intellectual message politicized in nature and corrosive to Islam.

There are those who argue that bin Laden's interpretation of Islam is just as valid as another Muslim's, because there is no central theological authority in Sunni Islam. It is important to be reminded of the important aspects of interpreting and applying Islamic law that al-Qaida ignores; it is this simplistic, fragmented, and ignorant methodology that makes Militant Islamist Ideology pseudo-intellectual.

Militant Islamists force their Muslim victims into a narrow reading of Islam, passing off opinions like those of Sayed Qutb as orthodoxy. Abdul-Hakim Murad, in his 1995 work, aptly describes a growing problem in the study of Islamic law and its application in Western democracies.[4] Murad comments that it "is common now to see activists prowling the mosques, criticizing other worshippers for what they believe to be defects in their worship, even when their victims are following the verdicts of some of the leading Imam's *fiqh*," He also points out that in the West, where individuals are taught to think for themselves and to challenge authority, it can be difficult for young Muslim activists to admit that they might not know something about their religion. This is so despite the cautions of such luminaries as Imam Malik, who founded the Maliki School of Sunni Islam, who, when asked forty questions about *fiqh,* admitted that he did not know the answers to thirty-six and then sought to research and ponder them.

To begin to understand the complexity of setting up sharia as the law of the land is the issue of its sources. They include the Qur'an and various commentaries, the *hadiths* (of which there are thousands, of varying quality and authenticity), *ijmaa* (which is the consensus of the Islamic scholars), and finally *qiyas,* or analytic reasoning, as well as precedence. Militant Islamists dismiss *ijmaa* and *qiyas,* though they know well that sharia is subject to interpretation. An added complexity is that sharia divides all actions into five categories:

- *Fard* (obligatory actions)
- *Mandub* (recommended but optional actions)
- *Mubah* (neutral or no opinion)
- *Makruh* (actions allowed but frowned upon)
- *Haram* (forbidden).

Examples include prayers (obligatory) and maintaining a beard (recommended but optional). Actions allowed but frowned upon include divorce, celibacy, and polygamy; forbidden actions include eating pork, alcohol consumption, theft, and murder. These details are lost in Militant Islamist discourse.

The issue of reconciling the separation of Islam and the state represents a crucial ideological debate in Islam today. Publicizing this key issue can undermine Militant Islamist goals and objectives and those who commit terror in the name of Islam to set up an unacceptable, intolerant, and totalitarian state in the Muslim world. It represents the counterargument to Militant Islamist movements, which yearn for the establishment of the caliphate in their own image, an image the world had to endure with the Taliban. We often talk of "Jihadist ideology," as compared to moderate Islamic teachings; this is a relative term that must be quantified by examples from the Qur'an, *hadith,* and Islamic history. As we have seen, the Qur'an and the Prophet's recorded sayings have little clear guidance on governance; what Muslims yearn for in a government based on the examples of Islamic history bears no resemblance to what al-Qaida proposes. In correct and constructive Islamic schools, Muslim children are taught the chivalric and compassionate aspects of Prophet Muhammad and the first four caliphs (Abu Bakr, Omar, Uthman, and Ali). The fact that when Omar conquered Jerusalem he purposely did not pray at the Dome of the Rock (which was then a church), because he knew it would be torn down and converted to a mosque, is held up for admiration. Another story admiringly told is how Omar would wander the streets of Medina at night to gain the measure of his people and sense their socio-political issues at the street level.

Of course, these men made political mistakes and also contradictions in the Qur'an to deal with crises. Such a case was the use by Ali (the fourth caliph and cousin of Muhammad) of the Kharijite movement (zealots who believed that Muhammad's progeny should succeed him) as shock troops, only to put the movement down. Madrassas that feed a particular Islamist political party with recruits negate the compassionate and complex aspects of Islamic history and precedent. It is considered enough for these students to believe that Muslims succeeded due to warfare only, and not because of any tolerance, compassion, knowledge, exploration, or disagreement.

In creating a serious counter-ideological argument to Militant Islamists it is vital to go back into the Qur'an, *hadith,* and key figures in the radicalist movement (like Ibn Abdul-Wahhab, Ibn Taymiyyah), and the rule of the first four caliphs of Islam. The style of the Militant Islamist leader is to out-quote scripture, without rationalization or discussion. It is a form of out-shouting your opponent, which is not debate at all.

Sharia, its study, and its interpretation differ among Muslims. Islam is one faith but with varying interpretations, doctrines, and social outlooks. The forty-eighth verse of the chapter al-Ma'ida in the Qur'an says: "If God so willed, He would have made you a single people, but His plan to test you in what He hath given you. . . . The goal of you all is to God, it is He that will show you the truth of the matters in which ye dispute." This undermines the forced compulsion of the Taliban, bin Laden, and Militant Islamists who wish to impose upon Muslims a single form of neo-fundamentalist belief.

Islam is first and foremost a religion and theological concept, but it is religion from which a political system can be extracted. But the Taliban under Mullah Omar failed to implement a just society and were unwilling to engage in the art of compromise as called for in verse 10 of al-Hujayrat: "The believers are but a single brotherhood, so make peace and reconcile between your two brothers and fear God, that ye may receive mercy."

Islam's founding documents, the Qur'an and the Prophet's sayings, do not have the concept of a full-time clergy, what is today known as *ulema*. When studying Prophet Muhammad's lifetime, along with those of the first four caliphs, we see that there were men and women more knowledgeable than others in religious affairs, but these persons had full-time trades or skills. It was only when Islam became urbanized, coming into contact with the bureaucratic and complex empires of Persia and Byzantium, that the concept of the full-time clergyman and Islamic judge evolved. But if there were no full-time clergy in Islam's founding years, what does this say about the legitimacy of theocratic rule as in Iran and the call for a theocracy seen in the Jihadist movement?

Under the Umayyad Empire (661–750), separate towns had different practices and methods of adjudications; there was pressure to unify Islamic practices and the judiciary. A recognized institution, the *ulema,* was formalized and developed to provide standard regulations for Muslim conduct. This was further developed by the Abbasid dynasty (750–935), and the *ulema* became a distinct class.

The Islamist cleric Hassan al-Turabi, who hosted bin Laden in Sudan from 1991 to 1995, said: "Islamic government is not total because it is Islam that is total. To reduce Islam to government is not Islamic. An omnipotent state is not Islamic. Government has no business interfering in one's worship or prayer or fasting."[5] Even such clerics as the infamous Yussef al-Qaradawi in Qatar, whose books and television show on al-Jazeerah have wavered between supporting the electoral process in Iraq and endorsing suicide tactics, writes: "There is no special class that possesses a monopoly on rationalizing Islamic texts and practicing *ijti-haad* [analytical reasoning]."[6]

The so-called rightly guided caliphs were complex political leaders who addressed various political problems, from the economic to the religious. They were not restricted to addressing religion, and none of these leaders claimed to be men of religion (the Prophet Muhammad, late in life, said: "You are better suited to decide upon worldly affairs"); all consulted with others to determine the course the new Islamic society should take. These men understood the Qur'an and had personally known the Prophet Muhammad, but their governments were by no means theocracies. They were governments of opinion, exchange, compromise, good and bad decisions, all with the understanding that God would approve of decisions made for *maslahah* (the public good or expediency). The caliphate was not a religious institution but one of political expediency, as we have seen. The caliphate was simply part of the political tradition *(turath siyasi)* of Muslim societies instituted after the death of Muhammad. Why is this early Islamic history important? It is to further understand and emphasize that the caliphate was a human institution for leadership born out of necessity and not a divine commandment, as argued by Zawahiri, bin Laden, and the Muslim Brotherhood today.[7]

Under the second caliph, Omar, the *diwaniyah* system evolved. Initially the caliph had around him a set of scribes known as *kutab,* who kept accounts and records on military and judicial affairs, public finance, correspondence, and much more. These scribes formed into *diwans* (literally "clusters"), and a primitive ministerial system was born. Again, this had nothing to do with Islam; Caliph Omar simply found utility in delegating powers in this *diwaniyah* system. When Muslims came into contact with complex civilizations, like the Persian and Byzantine empires, in the late seventh century, they absorbed Persian methods of accounting and bureaucracy. We see this clearly in the Umayyad (661–750) and Abbasid (758–1258) periods. Later civil-society developments in Islamic nations included the creation of the Majlis al-Shurah, Majlis al-Shaab, Majlis al-Nuwab, and Majlis al-Umma, all of which were twentieth-century adaptations of parliamentary representation, found in Egypt, Kuwait, Syria, and Saudi Arabia, with varying degrees of departure from single-party or -person rule. Another modern adaptation that was not commented on by Muslim scholars but considered in the realm of public good were that of trade guilds and unions for lawyers, doctors, and craftsmen. Usama bin Laden and his strategic guide Ayman al-Zawahiri do not take into account such complexities.

Democracy must be viewed in the same vein, as a tool of governance by which to take into account varying opinions, tribes, sects, and interests within a Muslim society. Sheikh Yussef al-Qaradawi, the Egyptian cleric based in Qatar, argues that the jewel of democracy is the right of people to choose their leaders and representatives; this and the freedom of the press and an independent judiciary are mechanisms that can be useful to Islamic society, not a form of ideology or political philosophy imposed by the West. The concept of *shura* can evolve into our modern concept of democracy. In addition, in Muhammad's early wars against the more powerful Meccans, although there were tribal political and economic considerations, his moral thought was guided by ensuring the freedom of religion and thought.[8] Prophet Muhammad was driven out of his hometown primarily because of his ideas of monotheism and his giving an opportunity for the unprotected (slaves, widows, and orphans) to join a new supertribe based on humanitarian principles considered alien in the harsh culture that was sixth-century Arabia. Jihadists today dishonor Prophet Muhammad by focusing solely on only one aspect of his life, that of warrior, and not the multifaceted life of Muhammad as arbiter, husband, father, observer, and leader. Islamic militants and the clerics that endorse them deliberately suppress the gentle and rational aspects of Prophet Muhammad and the daunting issues and questions he faced.

The perfect summation of Muhammad's path was expressed when his cousin asked him concerning his *sunnah* (way, path, or legacy). Muhammad answered: "Wisdom is my capital, reason the force of my religion, love my foundation, longing my vehicle, the remembrance of God my constant pleasure, trust my treasure, mourning my companion, knowledge my arm, patience my robe, contentment my booty, poverty my pride, asceticism my profession, conviction my strength, truthfulness my intercessor, obedience my argument, holy war my ethics, prayer my supreme pleasure."[9] These and many more sayings and verses offer a basis upon which to discredit Jihadist ideology and thought.

THE FATE OF SHEIKH ABDUL-RAZAK AND
HIS COUNTER-CALIPHATE ARGUMENT

After the initial publication of *al-Islam wa Usul al-Hukm* in 1925, there would be a second edition that same year, published by the National Library of Cairo. There would not be another edition until Razak's death in 1966, when a Beirut edition appeared, published by Dar al-Maktaba al-Haya, with a preface by Mamdouh Haqi. In 1971, the *Taliah* (Vanguard) magazine published excerpts of Razak's book to justify pan-Arabism and Arab socialism. A final Beirut edition appeared in 1972, published by the Arab Establishment for Publication and Studies.

In 1925, a censure committee for al-Azhar University was formed to adjudicate Razak's work. King Fouad used this action, which was solely within the realm of the clerics, to affirm the precedence of the caliphate and to arm his

Ummah Party with a religious affirmation of this political tradition. Razak's book energized political liberalists, like Salamah Mousa who called for a constitutional monarchy with power vested in a prime minister and parliament. The Wafd Party, which politically opposed the increased powers of King Fouad, argued that although they endorsed the right of the Higher Ulema Council to convene a censure committee, they were concerned for the preservation of the right of Sheikh Abdul-Razak to express his opinion freely. The Wafd Party also hoped that the council would not use this as a pretext for supporting the monarchy over parliament, and it viewed the Egyptian constitution as supreme over the monarch. The Wafd Party quickly saw this episode as a means for its rival the Ummah Party to score political points at its expense. (The Muslim Brotherhood did not exist until 1928, but its creator, Hassan al-Banna, followed the discourse with great interest.)

The Wafdist spokesman Abbas Akkad personally endorsed Razak's work and criticized both the convening of the Higher Ulema Censure Committee and its eventual verdict: "The time has passed when we engage in excommunicating people for coherent views and opinions." This was awkward for the Wafd Party, and its leader, the Egyptian nationalist Saad Zaghlul, rejected the book but declared that party members had every right to their opinions up to and including endorsing Razak's work. Razak, being a disciple of the Grand Mufti Muhammad Abdu, had been inspired by Abdu's view that the *umma* (Islamic community) had the right to create and depose a caliph. What became known as the "Rida Wars" were largely about asserting the caliphate of Mecca and Abu Bakr, not differences over Islamic orthodoxy. Aside from the clergy, the biggest political opposition was the Itihad (Union) Party, which along with the Ummah Party represented the avidly monarchist view of conservatives as a counterweight to the Wafd and Free Constitutionalists. Saad Zaghlul's Wafd Party as discussed did not present a united front regarding Razak's work. Within Wafd there were constitutionalists, nationalists, and anti-monarchist republicans. One can trace the political fight through the newspaper wars of each of the two major political parties, the Wafd's newspaper *al-Siyasa* and the Itihad's newspaper, which was named after the party.

Razak's censure committee would be convened by the minister of *Haqania* (censure or adjudication), Abdul-Aziz Fahmy Pasha, who was a full member of the Itihad Party and was a pro-monarchist. This minister was also in charge of enforcing any edicts issued by the Higher Ulema Council. One of Razak's nemeses was Rashid Rida, whose agenda and worldview were about defending Islam against secularism. Rida saw a chance to reconstruct the caliphate along Islamic and Arab lines. Rida incited people against Razak and used pejoratives like *ilhad* (dissenter), *ilmani* (secularist), *zandaqah* (heretic, but better translated as one who promotes sin using Islam), atheist, and *fitna* (someone who sows division among Muslims). He recommended that Razak be subjected to *itizal* (censure). Sixty-two al-Azhar clerics, placating King Fouad, went on to adjudicate Razak and his book. The sixty-two clerics cited provision 101 of al-Azhar Law Number 10, which made Razak subject to censure from the Higher Clerical Council. This law had been promulgated in 1911 when Egypt was under the rule of Khedive Abbas Hilmi II, to rein in the political power of clerics by subjecting them to adjudication for opposing the Anglo-Egyptian sharing of power over Egypt and the Sudan.

Let us now turn to Razak's discussion of the *sunnah* (Prophet's sayings and actions that supplement the Qur'an). When a man came to Prophet Muhammad and attempted to pay homage to him, the Prophet chastised him, saying: "I am a son of a woman of Quraysh that eats [like you] from the sustenance of Mecca."[10] Razak took from this that Prophet Muhammad never claimed divinity and that Islam first and foremost is a faith that binds humankind to God.

If one believes the caliphate is ordained, there are schisms within this radical Islamist and Militant Islamist notion. Which caliphate do you consider to be the prime example? For a Saudi Militant Islamist, it is that of the first four caliphs after the death of Muhammad; for the Syrians it is that of the Umayyads; for the Iraqis it is that of the Abbasids; and for the Turks, it is that of the Ottomans. When the Umayyads established their dynasty (661–750), they attempted the impossible by linking their rule to that of the Prophet Muhammad and, failing that, his close companions. This linkage necessitated the creation of such titles as *Khalifat Allah* (God's vice regent), *Amin Allah* (God's trustee), and even *Naib Allah* (God's deputy). These created titles then set the course for a merging of religion and state intuitionally within Islam. These are political traditions nowhere found in the religion itself. Such differences are useful in dividing Militant Islamist visions for the future. They also demonstrate the challenges of nationalism that undermine the pan-Islamism of al-Qaida's vision.

nine

Countering Militant Islamist Rhetoric Using Islam

> The purpose of intelligence analysis is to elevate the quality of discussion in this town.
>
> SHERMAN KENT, WORLD WAR II "FATHER OF INTELLIGENCE ANALYSIS"

If the United States is to cut through the confusion of Islamic terms misused by the adversary, policy makers and military leaders must gain insight into the language of Islam and delineate between constructive and destructive interpretations of the faith. Some misinterpretations of Islam lead toward a culture of suicide, death, and regression. One can confront injurious and evil ideology in two ways—hide and ignore it, or confront it. Confronting Islamist militant doctrine will be the job of Muslim intellectuals first, Arab regimes second, and the rest of the civilized world third. Bin Laden, Zawahiri, the late Abdullah Azzam, and Qutb collectively represent a threat. Their books, speeches, and ideas must be placed in historical context and exposed for the politically destructive agenda they present.

A central ideology that unites all Islamist militant groups, whether it be al-Qaida, Hamas in Palestine, or Abu Sayyaf in the Philippines, is the concept of *takfir* (accusation of apostasy, if Muslim, or infidelity, if non-Muslim). Some Islamist militant groups have even taken *"takfir"* within the name of their organization, such as *al-Takfir wal Hijrah* (Condemn and Excommunicate). *Takfir* is more than just excommunication. It carries with it the threat of violence and even death. The label of *kafir* (apostate, for a Moslem) led to the stabbing of Naguib Mahfouz (Egyptian Nobel laureate), the assassination of Sadat, and the killings and attempted killings of many public intellectuals in Arab public life. This concept must be met head on and countered by publicizing bin Laden and Zawahiri's hijacking of the seat of judgment, a role that is reserved for God alone. Bin Laden and *takfiris* (those who practice the declaration of apostasy against Muslims as well as non-Muslims) counter Quranic verses that ordain that judgment be left to God with the Quranic commands *"amr bil maruf wal nahy an al-munkar,"* enjoining believers to propagate what is right and prevent what is forbidden (Surah 9, verse 71). This concept of propagating what is right and preventing what is forbidden is known in Arabic simply as *al-hisbah*. There is a Militant Islamist website called *al-hisbah;* this is why some immersion in the Arabic of our adversary and its misuse is important. Their argument breaks down in the face of verses that declare *"laa ikrah fee al deen,"* there shall be no compulsion in religion (chapter 2, verse 256) and that moderation should be the key to all things in life. In addition, the verse "no compulsion in matters of faith" contradicts some Muslims who discourage the study of other religions. Muslims need to become outraged that the world's introduction to Islam comes at the hands of thugs, assassins, and suicide bombers, and it is up to the international community to assist in maintaining this outrage against Militant Islamists.

It is important to expose Militant Islamist rhetoric that suppresses and ignores aspects of the Qur'an that celebrate diversity, such as: "O you men! surely We have created you of a male and a female, and made you *tribes* and families that you may know each other; surely the most honorable of you with Allah is the one among you most careful [of his duty]; surely Allah is Knowing" (chapter 49, verse 13). What made Islamic civilization great in the ninth through the twelfth centuries was the lack of fear in the exchange of diverse ideas and public discourse. The scholars who made developments in philosophy, algebra, and anatomy were not above exchanging views with Jews, Zoroastrians, Hindus, and those with whom they came in contact with through trade and conquest.

It is this openness and embrace of humankind's diversity that is lost in today's Islamic world. Another Quranic verse in support of diversity is, "If your Lord had so willed, He would have made mankind one people, but they will not cease to differ, except those on whom Your Lord and Sustainer has bestowed His mercy, and for this did He create them" (chapter 11, verses 118–19). Regaining this candidness will not come through attacking Islam, but by countering the Islamist militants in the public arena with Quranic verses that undermine their arguments of

Jihad through warfare. One of the better books on how to handle diverse Islamic opinions in a constructive manner is entitled *The Ethics of Disagreement in Islam,* by Abdul Wahid Ali.[1] His work covers such topics as acceptable and unacceptable disagreements. Unacceptable disagreements cover al-Qaida and Militant Islamists who disagree in such a way that it causes discord and dissension and suppresses all concern for truth. The imposition of Islam by force goes against the Quranic injunction of not compelling persons to religion and against the verses that call for tolerance in human diversity and for special consideration for adherents to a revealed faith. A few modern clerics obfuscate and attempt to creatively justify terrorism as a form of forced *dawa* (proselytizing), a means to propagate the faith through violence. This should be exposed for the hypocrisy and the shallow argument that it is. *Dawa* can be achieved only through rational speech and thought. If propagated by violence and coercion, there can be no genuine acceptance of any Islamic idea. The concept of *dawa* in the end requires a rational, uncoerced discourse on faith, theology, theosophy, and history, in line with the Quranic injunction against compulsion in religion. This single verse has led to a line of reasoning that Islam's principal ideas are freedom of worship, which requires freedom of thought and freedom from compulsion by the state in matters of faith, that people should be able to cultivate their own relations with God without interference from the state, as compulsion is not true belief. Of course, Militant Islamists use the injunction *"al amr bil marouf wal nahee an al munkar"* (the duty to propagate virtue and prevent vice) to argue that the state has the ultimate responsibility of upholding this Quranic injunction. Militant Islamists use this issue of promoting virtue and preventing vice, reducing it to a state instrument, whose objective is to internalize fear. This tactic was used by the Nazis, through a practice called *sippenhaft,* the arrest of entire families for the crimes of one member of the family, and the *blockwart,* who was the neighborhood spy always listening for signs of criticism of the Nazi regime. The Taliban and Militant Islamists who control a neighborhood or even state employ these same tactics in the name of their version of Islam, robbing the Quranic injunction of preventing vice and promoting virtue of any moral quality.

The two opposing views of preventing vice and promoting virtue and the injunction of no compulsion in matters of faith demand a reconciliation through a moderate path. Although the point is lost on Militant Islamists, the Qur'an calls the Muslim community a moderate nation, or *umma al-wustaa* (chapter 2, verse 143). The famous Iranian philosopher Abdel-Karim Souroush took the "no compulsion in religion" verse to an interesting and basic conclusion. He postulated that since true belief in Islam (or any religion) can be attained only through free conviction and thought, there can be no true faith without freedom—does freedom, he asked, then overtake religion in significance?

First and foremost, it is important to recognize that neither the Arabic word for extremist, *tataruf*, nor for terrorist, *irhabi*, is found anywhere in the Qur'an or the Prophet Muhammad's sayings and deeds, *hadith*. Another word used to describe Militant Islamists is *zandiq*, from the adjective *zandaqa*, a heretic whose teaching becomes a danger to the Islamic community. However, the term was developed in Islamic jurisprudence in 742, a century after Muhammad's death, and was derived from a Persian term. Together the *hadith* and Qur'an make up the *sunnah*, the basic unit for Islamic jurisprudence. The terms *tataruf, zandiq,* and *irhabi* are modern Arabic constructions that are fluid in their interpretations. The closest comparison found in the Qur'an to describe this phenomenon of Militant Islamist Ideology in the Qur'an is *ghilu fee al-deen,* located in several verses; it refers to excesses in the practice of Islam, matters of faith, or religion. Whole commentaries have been written on how Muslims and non-Muslims can take religion to excess, derived from such Quranic verses as Surat al-Maida, verse 77: "Say: 'O people of the Book! exceed not in your religion the bounds (of what is proper), trespassing beyond the truth, nor follow the vain desires of people who went wrong in times gone by—who misled many, and strayed [themselves] from the even way.'"

This verse has led to Islamic debates over the Prophet Muhammad's meaning of what constitutes excess in religion. The canonical *hadiths* of al-Bukhari, collections of the Prophet's sayings undisputed by most Muslims, Shiite and Sunni, tell the story of Muaz ibn Jabl, who, while leading a communal prayer, utilized the longer chapter al-Baqara, which contains 286 verses. The Prophet Muhammad chastised him for this and encouraged the use of shorter verses in prayer, as many complained that the prayers had lingered beyond reason.

In the *hadiths* of al-Bukhari (the collection entitled *Book of Fasting*), a better example of the Prophet Muhammad addressing excessive zeal in matters of religion is that of Abdullah ibn Amru, who fasted all day and then elected to remain awake all night in worship. Muhammad learned of this and went to Ibn Amru, telling him to fast and then break his fast, to sleep and then awaken normally. "Your body has rights, your eyes have rights, your spouse has rights, and your society has rights." This saying of Muhammad has multiple meanings, from not conducting religious obligations at the expense of others or that cause harmful effects upon the body, to a focus on moderation, and finally to an emphasis on maintaining mind, body, and health for the moderate worship of God. This saying also calls into question tangentially the whole concept of suicide as a terrorist tactic. Although there are direct Quranic verses and prophetic sayings that call into question Militant Islamist methods, the adversary intentionally ignores the injunctions that condemn suicide in general. Militant Islamists attempt to create a distinction between individual suicide and suicide as a terrorist tactic that achieves an objective.

The issue of *ghilu fee al-deen* is of concern in the Qur'an because it places an undue burden on believers; divides society, nations, and neighborhoods; steers a person from moderation; oppresses the *karamah* (dignity) of the person, his family, and society; and causes *fitnah* (division) among Muslims.

An injunction against suicide is found in chapter 2, verse 195: "And spend of your substance in the cause of Allah, and *make not your own hands contribute to [your] destruction;* but do good; for Allah loveth those who do good." It is almost a certainty that bin Laden did not engage in such discussions with U.S. embassy bombers of Kenya and Dar al-Salam, and the 9/11 hijackers certainly skipped through this verse when they conducted what can only be called a crime against humanity. There are over 120 verses that are not part of the Militant Islamist discourse, such as Surat *al-Nisaa* verse 1 and Surat *al-Araaf* verses 26 and 27 of the Qur'an, which refer to humanity as *Bani Adam* (Children of Adam), meaning that we all derive from one mother and father irrespective of race, sex, creed, language, or religion. Another instance is chapter 2, verse 136, declaring that monotheistic faiths have similar goals of morality and come from a common strain. This humanistic theme is reinforced by sayings of the Prophet Muhammad that people are not true believers until they love for their brother what they love for themselves. A *hadith* collected by both Abu Daud and al-Tirmidhi has the prophet saying that all of human creation are children of God.

Bin Laden and those sympathetic to al-Qaida have not given careful thought to this verse. They tout paradise for those who follow their agenda, using the same Qur'an, but is this paradise assured when one has violated the injunction against excessiveness and to submit oneself to judgment before God alone? For neither bin Laden nor any cleric from Iranian ayatollahs to Sunni imams can promise the keys to heaven for walking through a minefield. They promise to Sunni militants eternal pleasures in the afterlife, but they can never guarantee that which only God can ordain for each man or women in the hereafter.

If Muslims should entertain the notion of al-Qaida sympathies they must reflect upon the by-products of *ghilu* in religion. The militant Jihadists have made it difficult for those Muslims wishing to exercise the obligations of their faith in the twenty-first century. Those who pray regularly or dress conservatively are suspect. The very act of paying *zakat* (alms) has been corroded by Islamist militants, who divert part of the funds for violence or abuse charity to maintain control over a populace by combining terrorism with social services. Gone are the days of simply placing donations into a collection box of a mosque. Now, one has to be concerned about whether one is financing humanitarian needs or terrorism or a combination of both. Muslims must assign a portion of the blame to Islamist militants who have increased the burden of those wanting to practice their faith and explore knowledge, content, rationale, and reason as discussed by centuries of Islamic thought.

This Islamic thought came into contact with Hellenistic ideas and many others. The Middle East's geography has made it the ideal melting pot of ideas that gave birth to early human civilization. Muslims living in the West must now concern themselves with whether the mosque and Islamic school is teaching Islam or politicized Islam that disengages young students from succeeding in the twenty-first-century globalized world. Another by-product of *ghilu fee al-deen* that Militant Islamists practice is that Muslims wishing to be observant are now suspected of radicalism or militance. In essence, al-Qaida has suppressed the freedom of religious Islamic expression through its militant actions. Perhaps the most tragic impact of Islamist militancy on Islam is the outright murder and suppression of constructive Islamic scholarship. This is a climate in which a Nobel laureate for literature, Naguib Mahfouz, suffered and barely survived being stabbed in the neck, and many others are silenced by threats.

Islamic militants also corrode the whole concept of *dawa*. The call of militants to Islam must be done without the taint of taking advantage of the individual or for personal material gain. The clerics who led the likes of John Walker Lindh and Adam Gadahn to the narrow path of Militant Islamist Ideology should read the Qur'an, Surat al-Nahl, verse 125: "Invite [all] to the Way of thy Lord with wisdom and beautiful preaching; and argue with them in ways that are best and most gracious: for thy Lord knoweth best, who have strayed from His Path, and who receive guidance." Instead the converts' lack of knowledge about Islam was taken advantage of during their initial conversion. They were only given a narrow microcosm of Militant Islamist theory and told that this was Islam and that any other form of Islam is apostasy. Adam Gadahn was used by al-Qaida senior leaders in October 2008 to spin a new narrative on the state of America's economy; pseudo-intellectually, he attributed the downturn to wars against Muslims saying:

> My dear brothers and sisters, today the Muslims are on the verge of a historic victory against the imperialism and tyranny of the unbelievers, and the enemies of Islam are facing a crushing defeat which is beginning to manifest itself in the expanding crisis their economy is experiencing—a crisis whose primary cause, in addition to the abortive and unsustainable crusades they are waging in Afghanistan, Pakistan, and Iraq—is their turning their backs on Allah's revealed laws, which forbid interest-bearing transactions, exploitation, greed, and injustice in all its forms, and demand the worship of Allah alone to the exclusion of all false gods, including money and power.[2]

Militant Islamist operatives are:

- Ignorant of the wide scope of the Qur'an and do not take the sharia (corpus of Islamic law) in its totality
- Ignorant of *usul al-deen,* meaning the deep historical, spiritual intent of the totality of Quranic verses (this comes from long study and rational discussion)
- Neither Islamic revivalists nor reformers
- Prone to react to global crisis and spin a narrative taking some form of credit for the crisis, independent terrorist action, and other upheavals.

The concept of balancing *deen* (religion) and faith with the daily affairs of this world is not new in Islamic discourse. What is new is the aggressive suppression in the twenty-first century of this debate by Militant Islamists who have hijacked, through the use of the information age and the Internet, Islamic scholarship and debate. The reference in Islamic scholarship of the twelfth century was *al-deen wal dawlah;* the concept of the *dawlah* (state) is not one that existed in the time of the Prophet Muhammad but had to be debated in later centuries. The theory is that humankind was placed on earth to praise and worship God and appreciate God's glory, known as *ibadah* (an Islamic concept that was found in the time of Muhammad). *Ibadah* cannot be achieved, which is a right that is rendered to God, if one elects to end one's life. If one transgresses the bounds and limits of endurance God has set and for instance commits the ultimate act of suicide, one not only forsakes trust that God will alleviate suffering but ultimately deprives God of his right to the veneration and worship of humankind, his creation. In delineating between *iman* (faith) and *ibadah* (the practice of faith or orthopraxy), one finds that *iman* is an individual choice and *ibadah* (fasting, prayer, pilgrimage, and alms giving) is designed to enhance the human collective spirit toward other people as well as toward God. Compare this to Militant Islamist Ideology, which divides the human spirit and discriminates even among Muslims, declaring the slightest difference in opinion, scholarship, dress, or expression of human dignity apostasy.

A counter-interpretation of Islam designed to contradict Militant Islamist Ideology is that the majority of the five pillars of Islam (specifically profession, prayer, fasting, alms, and pilgrimage) are fundamentally designed to increase a Muslim's ties emotionally and functionally to fellow Muslims, male or female. Militant Islamists and radical Islamist Salafi ideology (modernist interpretations calling for a return to the pious founders), through *takfir* and labeling ideas as heresy, have the opposite effect and isolate Muslims from their families, neighbors, society, the world at large, and finally from life itself. Muslim scholars of the ninth and tenth century who developed algebra, the algorithm, alchemy, astronomy, medicine, and much more by collaborating with Jews, Zoroastrians, Nestorian Christians, and Sabians did so because they understood the whole of earth to be a *mihrab* (prayer niche) of worship and that God reveals Himself through creation. This was the ultimate Islamic expression of embracing the globe and not withdrawing from it; this enabled the preservation of Greek and Roman classics in the ninth and tenth centuries, when Europe was in the Dark Ages. Muslims should take pride that their ancestors had these classics as a gift to the Renaissance. Instead bin Laden, Zawahiri, al-Qaida, Hamas, al-Qaida in Iraq, Abu Sayyaf, and many more militant personalities and organizations force us all, Muslim and non-Muslim, to look daily upon the destructive behavior of a microcosm of Muslims.

Another argument is one that Militant Islamists use to undermine such notions as secularism, democracy, and democratic institutions—and that can also be turned against them. Islamist militants follow the teachings of Sayyid Qutb, who postulated that all sovereignty belongs to God and that legislatures, parliaments, and democracy take away from God's sovereignty and in addition are *bida'a* (innovations) in Islam. One can take the *bida'a* argument and say that terrorism, suicide bombing, and murder in the name of Islam of Muslims and non-Muslims are additions to the religion of Islam and are also *bida'a*. The notion of Jihad (in the destructive warlike meaning) as a pillar of Islam is an addition to a religion that Muhammad declared was complete in his lifetime. Martyrdom as an essential pillar of Islam is nowhere to be found in Islam's original and only five pillars. Labeling a concept *bida'a* requires discussion, debate, and disagreement before a consensus is reached; today Jihadists simply post their labeling of *bida'a* on such websites as *al-Hisbah* and *al-Fajr*, and combine it with pseudo-intellectual arguments that do not have consensus support in Islam.

Today, Muslims confront a version of Jihad that proclaims martyrdom as its intent, raison d'être, and validation. Among Muhammad's sayings on the issue is, "He who has been killed to uphold the word of God has been martyred for his sake" (al-Bukhari, vol. 1, *hadith* number 223). Yet Muhammad also dictates that "a person whose intent is glory, booty [spoils], or females has no ties to God, and only God knows who strives for his sake" (al-Bukhari, vol. 6, no. 430). The second caliph and revered companion to Muhammad, Omar ibn al-Khattab, once chastised a group that was calling each of their war dead a martyr. Omar objected, "They should utter the Prophet's words; whoever died in the cause of God has died a martyr." Yet even this exhortation does not belie the historical significance of martyrdom, nor the fact that Jihad is always described as being "in the cause of God." Numerous *hadith* concerning martyrdom, intended to spur the believers to Jihad, are found in Malik ibn Anas's text, *al-Muwatta*. Malik ibn Anas (d. 796) was the founder of the Maliki school of Islamic law. Here we learn that Omar himself longed for death as a martyr: "Martyrdom in Your way and death in the city of Your Messenger" and defined the martyr as "the one who gives himself, expectant of reward from Allah."

The valuation of martyrdom in the Shiite tradition is even more deeply ingrained, reflecting the experience of the sect. One belief is that certain persons, like the prophets or martyrs, have the ability to intercede for the souls of Muslims as they proceed on the Day of Judgment. Intercession, or *shafa,* may be granted to martyrs for themselves and others, and also through grieving and shedding tears for the martyrs, Ali ibn Abi Talib and Hussayn ibn Ali. Moderates or Islamic liberals have been attempting to deconstruct the relationship of martyrdom and Jihad, particularly since 9/11. The difficult task of building counterarguments relies on the concept of *niyah*. It is important that disaffected youth or older supporters of the radicals separate the intent of struggling for Islam from a quest for martyrdom. Martyrdom may be "embraced" or accepted—as Muslims say, "submitted to"—without being sought out as an end in itself.

The *hadith* promising seventy-two virgins to the martyr is, for instance, a weak *hadith* of dubious quality. The chain of narrators linking this *hadith* to Muhammad is questionable. The saying is contravened by Qur'an 3:169: "Those killed in the cause of God are not reckoned dead but are fed a heavenly sustenance with their lord." Therefore proximity to God and not sexual or worldly pleasure is the reward for the martyr. Yet Militant Islamist clerics persist in using the saying of the seventy-two virgins to lure Muslim youth to their death, knowing full well its dubiousness. The issue of who is a martyr preoccupied early Islamic thinkers and entire volumes have been written on the subject, known as *Hukm al-Shahadah* (Rulings on Martrydom). The central theme of these works is that the answer to this question relies solely on the person's intentions, and these intentions are known only to God. Islamic scholars were once very concerned with *niyah* (intent). There is a *hadith* that the Prophet Muhammad called upon his followers to pray for a fighter who fell at the Battle of Khaybar (the Ditch), saying, "He raided livestock in God's cause, he was not a martyr."

The Quranic emphasis on *al-siraat al-mutaqeem* (the straight path) provides another means for ideological attack of Islamist militant ideology. The emphasis on straight path is a concept uttered numerous times as part of a chapter required in the Muslim daily prayer. It means not only the path of righteousness; *mutaqeem* (straightness) also means balancing mankind's spiritual, worldly, and physical needs. The embrace of the Jihadist lifestyle contravenes this balance and can be condemned using this Quranic injunction found in the first chapter *(al-Fatihah)* verse 6, a verse uttered numerous times in each of the five daily prayers. One must wonder if bin Laden is praying daily. Is he going through the motions, or is he truly reflecting on the words of this chapter of the Qur'an? It is presupposed that when mankind achieves it, this balance leads to contentment and happiness for all. Bin Laden and radical Islamist thought violates the intent of moderation, unity with God, and warnings for Muslims against divisions that *ghilu* (extremes of faith) can cause.

Muslims causing chaos and division within their own societies is addressed in the Qur'an in Ala-Imran, verse 103: "And hold fast, all together, by the rope which Allah (stretches out for you), and be not divided among yourselves; and remember with gratitude Allah's favor on you; for ye were enemies and He joined your hearts in love, so that by His Grace, ye became brethren; and ye were on the brink of the pit of Fire, and He saved you from it. Thus doth Allah make His Signs clear to you: That ye may be guided." Militant Islamists and Islamists use this same verse to call upon Muslims to unite against a perceived common enemy—against the infidel or apostate, quoting the first portion but not the entire verse—deemphasizing the interpretation of this verse that condemns the causing of divisions within Muslims, something that Militant Islamists are known for. Their practice of radicalism, *takfir,* and prejudices based on assessing who is a better Muslim all violate this verse. Militant Islamists, be it of the Muqtada al-Sadr militant Shiite variety or al-Qaida's Sunni Salafi variety, all reject the reality of diversity among Muslims. They also cause an intergenerational divide, preying upon youths and isolating them from their families. Many unknowing parents of suicide bombers have been documented in the public media. Al-Anam, verse 159, says: "As for those who divide their religion and break up into sects, thou hast no part in them in the least: their affair is with Allah: He will in the end tell them the truth of all that they did."

Richard Antoun writes in his 1989 *Muslim Preacher in the Modern World* on the subject of sermons in mosques.[3] He assesses the mosque sermons delivered in 1959–1966, in the Jordanian village of Kafr al-Ma. He finds that the Friday sermons (Friday is the Muslim Sabbath) emphasize not only Jihad as warfare but marriage law, justice, family obligations, treatment of parents, equality, fasting in Ramadan, education, pilgrimage, and much more.[4] One way of assessing whether a mosque is Militant Islamist is how much time it devotes to preaching militant ideology and the glories of martyrdom instead of a more holistic view of Islamic orthopraxy. Does a mosque devote its sermons exclusively to Jihad (in the Militant Islamist context of warfare)? If so, it is a politicized militant mosque; as long as it does not tangibly support violence by Militant Islamist groups, its members are Islamists. However, if there is probable cause that tangible support has been provided, it is subject to investigation and prosecution to the full extent of the law or, in the case of a military operation, to being shut down, preferably with the aid of local Muslim security forces. The Geneva Conventions do not protect religious sites used to support insurgents. Militant Islamists in Iraq have defiled the sanctity of mosques by using them to store weapons, maintain underground torture chambers, and use worshippers as human shields. This should outrage Muslims more than soldiers entering these misused mosques with their boots on to retake them and restore them to their proper roles as houses of worship.

RADICAL MILITANT ISLAMIST IDEOLOGY AND TRIBALISM

When Prophet Muhammad undertook his *dawa* (call) to Islam in Mecca, there were only a handful of Muslim followers. Only when he became leader of Medina did more individuals and tribes take an interest in this new monotheism he was proposing. Some became interested in Islam for spiritual reasons, others for tribal protection, and still others for the opportunity of plunder in the emerging crisis between the city-tribal confederacy centered in Medina and the more powerful Meccan oligarchy. What is clear in the early Islamic historical accounts is that the Meccans were uncomfortable with the concept of life after death and the notion of being held accountable for sin on Judgment Day. The Meccans, although aware of the Jewish and Christian traditions, primarily followed a religion based on animism. The Meccan oligarchic leadership did not consider the Judeo-Christian teachings of Arabia any more or less significant than other faiths found along their caravan routes to Yemen, Syria, and across the Red Sea in Abyssinia. The Meccans did, however, recognize a difference in Muhammad and, in particular, his preaching that began in 610.

Another intolerable threat he posed was the fact that he was from the tribal elite of the Quraysh, the city leaders of Mecca. His faith, combined with his status, provided those without tribal protection an opportunity to form a supertribe based not on blood ties but faith. The Meccan oligarchs, led by Abu Sufyan and Abu Jahl, could not allow this trend to continue, and their determination to eradicate Muhammad became even more urgent when the Prophet assumed leadership of Medina. The city Muhammad governed stood on the Meccan trade routes to Damascus and Jerusalem. It now became an economic necessity for the Meccans to rid themselves of Muhammad and the tribal confederacy he brokered in Medina. To say Muhammad established a military stronghold is an oversimplification; although he concerned himself with military matters, it is more accurate to say that he established a new social order, one that transcended tribalism.

Militant Islamists consistently stay away from such finer points of Islamic history and law, and they dismiss fourteen centuries of Islamic debate and writings. Militant Islamist clerics and self-appointed clerics in the streets inciting violence do not want Muslims to find out that they:

- Quote consistently from fragments contained in a half-dozen chapters in the Qur'an where the preponderance of war verses are located and neglect to reveal the complexities and intricacies of the Qur'an's 114 chapters as a whole.

- Quote war verses but only partially, repeating such verses as "fight in the cause of Allah those who fight you" but omitting the ending, "but do not transgress for God does not love transgressors" (chapter 2, verse 190).

- Shout slogans and fuse Arabic quotes from violent Abbasid caliphs or Ibn Taymiyyah's book on Jihad and pass it off as orthodoxy. (Even Ibn Taymiyyah's writings sow the seeds of counter-Islamist militant argumentation — for instance, his discourses arguing that Prophet Muhammad established a social order and not a government, or that all of Muhammad's actions were taken within the framework of his prophecy, which was the centrality of his mission, not the physical governing of society.)

- Do not want to delve into the historical context of even the verses they often quote, because it would reveal the defensive position in which Muhammad was placed in his struggle with the more powerful Meccans.

Militant Islamists and some clerics advocate the concept of *ahl al-hal wal aqd* (literally, "those who loosen and bind"), referring to a group that enables the emir to govern through achieving consensus between various factions. This group proposes leaders from among themselves to the Muslim public, to whom they would take a *bay'aa* (an oath of fealty). The fallacy of this argument is that this system, although couched in classical and legalistic Arabic, was derived at through *ijtihad* (analytic reasoning) as a means of dealing with the fractious Arabian tribes after Muhammad's death. As there is no clear Quranic guidance on the mechanics of Islamic government, institutions like the *khliafa* (caliphate), *ahl al-hal wal aqd,* and Khomeini's *veleyat al-faqih* (rule by supreme jurisprudent) are all innovations. Another problem is the misuse of *fard-kifaya* (optional obligation) versus *fard-ayn* (individual obligation) in the concept of the caliphate. *Fard-ayn* is an individual obligation that every practicing Muslim must undertake, like prayer or fasting. *Fard-kifaya* is an obligation from which, if enough Muslims undertake it, all other Muslims are exempt. An example of *fard-kifaya* is administering the burial rites; if enough Muslims participate, everyone else is exempt from this obligation. The application of this rule in the caliphate was that if enough Muslims showed up to take the *bay'aa* (oath of fealty), then the rest were exempt and must accept the authority of the caliph. This political tradition — and it is only a tradition — on obligations, couched in Islamic legalistic rules, creates an apathetic polity. Add to this the political tradition of not criticizing the caliph, in the name of

Muslim unity; this is a problem of inability to separate the person from the office, let alone the office from the cloak of Islam.

WHY DOES DECONSTRUCTING ZAWAHIRI MATTER?

There are 80,000 Arabs in the Kasbah. Are they all against us? We know they're not. In reality, it's only a small minority that dominates with terror and violence. This minority is our adversary and we must isolate and destroy it.

COLONEL MATHIEU, IN *BATTLE OF ALGIERS*, 1966, BY GILO PORTICOVO

To begin with, many Jihadist theorists have criticized Zawahiri, using Islamic argumentation that it erodes his influence in part of the Islamic community. That forces him to compete vigorously in the Islamic world of ideas. His reaction to Imam al-Sherif's book and interviews demonstrates his concern for image, the need to give the appearance that his method is the only correct Islamic means of redeeming lost Muslim glory. Joining the chorus of criticism is the Grand Mufti of Saudi Arabia, Sheikh Abdul-Aziz al-Alshiekh; while there is much in the sheikh's teachings that one can find objectionable, he has at least used Islamic argument to dissuade Saudis from traveling to Iraq and Afghanistan, taking a religious stance that causes young Saudis to think twice before letting emotionalism carry them away. Both have argued that al-Qaida has damaged Islam's image globally.

It is vital to encourage an intellectual deconstruction of Zawahiri's books and strategic visions, which are built upon a narrow, pseudo-intellectual view of Islamic law, history, and precedent. In Zawahiri's model we cannot explore the Muslim intellectual greatness of the ninth century, a historical period in which Islam was stimulated by the Quranic injunction of *ilm* (seeking knowledge). Al-Qaida wishes Muslims to take pride in violence and a culture of death, rather than in a culture that preserved the Greek and Roman classics until the Renaissance. A critique of Zawahiri, Qutb, and other militant thinkers should begin with the premise that they have reduced Prophet Muhammad to a simple warlord, when in fact his life, legacy, and example is richer and much more complex: he was a father, husband, civic leader, merchant, arbiter, negotiator, and judge. The ideological and intellectual line distinguishing Islamist militant versions of history and a more educated and encompassing view of Islam must be drawn by Muslim thinkers around the world. The fate of future Muslim generations and of the world depends on Islamically challenging al-Qaida, bin Laden, and Zawahiri.

The most important twenty-first-century Islamist militant thinker now alive is Abu Musab al-Suri, who is currently detained. His books call for multiple, independent, small-scale militant Jihadist attacks on organizations frequented by American citizens, instead of higher-profile targets, as a means of wearing down the United States. Fortunately, al-Qaida senior leaders appear not to endorse Abu Musab's strategy fully, still favoring the large-scale attack of the 9/11 type. It is vital that differences in strategy, tactics, and operations among Islamist militant groups be exploited and amplified in such media as the Internet. Other forms of discrediting al-Qaida, Hamas, and Hezbollah include Robert Pape's work *Dying to Win.*[5] In this book, Pape removes the mythology of suicide terrorism and reduces it to strategic, social, and individual logic. This removes the mysticism of terrorism and reveals al-Qaida, Hamas, and Hezbollah as opportunist organizations that pervert Islam for basic political gain—no more and no less.

Late 2007 and 2008 saw serious ideological challenges to al-Qaida in general and to Zawahiri specifically. The most significant was that a founding member, and first leader, of Egyptian Islamic Jihad Imam al-Sherief (also known as "Dr. Fadl"), whose book *Reconsideration of the Jihad* called al-Qaida tactics "misguided," labeled Zawahiri and bin Laden hypocrites and used Islamic arguments to tear down al-Qaida ideologically. This so worried Zawahiri that he dedicated time in his 2008 speeches to Dr. Fadl, a longtime associate after 1968, and issued a two-hundred-page rebuttal to Dr. Fadl's *The Exoneration.* It plainly concerns Zawahiri, judging from the time he spent crafting a response, when critics make rational Islamic arguments to counter his pseudo-intellectual and narrow views of Islam.

ZAWAHIRI'S DEMONS: HIS 2008 ANSWERS TO QUESTIONS

Ayman al-Zawahiri put out a call for questions from the public in late 2007, and he began to answer them in mid-2008. Among the most problematic issues that arose was the killing of innocent Muslims; Zawahiri dismisses it, saying the militants also grieve over Muslim lives lost. He also states that visas do not entitle a Westerner to protection; Fadl argues the opposite, and unlike Zawahiri, he has a Quranic passage on his side, Qur'an 9:6—"If one amongst the pagans asks thee for asylum, grant it to him, so that he may hear the word of Allah, and then escort them to where they can be secure." This verse is used by the Saudi government to justify the protection of foreign workers in the kingdom and to condemn al-Qaida in Saudi Arabia for attacks on foreigners. Zawahiri is also asked how he can issue fatwas in contravention to the clerical consensus, and whether he considers himself an *aleem* (singular for "cleric"). He replies categorically that he does not consider himself an *aleem* but follows their quotes and statements. This lack of clerical support and of a recognized clerical figure of the stature of Abdullah Azzam is problematic for al-Qaida; Zawahiri is left with the clerically obscure Abu Yahya al-Libi.

There were also questions on reconciling the roles of bin Laden, Mullah Omar, and Abu Umar al-Baghdadi; there is much confusion over the concept of who is "Commander of the Faithful." Zawahiri clarifies that bin Laden is a soldier of Mullah Omar and that Omar is the Commander of the Faithful. He also says hiding Abu Umar al-Baghdadi is necessary for his safety. The detaining of Rifai Taha, Talal al-Qasimi, and Abu Musab al-Suri, key ideologues in the twenty-first-century Militant Islamist movement is a problem for the movement, robbing it of key post-9/11 ideologues. Zawahiri in his answers to questions obsesses about the Muslim Brotherhood and cites aspects of the Egyptian constitution, court cases from the 1980s and early 1990s, that went over the heads of many young Militant Islamists. The instability of *takfir* becomes clear when he answers a question by saying he has never declared the former Grand Mufti of Saudi Arabia, Bin Baz, or the Saudi senior cleric al-Uthyameen, apostates. Zawahiri does say that the killing of government clerics is not useful and that the focus should be on Crusaders and Zionists. It remains to be seen whether al-Qaida cadres take Zawahiri's advice or ignore it, preferring to murder respected clergy. The Libyan Islamic Fighting Group (LIFG) and al-Qaida touted a public merger in 2006, yet Zawahiri says only elements of the LIFG have merged, meaning that the organization is splintered. On the 9/11 attack being a Jewish conspiracy, Zawahiri is angry with this characterization, saying that Hezbollah's al-Manar TV (Shiites in Lebanon) first spread this rumor and that it is without foundation. He seems to scoff at al-Qaida's being denied the glory of 9/11. In Zawahiri's mind Iraq does not have a Sunni minority, and he answers a question by saying that combining Kurds, Sunnis, and Turkomans forms a majority Sunni community in Iraq. This is delusional, for even with these minorities Sunnis would represent only 40 percent of Iraq, 60 percent being Shiite.

Zawahiri chooses not to answer questions he deems personal; in addition, he is limited in his quotations from clerics, preferring modern Islamist militant clerics of dubious quality, like al-Maqdisi and Omar al-Saif (who claimed to have earned his clerical credentials on the battlefield and was killed in Dagestan). Zawahiri laments not having a fully fledged Ulema Council within al-Qaida.

These insecurities need to be highlighted in the public domain, as Zawahiri is highly sensitive to public criticism, and it is in our interest to keep him ideologically on the defensive. When a woman asked what she could do for the Jihad, he advised against leaving her children behind to emigrate from apostate lands but to support the Jihad from within—this at a time when al-Qaida in Iraq out of desperation is resorting to the use of women as suicide operatives. Despite Zawahiri's copious public writings, speeches, and videos, he likely uses coded messages to communicate to his colleagues and operatives inner thoughts and operational writings. It is not beyond imagination that someone with Zawahiri's paranoia would use a sophisticated method of encoding messages, with the help of aides.

WHY IS THERE DISCOMFORT AMONG MUSLIMS OVER THE KILLING OF INNOCENTS?

The biggest image problem from among Muslims is that its operations kill many fellow Muslims. This appears frequently in blogs and was among the central themes of the questions posed to Ayman al-Zawahiri in 2007. Questions posed to Zawahiri on this topic could have been reinforced with actual Quranic verses and *hadith*. Zawahiri apologizes for the collateral damage and asserts that the al-Qaida intent is not to kill innocent Muslims but that the end justifies the means. The Muslim world must use this position to undermine Zawahiri Islamically. This can be done by showing that bin Laden, Zawahiri, and al-Qaida affiliates violate:

- Qur'an 5:35: "Whoever kills a person for any reason other than for sowing corruption in the land, it will be as if he had killed the whole of humankind." Are Zawahiri and al-Qaida sowing corruption on earth? Did they kill persons unjustly? These are the types of questions that start us toward fatwas that condemn not just al-Qaida but bin Laden and Zawahiri by name. Condemnations in the twenty-first century need to be less abstract and more specific, naming the Islamist militant leader and the group.
- Qur'an: 4:93: "And for one who kills a believer intentionally, his recompense is Hell, to abide therein; and the wrath of Allah is upon him and His curse, and a tremendous punishment has been prepared for him." Questions to Zawahiri based on this verse include: What constitutes a believer? Does the murder of thousands of Iraqi Muslims by al-Qaida in Iraq, an organization

he fosters, lead to God's wrath? If the martyr is rewarded with heaven, does this verse cancel out suicide operations that led to the death of Muslims in Afghanistan, Iraq, and other regions of the world where Muslims have been killed by al-Qaida operatives?

■ Prophet Muhammad, as reported in *al-Bukhari,* said: "A believer remains within the scope of his religion as long as he does not kill anyone unlawfully."

These verses and sayings of Muhammad demonstrate the hurdles and innovations that al-Qaida must overcome in an aspect of the organization's methodology that is perhaps most distasteful to many Muslims.

Another concept is that of declaring fellow Muslims apostate. This concept was not among the questions asked of Zawahiri, but it should have been, using Islamic argumentation. According to *al-Bukhari* and *Muslim* (two volumes of *hadith*), the Prophet Muhammad said: "Insulting the Muslim is wickedness and fighting him is unbelief." There can be no worse insult to Muslims then calling them disbelievers, a practice both Militant Islamists and Islamists engage in, although the Militant Islamist is more aggressive in prejudging Muslims. The Prophet also said, in the same two volumes: "Do not become unbelievers after I die, killing one another." Perhaps the most famous saying of Muhammad on Muslim-on-Muslim violence is, "When two Muslims draw weapons against each other they are at the brink of Hell. If one of them kills the other, they both enter it together. Someone asked, 'Messenger of God, this one was the murderer, but what was the fault of the murdered?' He replied: 'He was eager to kill the other.'"

Prophet Muhammad so abhorred tribal vendettas and blood feuds that he also said, according Abu Daud, "It is not permissible for the Muslim to frighten his brother." The issue of murder also extended to accomplices through this saying of Prophet Muhammad reported by al-Tabarani that said: "None of you should remain in a place where a man is being killed unjustly, for the curse [of God] descends on anyone who was present and did not defend him."

When Militant Islamists pass off a concentration of war verses and sayings of Muhammad that delve into warfare as the only means of becoming a worthy Muslim, one can counter by saturating the media with Quranic verses and the sayings of the Prophet that oppose this misuse and exposing such narrow readings of the Qur'an and Prophet's sayings. It is important to pose challenges to al-Qaida ideology in the language of the Qur'an and *hadith* and to encourage efforts by Arab governments to do so.

THE NEED TO LABEL QUTB AND ZAWAHIRI PSEUDO-INTELLECTUALS

Islamist militant theorists like Sayyed Qutb and Ayman al-Zawahiri reduce debates to pseudo-intellectual historical logic. For them the story is simple: the Prophet Muhammad was weak in Mecca, and only Jihad brought him victory, respect, and empire. There is no discourse among Militant Islamists or Islamists on the world of Muhammad's inner struggles, his complex character, and aspects of his life other than that of warrior. For this more Muslims should express outrage and withhold support for al-Qaida and other Militant Islamist groups. Free speech, democratic institutions, quality education, and freedom to pursue rational Islamic discussions will be the death knell of Militant Islamist Ideology, as Islamic diversity offers Islamists and Muslims of various political persuasions alternatives to violent political expression. It is vital that the international community, headed by Islamic nations, confront those who attempt to pervert Islam for violent and political causes.

There are clerics and intellectuals who can deconstruct Islamist militant rhetoric using Islamic history and expose the deliberate abuse of religious texts. These intellectuals include Dr. Khaled Abou-el-Fadl of the University of California at Los Angeles, a law professor who has written several books countering Islamist militant ideology using Islamic texts. The Egyptian social and political commentator Dr. Sayed al-Qamani has written many books in Arabic revealing as mythological such Islamist militant slogans as the restoration of the caliphate and the idea of democratic institutions "robbing God of his sovereignty on earth," describing them as incomplete ideologies that will only retard progress in the Islamic world. Dr. Wafa Sultan, a housewife who lives in Los Angeles, took on radical clerics on the al-Jazeerah news channel. These individuals represent the kind of intellectual voice in the Islamic debate that needs to be protected, fostered, and amplified.

Using Islamic legal terminology, terrorism can be categorized in two ways, as crimes of *hiraba* (terrorizing people for personal gain) and crimes of *baghy* (wars to divide people or rebellion), in which the *hadd* punishments are levied. *Hadd* means "limitations," and these punishments are designed to limit certain criminal acts, such as theft, murder, and *hiraba*. These concepts, combined with the Quranic injunction in Surat al-Maida verse 33 that warn of those who sow destruction upon the earth, were used to declare Iraqi tribes that sacked Mosul in the early eighteenth century as hypocritical. Hassan Pasha of the Ottoman Empire declared that the Prophet Muhammad had brought social order that was being violated by these brigand tribes, and he led a relentless, decadelong military campaign against them that did not end until 1714.[6]

Among the four *hadd* punishments sanctioned for those convicted of being brigands and marauders are: execution, by beheading; crucifixion, for those who murder to obtain property; amputation, for those who threaten bodily harm to gain property but do not commit murder; and incarceration for those who terrorize travelers without killing them or stealing from them.

Because al-Qaida combines people who join it for personal gain, thugs, and criminals, along with people who want to exact political change through violence, the label of *baghy* is also important. *Baghy* describes those who, through violence, cause an imbalance to the unity of Muslims or express dissent through violent means. Political gains made through violence, what we today call terrorism, in Islam falls legally under crimes of *baghy*. These are terms important for Muslims to rediscover in labeling Militant Islamists.

ten

Marginalizing al-Qaida

Utilizing al-Qaida Rhetoric and Actions

Creating the conditions for Muslims to delegitimize al-Qaida by exposing its hypocrisy must be a priority, beginning with Usama bin Laden's finances. Steve Coll's 2008 book *The bin Ladens: An Arabian Family in the American Century* reveals that while Usama bin Laden was condemning the international economic system as being against Islam, because of its prohibition of interest or usury, he gladly accepted his monthly stipend from the bin Laden business empire, funds held in trust for Usama, yielding a tidy interest rate. Other hypocrisies include Usama bin Laden criticizing the American troop presence during Operation Desert Storm (1990–1991) while his trust fund and shares that year in the Bin Laden Construction Company were doing very well; Usama accepted his share of the profits made by the Bin Laden Company, which was providing a myriad of services to U.S. military units evicting Saddam Hussein from Kuwait. Coll also points out the irony that one of bin Laden's elder brothers, attempting to attain his doctorate in economics, wrote a dissertation attempting to reconcile Islamic rules on the charging of interest with the modern economic system. We often forget that after a thirteen-month hiatus since his previous tape, Usama bin Laden released a January 2006 video that, if one looks past the Arabic embellishments and flourishes, was defeatist. Bin Laden's statement included attempts to reach a U.S. antiwar movement; threats that an attack would happen against the United States (which has yet to materialize, whether due to effective counterterrorism actions, failure to locate competent personnel, or his dependence on al-Qaida sympathizers); and an offer to uphold a truce with the United States, if America offers it (truces are temporary but usually mentioned in Islamic warfare, when one is in a position of weakness vis-à-vis one's opponent).

Sound bites need to be reshaped to expose al-Qaida's utter failures. Since Usama bin Laden undertook 9/11:

- Arab regimes have more power concentrated in their hands after 9/11, due in part to al-Qaida's actions.
- Al-Qaida has lost its safe haven and perhaps the only militant Salafi emirate ever to exist, Afghanistan.
- Their list of enemies includes the UN, the United States, Arab regimes, corporations, Shiite Muslims, Muslims who do not share their view, Muslims who participate in elections—the list goes on and on. It cannot convert its movement into a political mass mobilization.
- Al-Qaida has formed no tangible vision for the future.
- Many Islamist militant ideologues and even Muslim clergy have condemned al-Qaida's methodology as causing harm to Islam—voices that need to be amplified.
- Al-Qaida has killed many Muslim and non-Muslim civilians (the Zawahiri 2008 answers to questions posted online shows the single most troubling aspect of al-Qaida's methods is the killing of innocent civilians).

Counterarguments to al-Qaida can take any of several lines. They can portray bin Laden's 2006 suggestion of a truce as a sign of al-Qaida's failure. They can craft a message that as democratic institutions and elections occur throughout the region, they empower Muslims and preserve diverse Muslim beliefs (al-Qaida's vision is a regression toward totalitarian single-*shura* [council] rule of diverse Muslim and Arab populations). They can also make known that bin Laden's personal bodyguard, Nasser Ahmed al-Bahri (also known as Abu Jandal), has stated in the Arabic newspaper *al-Quds al-Arabi* that among his responsibilities was to kill bin Laden to prevent his capture alive by his enemies. Bin Laden may embellish this, according to Abu Jandal, as preferring martyrdom to capture, but this is simply a coward's way out, no different from Hitler's suicide in 1945.

The seeds of al-Qaida's destruction lie in its insistence that other Muslims are not pious enough, and this in turn causes *fitna* (dissension) among Muslims. Declaring one a *kafir*—an apostate if a Muslim, an infidel if a non-Muslim—has been a source of debate among scholars for centuries. Even Ibn Taymiyyah, the earliest inspiration for Islamist militant ideology, who used the practice widely, would be troubled by a saying of Prophet Muhammad that states: "If one declares another Muslim an apostate, then one of you is a liar, and it is usually the accuser." When Zawahiri first began his dissent into Islamist militancy, he used a bullhorn to disrupt prayers at a mosque in Cairo. He was confronted by the American Muslim journalist Abdullah Schleifer, who asked what he was doing and charged that he was causing *fitna* between Muslims. Zawahiri simply said, "You are right, Abdullah," and left.[1] Items to amplify in the war against al-Qaida's ideology lie within its own rhetoric and in Muslim criticisms. The Muslim Brotherhood, which offers an alternate means of attaining an Islamic state through the electoral process and grassroots social-welfare programs, is in direct competition with violent Jihad. Zawahiri by his own words demonstrates how elections drain the (violent) Jihad spirit. He is also critical of Hamas.

Violent Militant Islamist ideologues and practitioners, such as Dr. Fadl, the LIFG Noman Benotman, Salman al-Awdah and Muntasser al-Zayyat, and Sheikh Abu Bahseer al-Tartusi, have renounced al-Qaida's methods. This renunciation is coupled with compelling counterarguments written by militants in Egyptian prisons to violent Militant Islamist ideology. Most notable is the work of Egyptian social commentator Makram Muhammad Ahmed, who worked with a cadre of Egyptian Islamic Jihad (EIJ) and Gamaa al-Islamiyah (IG) members of the 1980s and got them to deconstruct Islamically their violent past. Since 2007, state-sponsored members of the clerical hierarchy have issued statements and fatwas condemning al-Qaida; this includes a fall 2007 fatwa of the Grand Mufti of Saudi Arabia, the Grand Mufti al-Azhar, and the Grand Mufti of Egypt, Sheikh Ali Gomaa.

The Grand Mufti of Egypt argues that the principles of sharia, Islamic law, have been applied and interpreted in light of changing realities, that Islamic jurists have traditionally sought to make the application of religion easier, not burdensome. He teaches a new generation of clerics in *al-makased,* a method of seeking to understand the purpose of law before applying it. He considers that Islamists like the Wahhabis toss out centuries of reasoned reflection and reduce the law to a narrow selection of the Qur'an and *hadith.*[2] Add to these clerics active Militant Islamist clerics like Sheikh Hamid al-Ali in Kuwait, who although inciting militant behavior has penned a scathing critique of the Islamic State of Iraq (ISI), arguing that not only was al-Qaida in Iraq not ready to establish a state, not having defeated the U.S. and coalition forces there, but that declaration of the ISI would have caused divisions that militant and violent Salafis could not afford in Iraq. Then there is Dr. Fadl, known as Imam al-Sherief, currently serving a Cairo prison sentence. The former mentor and leader of Zawahiri during Zawahiri's initial formation of Egyptian Islamic Jihad (EIJ), Dr. Fadl wrote a two-hundred-page critique of al-Qaida methodology and interpretation of Islamic jurisprudence. This so impacted Zawahiri that he issued a three-hundred-page rebuttal entitled *The Exoneration*. Zawahiri was no doubt concerned about the stature of Dr. Fadl and, more importantly, about his undermining of al-Qaida using Islamic argumentation and Jihadist language. These clamorous challenges to al-Qaida led to increased propaganda efforts by al-Qaida leadership, starting in 2007. All these combined efforts represent real ideological challenges to al-Qaida specifically, and Militant Islamist Ideology at large.

Is al-Qaida on the ideological defensive? That is a question asked by counterterrorism experts in 2007 and 2008. The last eight statements by al-Qaida leaders have focused on defending themselves ideologically and fending off questions about their methodology.

THE AMMAN MESSAGE: ISLAM AND ISLAMISTS SPEAK OUT AGAINST MILITANT ISLAMISTS

In 2005, King Abdullah of Jordan gathered two hundred leading Islamic clerics and leaders from around the world to sign the "Amman Message." The document recognized eight schools of Islamic thought among Shiites, Sunnis, and Ibadis, forbade the practice of *takfir* against fellow Muslims, and sought to address illegitimate fatwas. The Amman Message also declared that disagreement among scholars and diversity in Islam is a mercy. Former British prime minister Tony Blair praised the message, which received some media attention and then was forgotten—the public imagination thrives only on repeated sound bites. The Amman Message makes permissible the condemnation of Militant Islamist theory among more and more clerics and Islamic leaders.

Such efforts are commendable, and the United States should consider making elements of the Amman Message a talking point. Its two hundred signatories and three hundred endorsers include Iran's Supreme Leader, and the leader of Hezbollah; however, this document holds them accountable in the public image only for issuing irresponsible fatwas, one of the provisions of the Amman Message. Some may argue that for the United States to make statements about the Amman Message could undermine the document, but eleven signatories are those of leading American Muslim leaders and scholars; they could be utilized as a core group to publicize the Amman Message and help distinguish between Islam, Islamist, and Militant Islamist thought in the media, not only to counter Militant Islamist sound bites but also to educate the American public at large. Also, American Muslims in the U.S. government willing to act as spokespersons should be encouraged to do so.[3]

Finally, one way of looking at the list of over five hundred signatories of the Amman Message is as a statement of Islam and Islamists against Militant Islamists. Another missed opportunity to stay on message using wide condemnation of Militant Islamist methods and, by default, ideology is represented by the September 12, 2001, statement of the Organization of Islamic Conference (OIC) secretary general, who represents fifty-seven Muslim nations. He said: "We condemn these savage and criminal acts which are an anathema to all human conventions and values and the monotheist religions, led by Islam." What we must learn is never to let the significance of the Amman Message pass us by in creating a public climate that challenges Militant Islamist ideology and methodology. We must also take the next step and get a document signed by Islamists that condemns Militant Islamist groups, starting with al-Qaida and Usama bin Laden by name. Popular support is just as important to the adversary, as demonstrated by a 2005 letter from Zawahiri to Zarqawi lamenting the loss of the Taliban emirate in Afghanistan due to lack of popular support.

King Abdullah II of Jordan wrote the preface to the marvelous 2007 book *Lost History.*[4] The book is Islam at its best, discussing and bringing to life the theology and psychology of the scholars and leaders who helped advance human understanding of philosophy, the sciences, medicine, mathematics, and much more in ninth-century Baghdad and twelfth-century Spain. Like the unfortunate fixation with Jihad in our time, the book reveals the fixation in past centuries with the Quranic words *ilm* (knowledge) and *aql* (reason) by Muslims working with Jews, Zoroastrians, and Christians under the Islamic injunction, "The ink of the scholar is holier than the blood of the martyr." In 832, Caliph al-Mamun believed that to block out ideas, no matter the source, is to block out the Kingdom of God and the famous House of Wisdom. Al-Mamun dreamed that he was having a discourse with Aristotle, who came to him to answer his question: What is better for the affairs of man, reason or revelation, and which is the righteous way of the two?[5]

Aristotle answers: "They are not in opposition, reason is the portal to revelation."

Caliph al-Mamun: "Many claim to be holy and righteous who say true revelation comes not from the corrupt minds of men but from the pure divine heart."

Aristotle: "Such men have always been with us, be gentle with them, reassure them. Try not to have them fear their minds and ideas, which are sacred gifts from God and reflections of his divine mind. Turn all your resources to translating the great works of thought into Arabic, whether they be written in Greek or Latin or Persian or Sanskrit or any other tongue. Knowledge has no borders, wisdom has no race."

It is such history that Militant Islamists suppress, labeling these important ancestors as Hellenized; their hero of this age was Ibn Hanbal (founder of the Hanbali school of Sunni Islam), who antagonized Caliph al-Mamun. Even then Militant Islamists are selective about the writings of Ibn Hanbal, who argued that the caliph had secular authority to rule but that his powers in matters of faith should be curtailed. Caliph al-Mamun wanted to dictate both secular and religious life, and the two parties refused to compromise.

Among the interesting developments of 2008 in the world of fatwas was the declaration of Mufti Zainul Abdin, of the Pashtun Darra Adem Khel region in Pakistan's North-West Frontier Province, that the Taliban is "outside of Islam." He justified his fatwa because of the Taliban's violence, its failure to follow Islamic teachings, and its *takfir* of fellow Muslims opposed to its dogma. The Mufti writes, "The Taliban consider themselves superior to true Islamic principles and directives ordained by Allah"; he calls on fellow clerics to endorse this opinion and declare the Taliban "inhuman and immoral." The fatwa was issued when a Taliban religious leader of unknown credentials attacked the religious establishment of the North-West Province in a Taliban-issued CD. Islamic scholars have been afraid to criticize the Taliban publicly since the assassination of Maulana Hassan Jan after he declared suicide bombing un-Islamic. This 2008 fatwa is in the heart of the conflict zone between the Taliban and Pakistani forces.[6] This must be publicized and transformed into the moral high ground needed if Pakistani forces, the Afghans, and NATO forces are to expose the Taliban as ignorant brigands and murderers.

Other items for publicity are the scathingly critical book and series of interviews by former Taliban foreign minister Mullah Wakil Mutawakil, who is critical of bin Laden and his abuse of the hospitality extended by Mullah Omar.[7] This is echoed in interviews by former Taliban ambassador to Pakistan Mullah Abdel-Salam Daif.[8] The Grand Mufti of Saudi Arabia in March 2008 warned Saudis against giving money to an organization known for its evil, hurting the Islamic religion and its followers.[9] Mohamed Sifaoui, an Algerian author, journalist, and a person who infiltrated al-Qaida to write a book, *My Assassin Brothers: How I Infiltrated an al-Qaida Cell,* studied theology for four years. He says, "I would say that one must criticize Islamism. . . . I have always felt that it was a moral duty."[10]

The problem with categorizing the threat as Islam or Islamism is that this approach does not capitalize on the nuances between Islam, nonviolent moral supporters of al-Qaida, and political Islamists, and disaggregate them from Militant Islamists, who take the step of recruiting, providing funding, tangibly supporting, and operating in the name of violent Militant Islamist Ideology. However, many Muslims of various backgrounds, including former Militant Islamists, have felt it a moral duty to attack al-Qaida and its ideology. The tribes involved in the Anbar Awakening have come to the realization that al-Qaida is a subculture that needs to be isolated and eradicated.

There is also a U.S. homeland security aspect to advocating a clear definition between Islam, Islamist, and Militant Islamist: the clear delineation revolves on the constitutional guarantees to free speech and freedom of religion. Both Islam and various personal expressions by Muslims collectively and individually are protected under the U.S. Constitution; in many ways the United States offers a free expression to Muslim sects that remain hidden in their countries of origin. Islamist speech, no matter how abhorrent its conception of what an Islamic state should be, is protected by the Constitution. But the tangible support or actual undertaking of violence in the name of an Islamist ideology is not protected by the Constitution. In other words, *dawa* (Islamic proselytizing) and, *tarbiah* (education) are protected, based on certain state and federal restrictions, depending on sources of funding. There are no easy answers to this; however, it is important for state and federal law enforcement to focus on Militant Islamists instead of spending years monitoring a vocal Islamist group. The 9/11 hijacker Muhammad Atta and the eighteen other hijackers existed "under the radar"; focusing on Militant Islamists and disaggregating them from Islam and Islamist groups could prevent this in the future. Measures can be adjusted when Islamists migrate to Militant Islamist activity and back.

SHEIKH MUHAMMAD SAEED AL-BOUTI: A CLERICAL
COUNTER TO AL-QAIDA IDEOLOGY

Muhammad Saeed al-Bouti countered the Militant Islamist definition of Jihad in his book *Jihad fee al-Islam, Kaif Nafahamu? wa Kaif Numarisu?* (Jihad in Islam: How to Understand It? and How to Practice It?). The book, published by Dar al-Fikr Printing in Damascus and Beirut in 1995, makes a compelling argument as to the defensive nature of Jihad, holding that the first arena of Jihad is *dawa*. This is exactly the kind of nuanced argument al-Qaida leaders fear. Al-Bouti was born in 1929 and attained advanced Islamic degrees from Damascus and al-Azhar University. He also combined his theological degrees with a master's in education from al-Azhar, considered the premier institution for Sunni Islamic learning. In 1965, he attained his doctorate in Islamic jurisprudence and rose to become dean of Islamic studies at Damascus University. He delves into the nuances of Jihad that al-Qaida wishes to suppress, such as the complexity of when God sanctioned Prophet Muhammad to undertake Jihad. Bouti believes the view that Jihad was sanctioned after Muhammad fled Mecca for Medina is wrong, that in the Qur'an, verse 52 of al-Furqan, God called Muhammad to Jihad in the sense of calling the Meccans to Islam and a just society. Further, his subsequent persecution while he spread his monotheistic message was a form of Jihad.

Bouti's Complex Definition of Jihad

Bouti writes that Muhammad's Jihad occurred in phases, from calling people to Islam in Mecca and enduring the genocide of Muslims by the Meccans, to defending Medina from the military might of Mecca. More importantly, he says, to abrogate these phases of Jihad by stressing warfare, not struggling to call people to Islam, is pseudo-intellectual, because even when Muhammad was at the height of his influence he consistently called people to Islam through discussion and rational exchange. In addition, the Qur'an is very clear as to Muhammad's primary mission, which was to be a Messenger of God; every decision he made was meant to propagate this mission and his prophecy. Bouti writes that the first arena of Jihad is *dawa* and the propagation of virtue. Jihad as fighting is only a subset that supports the concept of ensuring freedom to conduct *dawa*. He uses the Quranic verses 21 through 24 of al-Ghashiah, verse 48 of al-Shuta, verse 40 of al-Raad, and verse 92 of al-Maida to justify his viewpoint. Much as Militant Islamists narrowly focus on war verses to justify a lifestyle of exclusive violence, Bouti offers a counterargument using select verses from the Qur'an. Just as Militant Islamists attempt to marginalize Quranic verses and Prophet Muhammad's sayings that are inconvenient to their agenda and justification of violence, Bouti writes that the Militant Islamist use of a saying attributed to Muhammad—ordering conflict until all bear witness that there is no God but God and Muhammad is his Messenger—is a weak *hadith,* with a weak chain of attributions. Sayings attributed to Muhammad are of varying degrees of authenticity: Is the chain of narrators broken or not? Who are the narrators, and are they reliable? Bouti also highlights that the Militant Islamist tactic of abrogating the Quranic verse "Let there be no compulsion in matters of religion" is a weak opinion—or, as Bouti writes, *gharib al-isnad.*

Bouti's Ideas on Democracy

Bouti's book holds that the goal of Jihad as fighting is the defense of land, of Muslims, and of public order. It argues that the remedy to apostasy is *dawa,* not compulsion to belief. Bouti, like many learned scholars, agrees that forced belief is not true belief; he uses the Quranic verse 8 of al-Mumtahina, which advocates religious coexistence. Bouti takes a wider and more correct definition of Jihad as struggle, not the narrow definition of Jihad as warfare only. This issue of freedom of conscience and thought to attain true Islamic belief is what Bouti utilized to justify democracy. If democracy ensures freedom of belief, freedom to propagate the faith without persecution, freedom to attain true faith, and justice, Islam has no opinion on the manner in which this is attained. In effect, he sanctions the democratic form of government, federalism, and institutions that freely allow the practice of Islam.

Bouti: Conclusion

The war against al-Qaida is not only a kinetic war of killing and capturing leaders and operatives but a war of language, ideas, and ideology. America's Foreign Area Officers specializing in the Middle East must immerse themselves in the nuances and competition of ideas that al-Qaida faces. Bouti's writings represent the kind of counterideological message and narrative that create a challenging environment for al-Qaida. It must be amplified by America's Muslim allies; the mechanism for amplifying these ideas on the complexity of Jihad linguistically, religiously, and historically allows for a serious way to dissuade those who attempt to make the transition from Muslim to Islamist and finally to Militant Islamist. This requires a higher level of nuance in America's national security debate about the schisms and disagreements inherent among Islam, Islamists, and even Militant Islamists. It also requires an understanding that language, ideology, philosophy, and historical narrative are weapons in this new arena of the global war on terrorism.

IDEOLOGICAL VULNERABILITIES OF AL-QAIDA
IN THE TWENTY-FIRST CENTURY

> Acts of violence don't win wars. Neither wars nor revolutions. Terrorism is useful as a start. But then, the people themselves must act. That's the rationale behind this strike: to mobilize all Algerians, to assess our strength.
>
> BEN M'HIDI, INSURGENT LEADER, IN *BATTLE OF ALGIERS,*
> 1966, BY GILO PORTICOVO

There are intergenerational tensions among Militant Islamist theoreticians that go back to Faraj, Sirriyah, Dr. Fadl, and Zawahiri. These new Militant Islamist thinkers possess a high level of secular education but no formal religious training. They have innovated new interpretations of Islamic concepts based on the objective of transforming Jihad not just as a Muslim obligation but a way of life that is all-consuming. One difference between Egyptian Militant Islamist theory and Saudi Islamist militant theory lies in the fact that the Egyptian model tends to be more inclusive and pluralist in its efforts to globalize and unite Militant Islamist groups. The Saudi models are more exclusive and center more on *tawhid* (monotheism). For them, unity is to be achieved not by compromise but through obedience; therefore al-Qaida requires oaths of fealty from al-Qaida in Iraq, al-Qaida in the Land of the Maghreb, and the Libyan Islamic Fighting Group.

Other tensions are emerging with the rise of anonymous leaders. An example is that the killing of Zarqawi in 2006 led to the rise of the relatively unknown Abu Umar al-Bahgdadi. Other tensions include that between battlefield scholars and those dubbed in Militant Islamist discourse as "armchair scholars." The Kuwaiti Militant Islamist cleric Hamid Ali has spoken against the declaration of the Islamic State of Iraq, not because he is averse to the concept but because he determined that conditions are not right. He also argues that the ISI would be more divisive among the Iraqi Sunnis and that unity among Sunnis is insufficient to declare an Islamic state. Hamid Ali also issued a March 2008 fatwa against those who issue religious rulings at the point of a gun. He is much resented by those on the battlefield, who feel that their fighting coalition forces in Iraq entitle them to make religious rulings.

Another internal disagreement is raised by Abu Musab al-Suri, author of the 1,600-page *Call to Global Islamic Resistance,* a leading strategic thinker of a post–bin Laden al-Qaida, and a rare critic. Abu Musab al-Suri wrote a letter to bin Laden criticizing him for not abiding by his agreement with Mullah Omar to refrain from interviews. Bin Laden had not only pledged to refrain from granting interviews but contracted Khalid Sheikh Muhammad to conduct the 9/11 attacks, thereby leading to the destruction of Mullah Omar's Taliban emirate. Sayf al-Adl, senior al-Qaida military operations chief detained in Iran, opposed 9/11, arguing that it risked the entire al-Qaida organization and destroyed the only Islamic emirate.

In post-Saddam Iraq, among the Sunni insurgency there are other stressors that undermine al-Qaida in Iraq (AQI), such as the tensions between the Islamic Army of Iraq (IAI) and al-Qaida in Iraq. The IAI struggles with AQI over the concept of this fight being for Iraq's Sunnis and not a wider pan-Islamist struggle; the IAI has narrower objectives than AQI. It is a tension between Jihad as *muqawama* (resistance) and Jihad for a wider pan-Islamist objective. In April 2007, the IAI, 1920s Brigade, and Anbar Awakening (Iraqi Sunni tribal confederation) would be labeled *majlis al-kuffar* (an apostate assembly). This caused Abdullah al-Jannabi, known within the insurgency as the Hero of Falluja, to break away from al-Qaida in Iraq and throw in his lot with Iraqi nationalist insurgents. In addition, AQI is undermined by the participatory Sunni political party in Iraq, Hizb Islami (the Islamic Party), an Islamist group with one of its objectives to represent Iraq's Sunnis in the provisional Iraqi government. It wants to limit al-Qaida's objective of widening the conflict and making Iraq the stage for a wider pan-Islamist conflict against the United States. Hizb Islami sees in al-Qaida's attempt to perpetuate Iraq as its stage to challenge the United States only a high cost in Sunni Iraqi lives. AQI accuses Hizb Islami of apostasy; that group counters by accusing AQI of abusing the Jihad and victimizing the Iraqi people. Hizb Islami is critical of the imposition of a stark choice of obedience or death that al-Qaida forces upon its members and the populace at large.

Perhaps the most revealing statement about the predicament of AQI in 2008 was made by Abu Turab al-Jazairi, a leader of AQI in northern Iraq who acknowledged the loss of several cities due to "a large number of tribal leaders betraying Islam," as well as al-Qaida fighters being "carried away with murders and executions."[11] We should not draw a false sense of security from this statement but infer that al-Qaida is under pressure but not totally eliminated in Iraq. The statement that some tribal leaders betrayed Islam should be challenged not as a betrayal of Islam, not even of Islamist political parties, but of Militant Islamist Ideology. Added friction on AQI comes not only from actual combat operations by the United States and the coalition but also the efforts of Col. Sean MacFarland of the 1st Armored Division, who assumed charge of Ramadi in 2006. Colonel MacFarland capitalized on the tribes, protecting their leaders and making the tribal leaders the conduit for American aid. This was a brilliant combination of American firepower, technology, and innovation with Arab tribal, cultural, and regional knowledge. Tribes were encouraged to be part of a winning confederacy, and Iraq's Awakening Tribes was born.[12]

Rumors and discord within al-Qaida, websites, and statements from al-Qaida's leadership are rife with divisions balancing militant pan-Islamist visions versus tribalism, nationalism, and differences in Muslim beliefs. Within the movement itself debates rage: Is Abu Umar al-Baghdadi, the designated emir of al-Qaida in Iraq, really in charge? The pressure to have him make public appearances beyond just audio tapes is omnipresent in Jihadist chat rooms. One impulse al-Qaida benefits from is the perception of its tenacious courage in the face of American forces. This is a perception that needs to be addressed and undermined in the popular media, by painting AQI as exploitative and divisive, whose warriors are barely trained and who now are so desperate they must use women, some of whom are mothers, as suicide bombers.

Another large tension is between al-Qaida and Islamists like Hamas and the Muslim Brotherhood. Zawahiri and al-Qaida have criticized Hamas for being elected through a Western democratic system, that it does not implement Islamic law in Gaza, that it is in indirect talks with Israel, that it accepts a cease-fire with Israel, and that it did not "go global." The Egyptian Brotherhood has not escaped Zawahiri's criticism; he openly says that elections distract the youth from Jihad. Such a statement reveals insecurity in Zawahiri's argumentation, if he sees Islamic political parties as a threat to his popular appeal.

The 2005 Amman Hotel bombings, killing of Shiites, and killing of Sunni tribal chiefs made al-Qaida for a time very unpopular. The challenge is to sustain this unpopularity against Militant Islamists using all elements of national power. This outrage over the killing of Muslims found expression in the 2008 answers to questions orchestrated by Zawahiri, in which, as we have seen, the killing of innocent Muslims featured prominently among the most problematic aspects of al-Qaida methodology. Acumen is needed to amplify these feelings and create a climate in which Islamist militants are subject to increased criticism, making them more controversial. The British strategist Colin Gray recommends that the United States and its functional allies show that terrorism fails and that moderate branches of Islam level the playing field considerably. Gray writes, "We can oblige al-Qaida to compete with its own expectations and promises."[13] He is on to something; however, he does not highlight the mechanics of how to do this—by exploiting diversity and schisms inherent in Islam, Islamist politics, and Militant Islamist groups like al-Qaida.

Such schisms are not new among Militant Islamists. As the Soviets began their 1989 withdrawal from Afghanistan there were deep divisions among the Arab-Afghans who surrounded bin Laden. Abu Musab al-Suri and Abu Walid al-Masri argues that Arabs needed to remain and develop Afghanistan; all the others returned to their countries of origin. Those who could not return or remain sought asylum in Europe. Abu Walid al-Masri recollects how different Islamist militant movements descended into doctrinal debates that eroded the Islamist militant movement's efficacy in Egypt.

Zawahiri laments not having a clerical council within al-Qaida. Also, most of the Islamist militant theoreticians known in the virtual and physical pulpits of the Militant Islamist movements are not colocated with al-Qaida; instead, they are located in London, Denmark, Palestine, Saudi Arabia, Kuwait, and Egypt. They include Hani Sibai (London), Akram Hijazi (Gaza), al-Tartusi (London), and Hamid Ali (Kuwait). Zawahiri today cites Abu Yahya al-Libi as a religious scholar—a debatable notion, as his religious credentials are not clearly known. Adding to this debate about the quality of scholars is Zawahiri's former mentor Dr. Fadl, who warned in 2007 that in Islam the end does not justify the means, to beware of Internet scholars, and that all actions should be based on knowledge, not attempts to make the Qur'an and Islam fit the action. He quotes verse 286 in the Qur'an citing that God does not place upon the soul burdens that it cannot bear. Dr. Fadl links this argument by saying that stealing to finance Jihad is a sin and that one cannot participate in Jihad without one's parents' permission. He outlines six reasons for prohibiting attacks on foreigners:

- There may be Muslims among them.
- Appearance is no longer a criterion as to who is a Muslim.
- Children, women, and priests are exempt from harm.
- Reciprocity—Muslims in non-Muslim lands are generally treated well.
- Animosity toward the government cannot be applied to tourists.

■ Those on visas do not come to fight but are secure in their persons by the concept of *aman* (safe passage).

Zawahiri's rebuttal, *The Exoneration,* read in the context of Dr. Fadl's book and statements, along with Zawahiri's answers to questions, shows deep insecurities in al-Qaida ideology. He cites thirty-seven so-called scholars like Tartusi, Abu Musab al-Suri, and Abu Yahya al-Libi, all questionable clerics of dubious credentials. Zawahiri cites no classical scholars and even neglects Sheikh Abdullah Azzam, who popularized the concept that Jihad is an individual obligation incumbent upon all Muslims, Islam being under siege. Azzam is the spiritual founder of al-Qaida, yet Zawahiri attributes the individual obligation of Jihad to a 1940s Egyptian cleric, Mahmoud Shakir. This oversight only fuels speculation that Zawahiri was involved in the murder of Azzam. In any case, if Zawahiri wishes to dredge up obscure Islamic clerics to bolster his position, we should do the same. Sheikh Mustafa Abdul-Razak (d. 1947) wrote *Tamhid li Tarikh al Fasafah al Islamiyah,* which postulates that the Qur'an encourages *nazar aqli hurr,* free rational thought; that literalist interpretations of the Qur'an are inadequate to its rational depth; and finally, that Islamic rationalism is intrinsic to Islamic revelation.

Such ideological pressures need to be maintained on Zawahiri, and the chorus of voices in the Islamic, Islamist, and Militant Islamist debate increased so as to drown out and reduce to irrelevance Zawahiri and bin Laden, as those with propensity toward Militant Islamist rhetoric seek other websites and media to listen to.

Trends in the Militant Islamist movement that need to be followed tend to radiate from the Arab world and among Arabs. In Indonesia the Militant Islamist movement has been energized by Yemeni immigrants. Ninety percent of Militant Islamist websites are in Arabic, the remainder in a plethora of other languages. Yet Islamist militant websites must not be confused with Islamist Muslim Brotherhood websites, which bear watching but not with the scrutiny that such sites as *al-Sahab* merit.

By delineating between Islam, Islamist, and Militant Islamist, we can begin to place people within a workable spectrum, as individuals who were Militant Islamists reform to become Islamists, and vice versa. In addition, Islamists frustrated and impatient with the political process can lapse into Militant Islamism. One methodology is the use of Militant Islamist terrorists who are promised glory in Iraq, trained, and compelled to undertake suicide missions against Algerian police stations. Or another use is revealed by an excellent Saudi TV show that interviews young teenagers who went to Iraq and returned with severe injuries and personal tales of deception, robbery, and trickery—placing people not wanting to undertake suicide missions unknowingly in suicidal situations. Examples include the native Saudi who insisted he wanted to partake in combat and not deliberate suicide missions; he was told to deliver a fuel truck that proved to have been wired to blow up. When it did, he suffered burns over a good portion of his body.

CONTINUUM OF MILITANT ISLAMIST ASCENDANCY: EBBS AND FLOWS

From an American national security perspective, these trends need to be viewed as part of a continuum, with ebbs and flows. If one maps out Militant Islamist movements from 1798, the arrival of Napoleon's legions into Egypt introduced the wider Islamic world to the reality that the West had overtaken Muslim civilization technologically, socially, and economically. In 1803, we see the ascendancy of the Wahhabi movement in Arabia, which propagated the faith through violence (i.e., Militant Islamist). By 1818, this movement had been subjugated by the Egyptians and Ottomans, and it would not again display Militant Islamist zeal until the creation of modern Saudi Arabia, which began in 1902 and culminated three decades later. The Saudi Kingdom as a government has tamed Militant Islamists and settled back to Salafi Islamist trends, spreading its peculiar and intolerant brand of Islam through *dawa* and not violence. With the denial of Arab national aspirations after World War I, we see the creation of the Muslim Brotherhood, which by 1939 and 1948 boasted its own special militia. Starting in 1954, with Nasser's purges, the movement settled into Islamist politics. The 1967 Six-Day War saw the ascendance of the Sahwa (Islamist Reawakening), which saw a spike in 1979 with the Iranian Revolution, the Mecca takeover, and its culmination in the Soviet-Afghan War. By 1989 Sahwa had begun a descent, followed by the creation of al-Qaida, which began an upward trend with the American embassy bombings in Kenya and Tanzania, the USS *Cole* attack, and 9/11.

Now some can argue it is ebbing, due to pressures from military operations, in the international community, and now clerics, as well as Militant Islamist ideologues, critical of al-Qaida. The following questions suggest themselves:

- What stimulated the ascendance of a Militant Islamist movement?
- How can we erode this ascendance?

- Is the Militant Islamist movement attempting to settle back to being an Islamist political group? Can it?
- What can the United States and international community do to increase the descent of a Militant Islamist group in terms of popularity and appeal?
- Is an Islamist group morphing into Militant Islamist methodology and justifying it through ideology?
- What forces locally can we capitalize on to accelerate the ebbs of a Militant Islamist group?

eleven

Ibn Taymiyyah

Unlocking the Origins of Current Militant Islamist Ideology
(1263–1327)

Ibn Taymiyyah was born in 1263, five years after the sacking of Baghdad in 1258—an event that is etched in Arab Muslim collective memory, as it destroyed the Abbasid caliphate and sowed the seeds of the slow decline of the Muslim world. The Mongols came from the east. Another pressure on the Muslim world—from the West—that Ibn Taymiyyah lived through was the Crusades. Ibn Taymiyyah's time was the midpoint of what would be a total of eight canonical Crusades. These two pressures shaped Ibn Taymiyyah's thought, leading him to begin the demonization of Shiites, Christians, Jews, and Mongols, as well as various forms of Islamic thought. He would completely discount the commonality of the heritage of Jews, Christians, and Muslims and the importance of Christians in early Islam, arguing that this history could be emphasized at the time of the Crusades. The Mongols had converted to Islam when Ibn Taymiyyah was preaching, but he argued that since they had not accepted Islamic law in its totality and still retained their tribal practices, they were apostates. Critics of Ibn Taymiyyah were many, and they offered counterargument that condemning all Christians was not just, that there were differences between Eastern Christians and the Western Christians who had perpetrated the Crusades. In addition, the Mongols, recent converts to Islam, could not be expected to abandon their customs immediately but only gradually—religion needs to be a process of gradual and rational realization. Ibn Taymiyyah's writings against the Mongols were timely for the Egyptian Mamelukes, who were fighting a titanic struggle against the Mongols for the control of the Levant. Ibn Taymiyyah's anti-Mongol message stimulated Egyptians to fight an intra-Muslim civil war (Militant Islamists today do not delve into such fine historical details). Ibn Taymiyyah would influence Abdul-Wahhab the found-

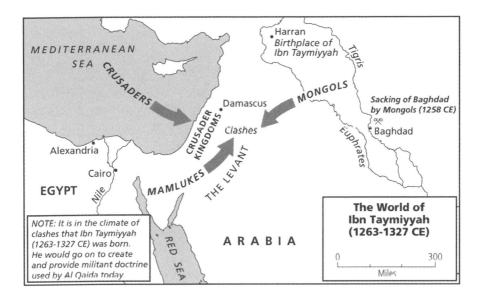

Harran
Birthplace of
Ibn Taymiyyah

MEDITERRANEAN
SEA

CRUSADERS

Tigris

MONGOLS

Damascus

Sacking of Baghdad
by Mongols (1258 CE)

Baghdad

Clashes

CRUSADER KINGDOMS

Alexandria

THE LEVANT

Euphrates

Cairo

EGYPT

Nile

MAMLUKES

NOTE: It is in the climate of
clashes that Ibn Taymiyyah
(1263-1327 CE) was born.
He would go on to create
and provide militant doctrine
used by Al Qaida today

RED SEA

ARABIA

**The World of
Ibn Taymiyyah
(1263-1327 CE)**

0   300

Miles

er of Wahhabism, parts of his writings would influence Khomeini, and his work is a foundational text for both Islamists and Militant Islamists. Another source of discomfort for Muslims critical of Ibn Taymiyyah is his uncompromising definition of what constitutes Islamic law, his contempt for any other school or form of Islamic law that conflicted with his interpretation of Hanbali Sunni Islam (one of four schools of Sunni Islam).

Today, the narrowness of Militant Islamist Ideology not only extends to their reading of the Qur'an, the *hadith* (the Prophet's sayings), and Islamic commentaries. It also takes a narrow reading of thinkers whom they hold up as ideal. Ideologues like Qutb and Ibn Taymiyyah contain contradictions to al-Qaida ideology. It is important to realize that Islamist militants pass off Militant Islamist thinkers and their manifestos as orthodoxy when they are in fact simply Islamic opinions on the state, belief, and military applications of Jihad. The goal of al-Qaida is to create not thinking scholars but pseudo-intellectuals, mechanically and violently imposing their agenda upon Muslims and non-Muslims alike. It should come as no surprise that they would suppress and deemphasize passages even within Ibn Taymiyyah that do not serve their purpose. Today's war against Militant Islamists aims to expose this hypocrisy and to begin portraying violent Islamist militant ideology as pseudo-intellectualism that belongs in the dustbin of history.

What Militant Islamist ideologues focus on in regard to Ibn Taymiyyah was that he viewed the state's chief obligation as to propagate virtue and prevent vice. This argument is found in his book *al-Hisbah fee al-Islam* (Accountability in Islam). He waged a vicious war against Sufis and Shiites, and he wanted the Hanbali School of Sunni Islam imposed upon all Muslims. Ibn Taymiyyah was also a sworn enemy of *bida'a* (innovation), but he could not distinguish between true intellectual thought and unconstructive sects such as the Assassins, whom he opposed. Ibn Taymiyyah believed that if the state is necessary, it must enforce the obligations of religion; this will make clear why the Taliban organized their polity around the fanatical enforcement of every minutia of Islamic orthropraxy.

Ibn Taymiyyah argues in such texts as *al-Siyasa al-Shariyah* (The Sanctified Polity) that the Prophet Muhammad established not a state in Medina but a social order that resembled a state. He makes this argument because the Qur'an and *hadith* do not prescribe or endorse a form of government, such as the caliphate or imamate. More importantly, all of Prophet Muhammad's actions are framed within the context of his prophecy. The Qur'an is clear that his mission is to be a Messenger of God; there is no mention of his being the leader of the growing city confederacy of Medina. The caliphate, imamate, and concepts of *wilaya* (state), he argues, came into being after Muhammad's death in 632. Therefore they are simply political traditions, which Ibn Taymiyyah accepts in the name of social order, but are not divinely ordained. When Muhammad adjudicated, sent military expeditions, and made tribal alliances, one could argue, these were the activities of a sovereign, but Ibn Taymiyyah holds that notwithstanding, to call him such is to detract from his true mission of *nubuwah* (prophecy). Muhammad's object—to build not an empire but a social order—is explicitly contained in Ibn Taymiyyah's political theory. On the *Khalifa* (the caliphate), Ibn Taymiyyah relies on the philosopher Ibn Hazm, arguing that it carries with it no political or religious significance but is merely succession over time. Ibn Hazm is uncomfortable with Islamic political traditions that delegate divine authority to man; Ibn Taymiyyah uses this line as a critique of Shiite views of the imamate and of the twelve imams, their infallibility, and concepts of a person being God's vice-regent on earth.

Ibn Taymiyyah wrote that *dawa* (proselytizing) is necessary before resorting to force, but he does unequivocally endorse the use of violence if *dawa* is exhausted. The debate among Muslims is whether al-Qaida has exhausted *dawa*. Have they damaged the climate for *dawa?* Reading Ibn Taymiyyah will boost our situational awareness of the adversary and expose how selective they are even in their quotations of ideologues they hold dear. Another lesser-known Militant Islamist theorist is Ibn Nuhaas al-Demyati (d. 1412), who wrote *Lessons to Those Who Shy Away from Fighting in the Way of Allah*. It is a concentration of sword verses combined with striving for God; striving has many meanings, but he focuses on fighting, postulating that this life means nothing compared to the hereafter.[1]

Lessons is a one-sided and imbalanced work, designed to compel violent action. These contradictions must be amplified in the public debate. One tactic is to portray Militant Islamists as being impatient with the duty to evangelize and bin Laden's call to Islam as damaging to the faith. If the United States suffers from a credibility gap, then bin Laden's credibility in calling people to Islam is nonexistent after his murder of thousands of Muslims and non-Muslims. Simply put, he cannot possibly be an acceptable ambassador for Islam, and this is something on which many Muslims and non-Muslims can agree.

twelve

Ibn Abdul-Wahhab (1703–1792)

The Founder of Wahhabism

Muhammad ibn Abdul-Wahhab was born in 1703 in the small village of al-Uyaynah, in central Arabia. He came from a family of *ulema* (clerics) and wanted to follow in the footsteps of his ancestors. He traveled to Mecca, Medina, and Najaf to learn Islamic jurisprudence, and during his travels he discovered that Muslims in Arabia were lapsing back into tribal customs and superstitions and calling it Islam. His personality was not that of a patient teacher but of a harsh and fiery preacher, and his observations were hidden by his style of delivery. Frustrated, he returned to central Arabia and over time linked up with Muhammad ibn Saud. Ibn Saud's tribal confederacy, centered on the town of Dir'iyah, was coming apart, and he saw in Abdul-Wahhab's mission to purify Islam in Arabia the means of energizing and then unifying the tribes of central Arabia under his own banner. In 1744 they entered into an alliance and would create the first Saudi state, which lasted from 1744 to 1818. They would create a tribal confederacy made up of the entire Najd (central Arabian) region by:

- Making promises for protection and money
- Intermarriage, whereby tribes married into the al-Sauds or the al-Sauds married into tribes
- Threats to have the cleric Abdul-Wahhab declare a tribe apostate and thereby making them subject to extinction through the collective warfare of all other central tribes and then making them his first two offers once again.

In 1803, the Wahhabis began raiding pilgrims on their way to Mecca from Egypt and the Levant. Their accusations of apostasy were simply covers for their

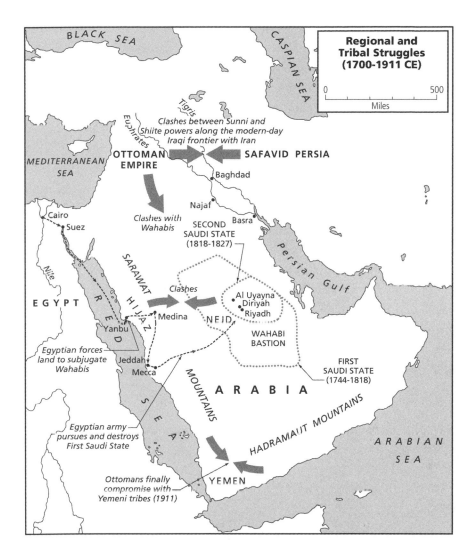

Regional and Tribal Struggles (1700-1911 CE)

0   500
Miles

BLACK SEA

CASPIAN SEA

Tigris

Euphrates

Clashes between Sunni and
Shiite powers along the modern-day
Iraqi frontier with Iran

MEDITERRANEAN SEA

OTTOMAN
EMPIRE

SAFAVID PERSIA

Baghdad

Najaf

Clashes with
Wahabis

SECOND
SAUDI STATE
(1818-1827)

Basra

Cairo

Suez

Nile

SARAWAT

Persian Gulf

HIJAZ

EGYPT

Clashes

Al Uyayna
Diriyah
Riyadh

RED

Medina

NEJD

Yanbu

WAHABI
BASTION

Egyptian forces
land to subjugate
Wahabis

Jeddah
Mecca

MOUNTAINS

A R A B I A

FIRST
SAUDI STATE
(1744-1818)

SEA

HADRAMAUT MOUNTAINS

ARABIAN
SEA

Egyptian army
pursues and destroys
First Saudi State

Ottomans finally
compromise with
Yemeni tribes (1911)

YEMEN

murder and plunder of travelers. The last of these murderous raids in the name
of purifying Islam would occur in southern Iraq in 1922. Amazingly, that same
year Iraqi Sunni and Shiite leaders and clerics convened in Karbala to condemn
the Wahhabi Ikhwan (Brotherhood) as brigands and engage in a common defense
with Iraqi Shiites to repel the Wahhabi raiders.[1]

In 1803 the Wahhabis also drew the ire of the Ottoman sultan Mahmoud II,
the Protector of the Three Holy Mosques. "Wahhabis" is an epithet created by the

Ottomans, akin to "papist" applied to Catholics by Protestants in the sixteenth and seventeenth centuries. The Wahhabis actually called themselves *Muwahiddun* (Unitarians, but implying excessive, obsessive, and destructive zeal for monotheism). The Ottoman sultan ordered his Egyptian viceroy, Muhammad Ali Pasha, to deal with this Wahhabi rabble. It took until 1818, partly because Muhammad Ali, the Egyptian viceroy, sent fellow Albanian officers to die on campaign against the Wahhabis, and his older son Tousson was defeated in the field. However by 1807, he sent his other son, Ibrahim, with twenty thousand troops and unlimited funds to deal with the Wahhabis. Ibrahim landed in the port of Yenbu, took Mecca and Medina, and then proceeded to use force, muskets, cannonade, and troops trained in the French style; offer monthly stipends to tribes that switched sides and rejoined the Ottoman and Egyptian fold; provide tribal protection with cannon and musket; and grant authority to tax on behalf of the Ottomans or Egyptians.

Ibrahim would undermine the fabric of the al-Saud tribal confederacy and in 1818 he arrived in the first Saudi capital Dir'iyah, where he captured the leader of the al-Sauds, Abdul-Aziz (not to be confused with the founder of modern Saudi Arabia of the same name), and sent him along as a gift to the sultan. The city would be leveled. Ibrahim Pasha became an accomplished military commander at sea and on land in the Balkans, fighting for the Ottomans in the Levant and in Egypt, as well as in Arabia and the Sudan.

Wahhabism is only one of many forms of Salafism (return-to-fundamentals movement) that have emerged in the Muslim world in different times and places. Wahhabism evolved in 1744; other Salafi movements include the Sannusis in Libya in 1859, Somali Sayyid Hassan in 1920, the Nigerian Uthman Fadio in 1817, and the Mahdi in Sudan in 1898, to name a few. Salafi movements are exclusively Sunni. Wahhabism is inherent in the fabric of Saudi Arabia and, as an Islamist movement, as we have defined that, is not an immediate threat to national security, as long as Wahhabi tendencies do not lead to violent actions and while those who espouse it stick to nonviolent, evangelical missionary work. But the origin of Wahhabism was tribal and violent. Wahhabism is not compatible with more cosmopolitan and urbanized Muslims, and it does not serve the interests of the United States. Saudis on the Red Sea coast and Eastern Province who retain their Sufi and Shiite heritage are suffering persecution and ostracism, but that problem is slowly being addressed by the current Saudi monarch, King Abdullah, who has recognized the corrosive impact of inter-Muslim accusations of apostasy. We cannot, however, be blind to the fact that Saudis have unfortunately been heavily involved in Militant Islamist groups, even volunteering to fight American forces in Iraq.

Youssef Choueiri, of the University of Exeter's Arabic and Islamic Studies Department, classifies the Islamic movement as "revivalist," "reformist," and "radicalist." The revivalists emerged in the eighteenth and nineteenth centuries and are primarily Salafi in outlook. Reformism is an urban movement of the nineteenth century, composed of state officials, military leaders, intellectuals, and *ulema;* it includes diverse views, from the liberal Taha Hussein to the archconservative Hassan al-Banna, and it was characterized by the open dialogue with European philosophy. In Choueiri's view, radicals are Militant Islamists who obsess about offensive Jihad and God's sovereignty, attempting to impose a totalitarian state using and misusing Islam.[2] Although Choueiri published his views in 1990 and one can disagree with his classifications, he is on the right path in delineating different nuanced strands within the debate over the future of Islam.

It is important to note that while the Egyptians were subduing the Wahhabis between 1803 and 1818, the United States was addressing through naval force another group that used Islam as an excuse to loot, pillage, and enslave—the Barbary Pirates. When John Adams was Minister Plenipotentiary to the Court of Saint James, he was invited to meet with his counterpart representing Tripoli. After an exchange of pleasantries, the Tripolitan ambassador explained that the Qur'an stipulates that Muslims are to make war upon nonbelievers. Adams sized up the situation and cut through the theological exposition, reporting back to Washington that the matter boiled down to simple "greed."[3] This Founding Father had the wisdom to assess the flowery talk and religious expositions and cut to the nub of the matter. Adams did not see this as a clash of civilizations or carry on about the incompatibility of Islam with Western society. We ought to embrace this sort of pragmatism and understand the heart of al-Qaida's expositions is the simple attainment of power through violent means. This is not a new phenomenon. The Wahhabis and Barbary corsairs looted, murdered, plundered, and raped, justifying it all by a narrow interpretation of Islam. But the Wahhabis settled into the pattern of *dawa* with the establishment of the Saudi kingdom in 1932 and went from Militant Islamist to Islamist. The Barbary corsairs could have been categorized as Militant Islamists, but in World War II their descendents fought in such battles as Mount Cassino on the side of the Allies and became stalwart supporters of the West in the Cold War.

thirteen

Hassan al-Banna and the Egyptian Muslim Brotherhood

The First Islamist Political Party

The Egyptian Muslim Brotherhood today represents the most significant organization that opposes the ruling regime in Egypt of Husni Mubarak and his National Democratic Party. One could classify this organization as Islamist, but its historical, ideological, and theoretical influences on Militant Islamist movements cannot be ignored. It has influenced Hamas, Hezbollah, and the National Islamic Front in Sudan, to name a few. The Ikhwan al-Muslimeen (The Muslim Brotherhood) was established by Hassan al-Banna in 1928. Al-Banna was not a cleric but a schoolteacher who taught in the port of Ismailiyah, overlooking the Suez Canal. He saw with disgust the way Egyptian laborers were treated by British and French engineers. This was grueling work, dredging and maintaining the canal; al-Banna would establish the Society of Muslim Brothers as a means of providing social welfare to the families of laborers. He modeled his organization after the Young Men's Christian Association, and on the eve of World War II it had no fewer than one million members in branches throughout Egypt. Al-Banna was a charismatic speaker, who as leader of the Muslim Brotherhood visited thousands of villages throughout Egypt, making them feel that their social issues were his. Photos show him embarking and disembarking from train stations during these village visits.

Al-Banna decided to transform this popular social movement into a political one. However, to participate in Egyptian politics of the 1930s, the Muslim Brotherhood had to compete with other political parties, such as the Wafd and the Young Egyptians. Egyptian politics under the reigns of King Fouad and King Farouk were not immune to nationalist and fascist influences from Europe; the Young Egyptians were modeled after Mussolini's blackshirts; they sported green shirts. To be able to compete the Muslim Brotherhood had to have street thugs, like other political parties in Egypt of the time. Al-Banna found that establishing an Islamic state would face opposition not only from several competing political parties and their thugs but also from the government, which sent in police to disrupt rallies and arrest Muslim Brotherhood leaders.

When World War II broke out in 1939, al-Banna issued an open letter to King Farouk calling for a ban on alcohol and for the segregation of the sexes—note the Islamist concern for public morals, not socioeconomic programs. His frustration with Egyptian politics would lead al-Banna and his Muslim Brotherhood to go underground, creating cells within the Egyptian army and police, gathering weapons, and attempting to put forth candidates in the teachers, doctors and engineers unions, known in Egypt as guilds. He would transform some of his sporting clubs into military training camps and undertake a process of collecting weapons, with which World War II Egypt was awash, as General Erwin Rommel's Afrika Korps threatened the Nile Delta. The object was to create a vanguard to usher in an Islamic state while simultaneously working with Egyptian nationalists to rid Egypt of British domination.

THE MUSLIM BROTHERHOOD, THE 1948 ARAB-ISRAELI WAR, AND NASSER (1948–1970)

Al-Banna would burst forth during the first Arab-Israeli War in 1948. With the Egyptian army went between five and seven thousand *fedayeen* (irregular infantry volunteers) of the Muslim Brotherhood, all of whom had received arms and rudimentary military training; some were incorporated into regular Egyptian army units. Egypt's defeat led to a return of discontented soldiers and Muslim Brotherhood *fedayeen*. Between 1948 and 1952 the Muslim Brotherhood would carry out bombings in Cairo and Alexandria and assassinate officials, including the prime minister, Nokrahsi Pasha. Judge Khizindar would declare the Muslim Brotherhood an illegal entity and would as a result be assassinated.

Al-Banna never lived to see the 1952 revolution that toppled the monarchy of King Farouk; in 1949 he would be gunned down by government agents in retaliation for the murder of the prime minister. Before his death some agreement was made between the Muslim Brotherhood and Nasser's Free Officers Movement. The details are sketchy and little known, but the agreement centered on Nasser's group and the Muslim Brotherhood both recruiting military officers. They were perceived to be undermining one another, and the Free Officers approached the Muslim Brotherhood, through Anwar Sadat, to lend their support to Nasser's effort. Al-Banna expected that this support would be rewarded by the imposition of an Islamic state in Egypt; however, Nasser understood that the majority of Egyptians did not espouse the Brotherhood's Islamic views and that 20 percent of Egypt was Christian. In 1952, Hassan al-Hudeibi, al-Banna's successor as "Supreme Guide," approached the Free Officers to congratulate them on toppling the monarchy and requested a government based on Islamic law. The Free Officers would offer the Brotherhood instead positions within the government in education and religious affairs; the group refused these tokens, and between 1952 and 1954 relations between the Free Officers and the Brotherhood took a turn for the worse.

In 1954, as Nasser was delivering a four-hour speech in Alexandria, eight shots rang out. All missed Nasser, and the assassin (Mahmood Abdel-Azeem) confessed to being a member of the Muslim Brotherhood's Special Apparatus. Nasser's wrath was immediate, and he set about purging the Muslim Brotherhood. So comprehensive was Nasser's purge that members of the Brotherhood sought exile in the Arab monarchies of Saudi Arabia, Kuwait, Jordan, and the Gulf States. These exiles would fill the ranks of the education system of Gulf nations and inculcate a generation of Saudi youth in Militant Islamist ideals.

It is here the Islamist Wahhabism of Saudi Arabia cross-pollinates with the Islamist agenda of the Muslim Brotherhood. Among the youths influenced by Muslim Brotherhood exiles were Usama bin Laden, whose high school teacher was an exile from the Syrian Muslim Brotherhood, and infamous ideologues like Muhammad Qutb, brother of Sayyid Qutb, perhaps the most influential Militant Islamist thinker of the late twentieth century. Another was Abdullah Azzam. The latter two figures taught at King Abdul-Aziz University in Jeddah when Usama bin Laden was a student.

Another result of Nasser's purges was a reexamination by the Muslim Brotherhood as to why it had failed in Egypt. The group retreated into two explanations; one rationalized that the fault was the Muslim Brotherhood's indulgence in the game of revolutionary power politics, abandoning the main focuses of *dawa* (proselytizing) and *tarbiah* (education), which had been the founding principles of the organization in 1928. This group further argued that change from the grass roots up was the methodology to be followed—a view that would evolve into the current Egyptian Muslim Brotherhood, a body of Islamists who represent Egypt's main opposition party to the ruling National Democratic Party. Another line was that society had failed to come to the aid of the Muslim Brotherhood and that this was an indictment of all society; the response, in this view, would be to impose *takfir* (declaration of apostasy) on society. This would be the logic followed by Militant Islamists. However, even among Militant Islamists the question of who would be labeled an apostate plagued the group. Was it certain individual Muslims (the ruler, ministers, etc.)? Every Muslim who worked for the government, whether civil and military? Or should it be society at large?

Arab monarchies provided asylum to the Muslim Brotherhood because they feared Nasser's propaganda calling for an end to feudal monarchies and the ushering in of a United Arab Republic. Nasser represents the heyday of Arab nationalism and pan-Arabism. He would fight a proxy war against Arab monarchies in Yemen from 1962 to 1967, known as "Egypt's Vietnam." It would tie up fifty thousand crack Egyptian troops and draw in an anti-Nasser coalition of Arab monarchies and clandestinely the Israelis, who saw in the Egyptian quagmire in Yemen the opportunity to keep elite forces thousands of miles away from the Israeli border with Sinai. Nasser would die suddenly of a heart attack in September 1970, Anwar Sadat would assume the presidency under tenuous circumstances, and a new phase of the Muslim Brotherhood would emerge.

SADAT AND THE MUSLIM BROTHERHOOD (1970–1981)

Anwar Sadat had immense shoes to fill; he was an unlikely candidate for Egypt's presidency. Nasser had made him vice president in late 1968, having been one of the few members of the Revolutionary Command Council to survive the debacle of the 1967 Six-Day War. Sadat was expected to be a placeholder until a stronger member of the RCC swept him aside and took control. Sadat's biggest threats were from Nasserists, leftists, communists, and pan-Arab nationalists. He could not openly criticize Nasserists or Nasser, due to the deceased president's popularity, and had very limited options in dealing with criticism on the street. Many of his security chiefs and commanders in the armed forces were avidly Nasserist. Sadat would break this political deadlock by granting amnesty to the Muslim Brotherhood and allowing a gradual entrance of Islamist political expression. This meant that Muslim Brotherhood, Nasserist, and leftist thugs battled it out on the streets, weakening the Nasserists. In essence, Sadat used Islamist politics to strengthen his position; he styled himself *Raees al-Mumineen* (President of the Faithful).

Sadat's presidency would be plagued by an initial informal pact with the Muslim Brotherhood. In 1971 he inserted a clause in the Egyptian constitution making Islam "a source" of legislation in the land; this was changed a decade later, replacing the "a" with "the." The partial freedoms granted the Muslim Brotherhood led to the group's taking over college campuses and imposing its brand of fundamentalism. Violent splinter groups would emerge from the Brotherhood, including al-Gamaa al-Islamiyah, al-Takfir wal Hijrah, and various cells in Egypt's colleges. One of these splinter groups would assassinate Sadat in October 1981 as he was reviewing troops on the anniversary of the 1973 Arab-Israeli War. Ayman al-Zawahiri would come of age during this period of experimentation with Qutbist theory, which is the subject of our next chapter.[1]

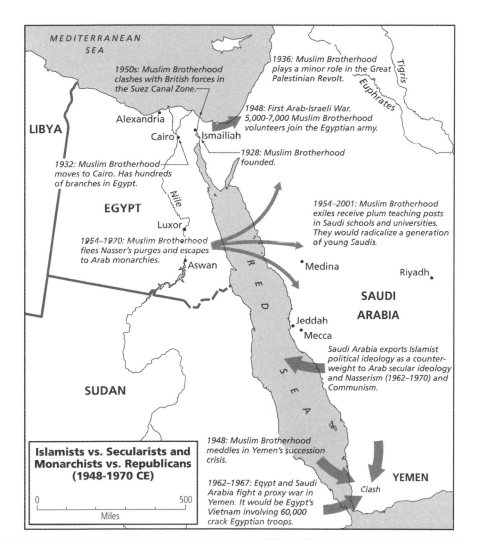

MEDITERRANEAN
SEA

1950s: Muslim Brotherhood clashes with British forces in the Suez Canal Zone.

1936: Muslim Brotherhood plays a minor role in the Great Palestinian Revolt.

Tigris

Euphrates

1948: First Arab-Israeli War. 5,000-7,000 Muslim Brotherhood volunteers join the Egyptian army.

LIBYA

Alexandria

Cairo

Ismailiah

1928: Muslim Brotherhood founded.

1932: Muslim Brotherhood moves to Cairo. Has hundreds of branches in Egypt.

Nile

EGYPT

Luxor

1954-2001: Muslim Brotherhood exiles receive plum teaching posts in Saudi schools and universities. They would radicalize a generation of young Saudis.

1954-1970: Muslim Brotherhood flees Nasser's purges and escapes to Arab monarchies.

Aswan

R E D

Medina

Riyadh

SAUDI

ARABIA

Jeddah

Mecca

Saudi Arabia exports Islamist political ideology as a counterweight to Arab secular ideology and Nasserism (1962–1970) and Communism.

SUDAN

S E A

Islamists vs. Secularists and Monarchists vs. Republicans (1948-1970 CE)

1948: Muslim Brotherhood meddles in Yemen's succession crisis.

0   500

Miles

1962–1967: Egypt and Saudi Arabia fight a proxy war in Yemen. It would be Egypt's Vietnam involving 60,000 crack Egyptian troops.

YEMEN

Clash

fourteen

Sayyid Qutb

Twentieth-Century Theoretician of Militant Islamist Ideology
(1906–1966)

If we are going to stay in there [Vietnam], if we're going to up the escalating chain, we're going to have to educate the [American] people, Mr. President. We haven't done so yet.

DEFENSE SECRETARY ROBERT MCNAMARA, PHONE CONVERSATION WITH
PRESIDENT LYNDON JOHNSON, JUNE 1964

It is impossible to understand Ayman al-Zawahiri or many other Islamist and Militant Islamist figures without delving into Sayyid Qutb. His political manifesto *Milestones along the Road* ranks among the required reading of many Militant Islamists. Qutb's case is also an interesting study into the radicalization process from intellectual and social critic to ardent Egyptian nationalist, to Islamist, and finally Militant Islamist. Qutb was heavily influenced by the Islamist political theories of Abu al-Ala' al-Mawdudi (d. 1974). Mawdudi is considered one of the founding fathers of Pakistan.

Born in 1906 in the village of Qaha, in Assuit, Qutb came from humble peasant origins and was the first of his family to attain a university education. His mother encouraged his education, scraping together funds for him to continue beyond Quranic memorization. At thirteen he entered Dar al-Uloom Teachers College in Cairo and became noted for his poetry and literary criticism. The year was 1919, and he would witness the great revolt in which Egyptians protested British indifference toward independence after World War I. Qutb underwent four intellectual phases during his lifetime, in this order: literary, social, philosophical, and political.[1]

Dar al-Uloom was established to amalgamate the Islamic traditions with European learning and philosophy. Here Qutb would thrive and begin his mixing of Western and Islamic ideals to weave a militant philosophy that would inspire generations of Militant Islamist groups, including al-Qaida. The college was designed to be a moderate alternative between Islamic traditional learning at al-Azhar and Cairo Universities' immersion in the European style of learning. Qutb would also follow with interest the caliphate debates of 1925, as a result of the abolishment of the caliphate by Kemal Ataturk in 1924. About 1933 he graduated from university, serving as a teacher and landing a Ministry of Education posting as a minor bureaucrat. While Qutb was teaching he would turn against his mentor Abbas Mahmoud al-Akkad, who led a moderate Western and Islamic course of study, siding instead with the 1930s Islamist writer Mustafa Sadik al-Rafaee. Qutb would see in al-Rafaee an intellectual who had risen from similar humble origins like himself; his former mentor, al-Akkad, came from Egypt's elite families, and Qutb at the time was attracted more by al-Rafaee's class than his ideas. Qutb saw in al-Akkad, Ahmed Shawky, and Taha Hussein the inability of the Egyptian intellectual youth to innovate on their own and make their own marks on society, so he began to attack them and their emphasis on Western values.

By 1942, Qutb had risen to become a noted writer of literature and poetry. There is speculation that Qutb abandoned his dream of being a great poet due to feelings of inadequacy among the giants of Egyptian poetry of the period, like Ahmed Shawky and Hafez Ibrahim. He would never abandon the poetic style, however, even in his Militant Islamist writings. Qutb would make his mark in social and political criticism. What made 1942 a pivotal year was the Sir Miles Lampson incident: a government was dictated to King Farouk at the point of British armored regiments by the British ambassador, Lampson. This was done to ensure once and for all the Egyptian monarch's commitment to the Allied cause in World War II. However, this incident planted the seeds of the Free Officers Movement under Nasser and discredited the monarchy. Qutb began a scathing critique of the monarchy, and by 1947 he would come to the notice of the Egyptian regime. The incident also gave momentum to the Muslim Brotherhood and gave credence to its line that Islam was the solution to such problems as a corrupt and British-controlled monarchy. Qutb's admirers found him a two-year fellowship in the United States, from 1948 to 1950; it was hoped that with the passing of time the ire of the Egyptian regime would subside and Qutb's radical Egyptian nationalism would cool. The interlude would have the opposite effect, drawing him closer to the world of Militant Islamist theory. It is likely that it was because of complex contradictions within Qutb that he was able to explore freely the Islamist radical option as the only salvation for Egypt and the Middle East.

Qutb may have already formed a hatred of the United States before arriving on America's shores. He had never been outside Egypt, and as he made his way to the United States, he would undergo an inner struggle that centered on the question: Do I indulge in every pleasure America has to offer, or do I become an upstanding Muslim and resist temptation? He would choose the latter, living a relatively isolated life in which he observed Americans and commented on American society. Qutb would comment on race relations, women's freedom, dress, church services, and materialism; he had utter contempt for American society, which he viewed as decadent. Qutb would write a friend, the author Tawfik al-Hakim, a letter ranting about the great industrial factory called the New World, which has no soul, and how a PhD student had presented a dissertation on the best means of washing dishes, snidely writing this was more precious in America than research into the meaning of the Bible. He would travel from New York City to Washington, D.C., and across the country, settling for a year at North Colorado Teachers College in the town of Greeley. There he would pen *Islam and Social Justice,* his first book, and begin exploring his ideas on radical Islamist political thought. This book would be the first of twenty-three that Qutb would write. In America he would read and comment on the Kinsey Report, *Sexuality in America,* and would experience racism when his friends were not allowed into theaters or barbershops because of their race. He would listen to Billy Graham's sermons and wonder how Islamic proselytizing might be used as a bludgeon against communism and nationalism.

Qutb's views on America and his narrow pseudo-intellectual outlook can be best understood by his reductionist view of the United States and its history. He tells readers that the essence of American history is one of competition that needs to be fed by constant warfare. In his view, the founding of the country in 1776 was an unwarranted revolt against the mother country, England. The need to sustain this warlike mentality extended into the American Civil War, a war of dominance over the South. Qutb postulates that America's entry into World War I and II were matters of choice and during his own visit to the United States, between 1948 and 1950, the Korean War was an optional conflict designed to sustain America's military-industrial complex. In Qutb's view, Jefferson's ideal of the pursuit of happiness superseded, and was at the expense of, the collective good. This steeped

Americans in a culture of cheating and deception. Finally, the greatest tragedy was that the United States wished to turn the world into a global factory, which if accomplished would be the greatest human catastrophe. Qutb completely missed the details of American history—of taxation without representation, the War of 1812, the influence of the French Revolution on American politics. His simplistic thesis on the American Civil War made no mention of the events that led to the conflict, from slavery to states' rights. As to World War II, surely the United States had no choice after the attack on Pearl Harbor on December 7, 1941, and the declaration of war on the United States by Hitler a few days after. Qutb was selective in what he observes and hears in his synthesis of the Korean War; also, there were no details on containment, American efforts to challenge the Soviets in Iran or Greece, even in Qutb's neighborhood, in Libya. His selective view even extended to those with whom he interacted. He wrote to a friend, "I want to talk to someone here [the United States] about the soul, philosophy, not cars and the dollar." With whom did Qutb, the recluse, actually interact? He may have suffered from such egotism that he could not move in the campus intellectual scene. Also, maybe his spoken English was not good enough to carry on theosophical discourses with American graduate students or professors.

Among Qutb's many books his most infamous one is *Maalim fee al-Tariq* (Milestones along the Road). His books *Islam and Global Peace* and *Islam and Capitalism* are anti-American diatribes that are receiving a revival today, along with such Qutbist themes as that Islam is engaged in a global struggle against the United States. He also advocates that for the United States "global peace" is a cover for world domination. Individuals like Abdel-Fatah Khalidi, in his 2003 *al-Harb Al-Amriki bee Manather Sayid Qutb,* which revised an 1985 book, re-introduced Qutb on the Arab street, in order to justify a total war against the United States on the eve of Operation Iraqi Freedom. Khalidi's book, published in Amman, Jordan, by Dar al-Uloom, established Khalidi as a major keeper of Qutb's legacy. Khalidi has produced over forty books on Islamist radical theory, at least eight of which delve into Qutb and his theories.

Although Qutb had a destructive obsession with the United States, he was even more venomous toward the Soviet Union. Writing that the Soviets possessed a naked and uninhibited hatred for Islam, Qutb reminded readers that the USSR recognized Israel even before the United States. (Qutb never explained Stalin's reason for doing this, which was to undermine Britain—Stalin misjudged the threat and revised his stance in later years to focus his efforts on the United States.) In

Qutb's view, both the United States and Soviet Union victimized Islam and Muslims. Khalidi argues that Qutb's most prescient explanation of what is happening today was that "the wars between the Soviets and United States will occur in our lands, in Turkey, Iran, Iraq, Syria, Egypt, Pakistan, Afghanistan and North Africa. It will be waged in the petroleum fields of Iran and Arabia. It will destroy our [Muslim] exports, ruin our lives and sow destruction on our own lands."

Qutb would return to Egypt in 1950, and having become even more radicalized, he would be unable to continue at the education ministry. Leaving the ministry he drifted toward the Muslim Brotherhood, where he served as editor of the newspaper *al-Ikhwan* and would involve himself in the intrigues that led to the 1952 revolution that established the Egyptian Republic. This work included inciting attacks on the Suez Canal and making overtures to the Free Officers Association. Qutb would serve as a liaison between the Muslim Brotherhood and the Free Officers, led by Colonel Gamal Abdel Nasser. However, the Free Officers and the Muslim Brotherhood were on a collision course that led to the 1954 assassination attempt against Nasser in Alexandria. This incident, known as the Manshiah incident, after the area where Nasser was delivering his speech at the time, is controversial. Some consider it to have been created by Nasser, staged as a pretext to crush the Muslim Brotherhood. For others it was indeed a Muslim Brotherhood plot, as relations between the two were deteriorating rapidly; in this view it was an attempt to remove Nasser and bolster General Muhammad Neguib. The end result was that from 1954 to 1970 Nasser would purge the Muslim Brotherhood. This would begin Qutb's fifteen years of imprisonment, torture, and further radicalization. Qutb would produce his major Militant Islamist works in Nasser's jails amid torture and violence. Ibn Taymiyyah would also write his militant works in prisons, a victim of the *minha* (inquisition) of the Ghazali Islamic thinkers that dominated the Levant and Egypt at the time. It is unclear, but there is speculation that Qutb identified himself with Ibn Taymiyyah.

QUTB'S FINAL YEARS

The story behind Qutb's execution is important in the elevation of this man's ideas on the street. When an Egyptian judge passed the sentence of death in 1965, Qutb exclaimed, "Praise be to God, for I have spent fifteen years to earn this martyrdom!" Calls began to arrive for Nasser from Arab leaders, who, aware of the popularity of *Milestones along the Road*, argued that his execution would make matters worse and that he should be exiled or serve a life sentence. Jailers entered

Qutb's cells and attempted to get him to leave, to seek asylum in Saudi Arabia, Kuwait, or Jordan. Qutb refused. His sister was brought to convince him to leave the jail, but he told her that his martyrdom was not to be denied: "My words will have more meaning if they execute me!" In February 1966, he was executed.

Qutb's *Milestones* became the manifesto for the *al-Sahwa* (Islamist Reawakening), which emerged in the aftermath of the 1967 Six-Day War. He would stimulate a string of Militant Islamist ideologues, including Muhammad Abdel-Salam Faraj (the dialectic in "near" versus "far" enemy), Ayman al-Zawahiri, Usama bin Laden, Omar Abdul-Rahman ("the blind cleric"), the late Abdullah Azzam (spiritual founder of al-Qaida), and Ahmed Yassin (founder of Hamas).

QUTBIST THEORY: THE FOUNDATIONS OF TWENTIETH-CENTURY MILITANT ISLAMIST IDEOLOGY

Among Qutb's theories was that all of Muslim society in the twentieth century was in a state of *jahiliyah* (ignorance) and that the example of Prophet Muhammad needed to be followed, to shift away from this *jahili* society and establish a true Islamic society from which a vanguard would emerge and incite an Islamist revolution. This is a pseudo-intellectual interpretation of Prophet Muhammad's example, as it ignores the details on how he became leader of Medina, how he left Mecca after ten years of preaching his message. Qutb reduced Muhammad to a simple warlord. This notion of *jahiliyah* as interpreted by Qutb is a powerful concept, however; he argued that Islam was under assault by external and internal forces, from outside and from within, by the West and by fellow Muslims ignorant of their own obsession with materialism, and that therefore Islam had to be saved by any means necessary. Muslims, according to Qutb, needed to rise up against the leaders who allowed this *jahiliyah* and free Muslims from this disease. It is a Militant Islamist, existential concept that empowers the chosen few to do God's work on earth. However, in the Qutbist view of Muhammad's example, Muslims must withdraw from this corrupt society to an emirate, there to perfect Islam and produce a vanguard that can bring in the Islamic revolution.

In addition, Qutb's call for Muslims to isolate themselves contravened the Islamic notion of humans as social beings. In the Qutbist view, modern Arab society is steeped in paganism and cannot be reformed but must be completely destroyed and a new Muslim society built. This view is not in line with the Muslim Brotherhood position, which wants change toward an Islamic society through *islah* (reform) and not *thwarah* (revolution). He likely derived this merciless condemnation of modern Muslim society from the brutality meted out upon him and his fellow prisoners, especially an alleged prison massacre in 1957 in which prisoners were summarily executed in their cells.

Qutb argued that all sovereignty belonged to God and that legislatures and parliament share sovereignty with God and are therefore apostate. In essence, he argues for anarchy, in which to usher in an Islamic society. This notion was known as *hakimiyah*, and it begins to make clear how the late Abu Musab al-Zarqawi ideologically justified the use of violence to keep Iraqis from voting. Qutb also wove fragments of Western philosophy into his Militant Islamist discourse. For instance, he was impressed with the writings of Alexis Carrel's *Man: The Unknown,* a critique of individual value and spirituality in Western civilization.[2] He would listen for hours to Billy Graham's sermons, attempting, as we have seen, to synthesize ways in which Islam could be used as a bludgeon against communism. Qutb postulated that Western civilization had Roman slavery, feudalism, capitalism, Marxism, and Nazism as its roots and that all these have exploited and undermined humanity.[3] His critique was based on fragments of Western civilization Qutb pulled together to synthesize his thesis. There is no commentary on the Reformation, Renaissance, the rise of nationalism, or the triumph of democracy against fascism. The material is further reduced into sound bites for the Islamist Militant foot soldier—that only Islam can isolate Muslims from the infection of Western liberalism, that it is up to this vanguard to force Muslims into Islam. The problem is that there can be no true belief without freedom of choice; Militant Islamists run up against the Quranic injunction "Let there be no compulsion in matters of religion," a verse they conveniently marginalize. Islamist Militants take fragments of Islam to weave a violent political ideology, much as Marx wove together his argument of the stages of history, the dialectic.

Qutb, in *Milestones,* disaggregated Prophet Muhammad's life, separating the Meccan from Medina periods, and focused on nothing but the phases that led to the Prophet's taking up the sword. His exposition of Muhammad's life led to his central thesis that Jihad (in the sense of fighting) is an inherent necessity of Islam. He argued that the faith could not have been spread through proselytizing, preaching, or other peaceful means. Qutb's main source was Ibn Qayim (1292–1350), a disciple of Ibn Taymiyyah (1263–1328). Qutb quoted from Ibn Qayyim's book *Zad al-Ma'ad,* focusing narrowly on the chapter entitled "The Prophet's Treatment of the Unbelievers and Hypocrites from the Beginning of Messengership until his Death," which reduces the Prophet to a warlord.[4] Ibn Qayyim provided

Qutb an opinion and model that broke apart the Prophet's life and picked those aspects that fit his militant worldview and that justified violent direct action. In the case of Ibn Qayyim it was the Crusaders, Shiites, and Sufis; for Qutb it was the West, Arab regimes, and the Muslims who enable both. This is the pattern of Militant Islamist theory, a distillation that does not take a holistic view of Muhammad's life. Suppressed by Militant Islamists is Ibn Qayyim's work as an astronomer and alchemist; he postulated that the Milky Way comprised tightly packed stars and theorized that distant stars are larger than the visible planets. Again, Militant Islamists narrowly focus on aspects of the disciples they quote from; their theory is pseudo-intellectual and selective.[5]

Aside from *Milestones along the Road* (sometimes translated as *Guideposts along the Road*), Qutb published a multivolume commentary on the Qur'an, entitled *Fee Zilal al-Qur'an* (In the Shade of the Qur'an), a detailed analysis of the entire Qur'an, written in Nasser's prisons. *Fee Zilal* is important because in it Qutb argues that Muslims have not understood the Qur'an as a dynamic, battle-oriented document.

Qutb's *Islam and Capitalism* today is being used to give him the aura of a futurist who predicted Islam's struggle with the United States. Militant Islamists of the 1970s and 1980s who attempted to operationalize Qutb's theories include Muhammad Abdel-Salam Faraj, a lead conspirator in the plot to assassinate Anwar Sadat. Faraj, an electrical engineer, would postulate the theory of the "near" and "far" enemy. The near enemy comprises Arab regimes, and the far enemy the United States and other Western democracies. His booklet *al-Farida al-Ghaiba* (The Missing Obligation) postulates that Muslims (Militant Islamists) need to focus their Jihad on the near enemy and then on the far enemy. This trend would be reversed by Usama bin Laden and Ayman al-Zawahiri with the 9/11 attack, causing much consternation among Militant Islamist circles.

It is easy to see in Qutb the trappings of intellectualism and deep philosophical thought. One cannot deny that he is well read and that he thought deeply about Islam, the Qur'an, politics, society, economics, and philosophical matters. However, his theories and attempts to put them into practice clearly expose his pseudo-intellectualism. One cannot be deluded by impressive thought and lofty language or be blind to the essence of Qutb's proposals and the damage they have done to the Muslim world and the disagreements they have caused even among Islamists. Qutb ignored the complex political relationships and treaties that Prophet Muhammad himself engaged in and the long history of alliances and practical politics engaged by the caliphs over centuries. Qutb simply advocated the isolation of all Muslims from the world, hoping this isolation would encourage violent radicalism directed against the United States, the former Soviet Union, and Europe: "Nations should withdraw into the salvation of Islam, by applying its laws in government." Aside from an unhealthy and irrational call for global isolationism, Qutb called for governments to institute Islamic laws but deliberately sidestepped the questions of who would interpret these laws and whose Islam they would interpret. Qutb summed up that Muslims united could oppose Cold War superpowers and that an Islamist bloc should be created as a counterweight to the capitalist and communist blocs. We will see what Qutbism wrought in the twentieth century and now in the twenty-first.

QUTBIST THEORY AND THE MUSLIM BROTHERHOOD: CONSTRUCTIVE OR DIVISIVE?

Sayyid Qutb's Militant Islamist theories would create a schism within the Muslim Brotherhood. The late Supreme Guide of the Brotherhood, Hassan al-Hudaybee, wrote a book entitled *Duaa wa la Qudaa* (Preachers and Not Judges) that refuted Qutbism generally, though not Qutb by name. Hudaybee argued that no person has the right to tell other Muslims that they are apostates and outside the faith. Hudaybee argued that this right is God's alone; he used this to deconstruct Qutb's condemnation of modern Muslim society as *jahili* (ignorant). This rejection of the concept of *takfir* (declaration of apostasy), postulated by Qutb, led many ardent Qutbist members to split into such Militant Islamist groups as Gamaa al-Islamiyah and al-Jihad. One of the conditions of being a member of the Brotherhood is *al-samaa wal taa* (to listen and to obey); one cannot undertake violent actions without leaving the Brotherhood. Militant Islamist splinter groups like al-Jihad and Gamaa al-Islamiyah provide a venue for this violence.

However, the complication is that the Brotherhood does not clearly dissociate itself from members who stray into Militant Islamist groups. In many ways this schism between Islamists like Hudaybee and Militant Islamists like Qutb continues today. Hudaybee's and Qutb's views are being fought over in websites and pamphlets, as well as violently in Iraq, Egypt, and in the Levant. Muntasser al-Zayat, a reformed Militant Islamist who has turned toward Islamist politics, and who shared a cell with Zawahiri, wrote in a 2005 autobiography, *al-Gamaat al-Islamiyah Ruaa min al-Dakhil* (Islamist Groups Observations from the Inside), "I was seriously impacted by Qutb, mainly *Milestones* and *In the Shade of the*

Qur'an." He describes Qutb as giving the Qur'an relevance to the pain and suffering of Egyptians today.[6] For instance, Zawahiri condemns Islamist groups like the Muslim Brotherhood and Hamas for participating in the electoral process. An interesting phenomenon is the discontent of former Militant Islamists and Islamists with the Muslim Brotherhood, who, combining with advocates of a secular state with an Islamic character that has room for diverse Muslim views, have formed the Wasatiyah (Moderate) Party in Egypt.

THE FAILURE OF MILITANT ISLAMIST IDEOLOGY

Another indication of twenty-first-century failure of Militant Islamist Ideology and practice is the group Fatah al-Islam in the Lebanese Nahr al-Barid Palestinian refugee camp. This group openly endorsed al-Qaida's program and was abandoned by organizations such as Fatah, Hamas, and other Palestinian rejectionists (that is, of the West and its culture); the Lebanese Armed Forces dismantled the group in 2007 by force of arms. In the Horn of Africa, tribalism, differences between Islamist and Militant Islamist theories, and pressures from government forces have led to difficulty in establishing any effective al-Qaida franchise. The Muslim Brotherhood has denied and distanced itself from the actions of Gamaa al-Islamiyah, the group that assassinated Anwar Sadat in 1981. This can be seen in the attempts of Islamists to distance themselves from Militant Islamists and of Militant Islamists to distance themselves from the cell that planned and undertook that act of political violence. One lesson learned and discussed by Abdullah Anas, a reformed Algerian Militant Islamist, the son-in-law of Abdullah Azzam, is how the Egyptian Militant Islamists and those espousing Qutbist theory galvanized the Arab-Afghan movement against the Soviets. This would play itself out in the struggle between Abdullah Azzam and Zawahiri over the future of the Arab-Afghan movement after the withdrawal of Soviet forces from Afghanistan. Islamist Militants began arriving from the jails of the Middle East, released by Arab governments as a means of sending them on a one-way trip to their maker, fighting the Soviets. Azzam would be assassinated along with his two sons by a massive vehicle-borne explosive device. The leading suspect is Zawahiri: was Azzam veering from Militant Islamist to Islamist? If so, this was an unacceptable use of the momentum of Arab-Afghans in the aftermath of the withdrawal of the Soviets. In Iraq, the declaration by al-Qaida in Iraq of an Islamic State of Iraq and the disagreements among Militant Islamists on this decision had much to do not only with foreign fighters (non-Iraqis) leading Iraqis in their own country but also the declaration of an Islamic state with al-Qaida's special brand of *fiqh* (Islamic jurisprudence).

Islamists and Militant Islamists take fragments of Islam to justify their nuanced agendas, group one through political and grassroots means, the other through violence and intimidation. However, the nuances must go deeper, and in many ways those who conducted the 9/11 attacks took fragments of Islamist ideology and Islam as well as Militant Islamist theory. The Egyptian Muslim Brotherhood, an Islamist group, has a great challenge in the twenty-first century. Qutb came from within the ranks of the Muslim Brotherhood and developed a distinct radical Militant Islamist Ideology; the condemnation of Qutb by the Muslim Brotherhood must be vocal and frequent. Another complexity is that Militant Islamists like bin Laden were educated by members of the Muslim Brotherhood in exile, escaping Nasser's purges; they represented a disaffected Islamist revolutionary group that would introduce a generation of Saudi and Arabian Gulf youth to fragments of Islamist ideologies, starting with Qutb's Militant Islamist theories. In addition, a former Supreme Guide of the Muslim Brotherhood, Mustafa Mashoor, endorsed a printing of the late Brotherhood member Hassan al-Jamal's memoirs detailing the Brotherhood's insurgency tactics against British forces in the Suez Canal and the 1948 Arab-Israeli War—*Jihad Ikhwan al-Muslimeen fee al-Qanaa wa Filisteen* (Jihad of the Muslim Brotherhood in the Canal and Palestine), published by Cairo's Dar al-Tawzea wal Nashr al-Islamiyah in 2000. It glorifies the methodology of Jihad, although in fact the Muslim Brotherhood volunteers fighting in Palestine and the canal had a negligible combat impact and were a tactical failure, returning to incite violence in Egypt in the late 1940s and early 1950s.

Another problem is commenting on past statements of Muslim Brotherhood Supreme Guides, reconciling the tolerance of Brotherhood founder Hassan al-Banna for Shiites with the anti-Shiite chapter of Supreme Guide Omar al-Tilmisanee's memoirs. Among the divisions between Islamists (not Militant Islamists) are statements by the late Grand Mufti of Saudi Arabia, Sheikh Bin Baz, and the late Grand Saudi Imam Sheikh al-Uthaymeen, who both cautioned that the Muslim Brotherhood should not stray from the main focus of calling people to *tawheed* (uncompromising monotheism). These divisions between the Islamist Muslim Brotherhood and Wahhabis are subtle but exist under the surface.

However, it is also necessary to be aware that Zawahiri attacks by name Islamist clerics like Sheikh Yusuf al-Qaradawi who, while endorsing the tactic of suicide bombings against coalition forces, issued a ruling allowing Muslim-American service members to fight al-Qaida. This is a vivid example of someone who is a friend of neither the United States nor al-Qaida but offers a competing ideology to Zawahiri. In essence, while Zawahiri is the purveyor of Sayyed Qutb's legacy, Qaradawi views Qutb within the overall context of the Muslim Brotherhood and ranks among the keepers of the legacy of Muslim Brotherhood founder Hassan al-Banna. Here is a sampling of statements demonstrating the difference between the Militant Islamist ideologue Zawahiri and the Islamist ideologue Qaradawi. Zawahiri stated, "God has implanted perpetual animosity between Muslims and those of other faiths and is on this basis fighting must commence." Qaradawi's statements include, "Our enmity between the Jews and us [Muslims] is one over land only not faith." Islamist leader and current Muslim Brotherhood Supreme Guide Mahdi Akef says that "we stand not against the Jews but Zionism."

What does not help the Muslim Brotherhood in maintaining its Islamist distinction from Militant Islamists is a set of 1980 children's books calling Jews the perpetual enemy of Islam. Of course, Akef was not leader of the Muslim Brotherhood in 1980, but for him to repudiate such books as going against his public statements and those of other Brotherhood leaders would be a useful step. The United States should be able to counter statements by Akef like, "Without a shadow of a doubt [bin Laden] is a Jihad fighter. . . . [M]ay he be praised and extolled." Another outrageous statement was that he supports al-Qaida's activities against occupation but not against civilians.[7] Akef needs to elaborate on the moral dilemma: Who exactly are the occupiers? Do they include the Islamic Party (i.e., Sunnis who have a quasi–Muslim Brotherhood platform), which works with the Iraqi government? What is the Islamic consequence for al-Qaida's victimization of civilians? That does not help the image of Islamists in separating themselves from Militant Islamists. Finally, he needs to be asked if these statements undermine the Islamist platform and whether these outrageous statements reflect his personal views or those of the Muslim Brotherhood.

Zawahiri also issued a scathing criticism of Shiite cleric and secretary general of Hezbollah, Hassan Nasrallah. He may have done so due in part to the street popularity Hezbollah is enjoying as defenders of Palestinian rights and the image it has cultivated as having militarily challenged Israel and survived during their 2006 clash. Zawahiri's writings and numerous statements betray his innermost desire to be viewed as an Islamic visionary who has taken Qutbism to the next level, holding that *jahiliyah* had so infected Muslims that only violence can shake them out of their stupor and get them to look at their religion in a new way defined by Zawahiri and Militant Islamist ideologues. In essence, it is an "us versus them" mentality, in which the end justifies the means—since the ends are noble, one can kill as many Muslims (after all, they are not really Muslims, having by their passivity consented to corrupt regimes) and non-Muslims alike until a (delusional and elusive) pristine Islamic government is established. We have seen the logical conclusion of this formula in Algeria. One of the most bizarre Militant Islamist communiqués was issued by Antar Zawabri, the late leader of the Groupe Islamique Armée, declaring the entire Algerian population infidels deserving of death, except for his small band of followers.[8]

This declaration represents a reductio ad absurdum of Militant Islamist Ideology. What opportunities then exist for the United States and its allies to amplify these divisions, to marginalize and isolate Militant Islamists ideologically, in the media, covertly, and overtly, utilizing all instruments in the national power?

KEY DATES IN ISLAMIST MILITANT THEORETICAL DIALECTIC

The key dates of recent history that pervade the Militant Islamist imagination start with 1798 and the invasion of Egypt by Napoleon. Why is this significant? Simply put, Muslim leaders had begun understanding that their civilization was in decline vis-à-vis Europe starting in the mid-seventeenth century, but the wider Muslim masses came to this realization only when Napoleon's battalions landed on the shores of Egypt and swept away the Mameluke forces with thirty thousand troops and modern military tactics. To add insult to injury, it took a British naval force, under the command of Admiral Horatio Nelson, to evict the French from Egypt.

This would lead to wider questioning by Muslim masses as to the reasons for the decline of Muslim civilization. A civilization that had brought philosophy, science, and mathematics and led the way in human development in the ninth and twelfth centuries now had to import technology. What was the cause, what was the remedy? Was it because Muslims were not Islamic enough? Had God forsaken the Muslims? Was the problem unwillingness to die for God? Was the answer to emulate Western ways? The questions and proposed remedies continue to this day.

The British occupation of Egypt in 1882 would see the crown jewel of the Ottoman Empire a protectorate of the British Empire. This would further add to the humiliation of Muslims. The Sykes-Picot Agreement of 1916 would divide the Arab dominions of the Ottoman Empire into French and British spheres of influence, break promises made to those who had rebelled against the Ottomans, and deny Arab self-determination at the Versailles Peace Conference. The 1948 Arab-Israeli War and the creation of Israel would be significant, but it was the humiliating defeat of the 1967 Six-Day War that truly discredited pan-Arabism and Nasser.[9]

Thousands attempted to make sense of the defeat through Islamist politics and Militant Islamist groups—this movement was called *al-Sahwa* (The Islamist Reawakening)—and it would bring in many noted figures in Islamist Militance, including Zawahiri, bin Laden, Azzam, Sheikh Yassin, Juhayman al-Otaibee, and many more—the *Sahwa* generation. Abu Musab al-Suri, the twenty-first-century Clausewitz of al-Qaida, views the Militant Islamist movement in intergenerational terms, the first generation being this *al-Sahwa* movement of 1967 through the Soviet-Afghan veterans of 1989, the second generation the one after the Soviet-Afghan War, and third generation the post-9/11 cohort.[10] We too must view Militant Islamists from an intergenerational perspective.

The year 1979 would be a banner one for the *al-Sahwa* generation. In February Khomeini toppled the U.S.-sponsored shah and imposed an Islamic Republic in Iran. In the minds of Islamists and Militant Islamists it became possible to overthrow a U.S.-backed regime. In November 1979, Arabs influenced by the *al-Sahwa* and the imagery of the Iranian revolution took over the Grand Mosque of Mecca and held Saudi security forces at bay for two weeks. Saudi security forces would take over the Grand Mosque after vicious hand-to-hand fighting; however the result was a more conservative Saudi society. On Christmas Eve of 1979 the Soviets would invade Afghanistan and bring the *al-Sahwa* generation into the common experience of donating, volunteering, and, for some, fighting in the Jihad against Soviet forces occupying Afghanistan.

fifteen

Inside the Soviet-Afghan War (1979–1989)

A Militant Islamist Perspective

The most significant figure of the Arab-Afghan movement was a cleric, Abdullah Azzam, born in Jenin, Palestine, in 1941. He would be known as "the Fighting Cleric." His central obsession was to wage offensive Jihad for Muslim glory and to return to his village of Jenin at the head of a conquering Islamic army. He was steeped in the Muslim Brotherhood of Jordan, Syria, Palestine, and Egypt. Azzam would attain the highest levels of clerical training, achieving a doctorate in Islamic jurisprudence from Egypt's al-Azhar University, along the way cultivating friendships and networks of clerics and eliciting the patronage of senior clergy. This extraordinary (from an adversarial perspective) Militant Islamist cleric would:

- Create Maktab al-Khidmat lil Mujahideen (Special Services Office, for Arab-Afghans) to greet and process Arabs showing up to fight the Soviets in the Afghan-Soviet War.
- Transform Usama bin Laden from a donor to someone who through Maktab al-Khidmat would maintain a more permanent presence in Pakistan and Afghanistan. Usama bin Laden energized Azzam's organization with donor money, bringing to bear the resources of the Bin Laden Construction Company. The company's expertise in arranging for the importation of thousands of laborers and the processing of airline tickets, visas, and passports would produce a pipeline for Jihadists from North Africa, Egypt, Arabia, and the Levant to Pakistan.
- Craft a new way of justifying the theories of Jihad, arguing that the age of air travel and an Islam-wide state of siege made Jihad an individual obligation,

incumbent upon all Muslims, and not *fard kifaya* (a collective obligation), limited to those under direct assault only. If, Azzam tried to convince Muslims, Islam was under siege and Jihad was *fard ayn* (an individual obligation), then the obligation of Jihad was no different from prayers or fasting. You do not need the permission of your parents or superiors to pray, and so you do not need anyone's permission to wage Jihad. This goes against the injunctions of Prophet Muhammad that a Muslim's first responsibility is to parents, before undertaking Jihad. Azzam would craft his fatwa (religious edict) into a book and bring together the network of clerics to endorse his religious ruling under the shadow of the Soviet-Afghan War. Abdullah Azzam probably never discussed the Prophet Muhammad's saying, collected by Ibn Majah, that *ilm* (seeking knowledge) is an obligation on every Muslim. That, after all, would detract from perpetual fighting.

- Formulate theories of *al-Qaida al-Sulba* (the Firm Foundation) that would make him the spiritual founder of al-Qaida. The meaning is found in Azzam's books; it refers not exactly to "base," and definitely not "database," but to "foundation," which can mean a base of operation but also a financial foundation that helps Muslims in need with money, as well as technical or military aid.
- Cofound Hamas, with Sheikh Ahmed Yasin.
- Two years before his assassination, follow the example of Hezbollah and bring Militant Islamists to the United States to raise funds, hold conventions, and recruit, out from under the omnipresent gaze of intelligence and internal security apparatuses of the Middle East. Major Militant Islamist conventions would be held in Houston, Jersey City, Kansas City, and many more cities within the United States.

In November 1989, Azzam and his two sons (Muhammad and Ibrahim), on their way to Friday prayers, were killed by a massive vehicle-borne explosive. A few months previously, an explosive had been placed inside the *mimbar* (stepped podium) where he was to deliver the Friday sermon at his neighborhood mosque. That attempt was not carried out, and the bomb was discovered by Azzam's followers, but the vehicle-borne attempt succeeded. His murder remains unsolved; the list of people wanting to assassinate Azzam was long. Top on this list was the Israeli Mossad, Saudi intelligence, the Soviet Committee of State Security (KGB), Pakistan's Islamic State of Iraq, Afghan factions, and Militant Islamist factions. Between 1988 and 1989, the Pakistani government had begun closing down mujahideen training camps. Restrictions were being tightening on the Arab fighters, and Azzam was an open critic of the Pakistani government.

But the leading contender as Azzam's murderer is Ayman al-Zawahiri. Among Militant Islamist circles it was well known that Zawahiri and Azzam despised one another and had spent the better part of a year arguing where to take the Arab-Afghan movement. Azzam had wanted to perfect the "firm foundation" in Afghanistan and then take the Jihad to specific locations, concentrating on one conflict at a time, such as the Soviet Islamic republics, the Philippines, or Palestine. Azzam did not feel that the movement had the strength to attack Arab regimes at this juncture and felt that Militant Islamist zeal needed instead to be directed to conflicts on the periphery and then work their way inward. Zawahiri, however, wanted fighters to return to their respective countries and energize the Islamist and Militant Islamist movements in Egypt, the Gulf, North Africa, and the Levant. In addition, both were competing for the support of bin Laden. Azzam had broken ranks with certain factions of Afghan mujahideen, supporting Ahmed Shah Masood over the Militant Islamist mujahideen faction of Gulbuddin Hekmetyar and Abdul-Rasul Sayyaf. His murder would decide the course of the Arab-Afghan movement, and his theories and legacy would be foundational for al-Qaida.

At the end of the Soviet-Afghan War, Arab-Afghan fighters split into three groups: those who remained in Pakistan/Afghanistan; those who returned to their respective countries; and those who seized the opportunity and sought asylum in Europe, Scandinavia, or the United States. This dispersed network of Arab-Afghans would be capitalized upon by bin Laden to form the basis of a transnational organization known as al-Qaida.

SHEIKH ABDULLAH YUSUF AZZAM:
THE SPIRITUAL FOUNDER OF AL-QAIDA

No study of Militant Islamist ideologues and the cleavages between Militant Islamist and Islamist groups can be complete without delving into the life, actions, theories, and legacy of Abdullah Azzam. Militant Islamist operatives take the nom de guerre "Abu Azzam" in his honor.

A witness to increased Jewish immigration into Palestine in World War II, Azzam was reared on the stories of resistance by the Izz al-Din al-Qassam Brigade, which led guerilla raids against the British and then Jewish settlers. He came from a family of farmers, attached to the land and tradition. Azzam was seven when the first Arab-Israeli War broke out in 1948 and was seared into Arab and Islamic collective memory as *al-Nakbah* (the catastrophe). In the late 1950s, Azzam began his clerical studies in Syria, attaining a Master's degree by 1966. He also would be heavily drawn into the activities of the Syrian Muslim Brotherhood, joining in the criticism of pan-Arabism and calling instead for pan-Islamism. The 1967 Six-Day War, a humiliating defeat for five Arab armies—with Egypt losing the Sinai, Syria the Golan Heights, and Jordan Jerusalem—discredited Nasser and pan-Arabism. The Islamists received a boost, in the form of thousands seeking answers in Islamist politics and a return to religion, in a movement known as the *sahwa al-Islamiyah* (Islamist reawakening), or simply *al-Sahwa*.

After 1967, Azzam never returned to his hometown of Jenin, and the Six-Day War would push him toward more radical Islamist politics. To Azzam, Jihad was fighting, fighting with a gun or with a sword, no more and no less. He would at some point join the Palestinian *fedayeen,* become a Fatah fighter, and train in military camps set up jointly by the Muslim Brotherhood and Fatah. This combination of the secular Fatah and its resources, weapons, and camps with Muslim Brotherhood and Islamists provided an alternative for Islamists and Militant Islamists wanting to undertake military training.[1] Among his observations during his training in Palestinian camps was the need to create an Islamist fighting unit that would be uncorrupted by the ideas of secular Palestinian groups like the Marxist Popular Front for the Liberation of Palestine (PFLP) and Fatah. This would allow for indoctrination in a purely Islamist radical model. This was a Machiavellian world in which pan-Arabist or secular groups were more than willing to undertake guerilla operations at the expense of Islamist radicals wanting martyrdom, only to claim the victory for themselves—a lesson not lost on Azzam.

Soon after 1967, and through his connections within the Syrian, Egyptian, and Palestinian Muslim Brotherhood, he obtained a scholarship to obtain his doctorate in Islamic jurisprudence at Cairo's prestigious al-Azhar University. He would study, cultivate his clerical network, and develop his theories of Jihad as incumbent upon all Muslims. Azzam would undertake a careful study of Islamists and Militant Islamist writers like Ibn Taymiyyah, Abdul-Wahhab, and Sayyid Qutb. His initial idea was that the only way to liberate Palestine was through violent Jihad; he took the Qutbist view that Islam was under siege by the West, culturally, militarily, and economically. He would witness Sadat's amnesty of jailed Muslim Brotherhood members to neutralize the threat from leftists, pan-Arabists, and Nasserists. Azzam would be immersed in this clash between Islamists and pan-Arabists. From Egypt, Azzam traveled to Jordan, where he was fired within a year from the faculty of the University of Amman for his increasingly radical

Islamist views. Azzam would arrive in Jeddah, Saudi Arabia, in the mid- to late 1970s, teaching at King Abdul-Aziz University and joining a cadre of other Muslim Brotherhood members in exile, including Muhammad Qutb, brother of Sayyid Qutb. Usama bin Laden, a student at this time, attended Azzam's fiery lectures on the need for Jihad. Azzam had also woven himself into the good graces of Sheikh Muhammad Bin Baz, the Grand Mufti of Saudi Arabia, and the clerical hierarchy of Saudi Arabia.

In 1979, the Soviets invaded Afghanistan, and by 1981 Azzam had accepted a position at the Islamic University at Islamabad to be close to the Soviet-Afghan War. He would be the Muslim Brotherhood representative in Pakistan, relied upon to handle, as needed, the affairs of the Brotherhood in Peshawar, Islamabad, and Karachi. Azzam realized that no one was greeting at the airport many Arab youths who were showing up to fight, that the Arab effort in the Soviet-Afghan War lacked any real organization. Creating the Maktab al-Khidmat around 1982, he would travel from Peshawar to Saudi Arabia, marketing the Jihad against the Soviets, soliciting donations, and recruiting. Azzam also established contacts with wealthy Saudi sponsors, one of whom was Usama bin Laden, who, until becoming involved in Azzam's project, had been known as a financial donor and organizer for the Afghan Jihad against the Soviets. Bin Laden benefited from an organization that allowed him to remain in Peshawar and play a more direct role in the Soviet-Afghan War, and Azzam benefited from bin Laden's money, organizational expertise, resources, and access.

Bin Laden worked the operational side of Maktab al-Khidmat; the organization would expand as thousands of Militant Islamist and Islamist Arab youths, many released from jail, would be dumped in Pakistan to fight the Soviets. It was hoped by the nations that sent them that they would never return but would fulfill their ardent wish for martyrdom. Azzam used the power of media, mythology, and narrative. He began to publicize the Soviet Jihad for fund drives and recruiting, and many who had the impulse to volunteer for Jihad in Afghanistan but did not know how to travel to the area would seek out Azzam's Maktab al-Khidmat, which could be contacted through the Muslim Brotherhood. Azzam encouraged not only fighters but professionals, like engineers, doctors, and teachers, to help in refugee camps.

EXAMINING AZZAM'S THEORETICAL VIEWS ("THE FIGHTING CLERIC")

Azzam wrote in *Ayyat al-Rahman fee Jihad al-Afghan* (God's Signs in the Afghan Jihad), "The Afghan [-Soviet War] issue is the story of Islam wounded in every part of the globe. Where nation-states have ripped it [Islamic nations] apart in every age and every era." He explained that the Soviet-Afghan War was the same as the situation in Palestine, Chad, Philippines, Syria, Lebanon, and Egypt. "Those [Muslims] who prefer imperial enslavement to foreign rulers; instead of God's glory," Azzam proclaimed. All Jihads, in Azzam's definition, were sacred warfare and "are interrelated and form a singular chain from which the next operation, war or conflict will be born." In other words, Azzam looked upon Afghanistan as only the start of a Jihad of perpetual conflict. Azzam wrote that the Soviet-Afghan War, at a minimum, gave the Palestinians something to look up to and aspire to. The Afghan Jihad was related to the Palestinian one, in that Azzam labels both as *fard ayn,* incumbent upon every Muslim. The Muslim warrior, Azzam urges, must not surrender or lose faith but go from area to area, from trench to trench, to keep his spirit and self alive. Of note, the Algerian Abdullah Anas was brought into the Soviet-Afghan War first through Azzam's fatwa and then by meeting Azzam in Mecca, from where he was expedited to Pakistan and then Afghanistan. Anas would become Azzam's son-in-law and a major critic of Zawahiri, claiming that he may have been involved in Azzam's death.

AZZAM, THE APOSTLE OF *TAKFIR* AND JIHAD: A CLOSE EXAMINATION OF HIS FATWA ON JIHAD

Azzam viewed Prophet Muhammad through one lens, that of warrior; he does not write about him as a father, merchant, arbiter, city leader, youth, or husband. His books are saturated with Jihadic verses and sayings of the Prophet uttered during his struggle for the survival of Islam against the more powerful Meccan oligarchy. Azzam focused on these verses and sayings, quoting liberally from about a dozen chapters of the Qur'an (the Muslim divine book contains 114 chapters), because it is in these few chapters that the heaviest concentration of sword verses are found. He used these sword verses to argue that "the use of the sword and the spear was to compel [humankind] toward the worship of God alone and is a form of *dawa* [proselytizing]." Azzam ignored Muhammad's lifesaving relations with Christians and the Prophet's interactions with the Jewish tribes of Khaybar and Medina. He also ignored the Quranic verse "Let there be no compulsion [in matters] of religion." His Palestinian experience betrayed his obsession with sword verses. He declared that whoever oppose him was among the disbelievers, then delved into *Takfir,* declaring all Muslims and non-Muslims who stood in his way apostates and deserving of death. (This is a concept that has killed Muslim intol lectualism and favors the Islamist militant. *Takfir* is a key ideological weapon among the tools of militant Jihadists today, one that must be exposed and discredited as unacceptable in the information age.)

Azzam then laid out a Manichean argument, a struggle of good and evil. He advocated the concept that (religious) truth requires strength to protect it and that there are those willing to sacrifice themselves to fight people who spread dissent and evil. Azzam's books make it clear that "the evil" was the Soviet Union, Israel, and the United States. He saw Jihad as a duality, that of personal struggle and the ultimate sacrifice for God. The most important *fard* (obligation), and that which Azzam said is missing for Islamic greatness, is Jihad (not struggle but fighting in the cause of God). He wrote and preached that "Jihad has left the common consciousness of Muslims today," meaning that the remedy for Islamic decline was a return to fighting and dying for God. He then outlined the warfare aspect of Jihad as having two aspects.

First, when Muslims are a persecuted minority Jihad becomes *fard kifaya* (an optional obligation), in which the imam authorizes annual expeditions into *Dar el Harb* (the Abode of War), lands considered not under Muslim dominance. To better understand *fard kifaya,* let us look at another application of the concept, the Islamic prayer of the dead. Typically, Muslims are buried by the day after they die, and prayers over their souls are said after the fifth and last prayer in the evening. If you can gather enough Muslims to stay after the final prayer to pray for the dead person, the rest of the congregation is excused. If Jihad is conducted by enough Muslim fighters to defend the homeland, the rest of the community is excused from that obligation as well.

Second, the issue of Jihad as *fard ayn* (individual obligation), Azzam wrote, arises if the infidel enters Islamic lands, if an infidel army masses on an Islamic border, if the infidel takes Muslim prisoners, and finally if the imam's warning to the infidel to leave Islamic lands goes unheeded. Then Jihad becomes an individual obligation, incumbent upon every Muslim and not requiring the permission of husband, creditor, or father. Azzam was in effect removing any authority or restraints upon Jihad, which is a simplistic formula. Islamic history is replete with examples of caliphs, tribal chiefs, or *ulama* (clergy) negotiating and consulting before a declaration of war. Even Muhammad Abdul-Wahhab, the founder of Wahhabism, an ultraconservative strain of Sunni Islam, was concerned about the use of Islam to satisfy the demands of tribal warfare as opposed to what he considered warfare for the faith.

AZZAM'S INTERPRETATION OF JIHAD AS AN INDIVIDUAL DUTY

Azzam opens his book *Jihad Shaab Muslim* (The Jihad of the Muslim Nation) with discussions with Sheikh Bin Baz, the late Grand Mufti of Saudi Arabia. The sheikh had told Azzam that he did not expect the Afghan mujahideen to last seven days against the Soviet onslaught. Azzam was more optimistic. Centuries of fighting in Afghanistan, beginning with the Mongols and Persians, had evolved into a Jihad against Hindus and then a war against the Sikhs. Although Azzam had read about the "Great Game"—the competition between regional powers and Britain for control of Afghanistan—he viewed it only through the lens of Muslim victimization and triumph. He did not mention the struggle between the royal families of Europe and the ensuing fight between Bolshevism and British liberalism that also played out in Afghanistan. Azzam discounted centuries of Islamic debate on the nature of warfare and Jihad, providing a fresh interpretation of Jihad as individual duty. He used images of Afghan suffering and portrayed the Afghan fighter as David versus Goliath, the Soviet war machine. When Jihad becomes a collective obligation, Azzam says, no permission to participate is required. For example, the rules of husband over spouse, of father over child, and of the *mihrim* (guardian) are suspended. Azzam uses Ibn Taymiyyah's fatwa to argue this point, which was pivotal to recruiting efforts during the Soviet-Afghan War. The problem, of course, was that Ibn Taymiyyah represented a narrow view of Islamic jurisprudence. His fatwa was designed to condemn Christians and Jews for the Crusades, to label the Mongols (who had embraced Islam) as apostates, and to further the ambitions of the Mameluke rulers of Egypt, who were locked in a titanic struggle with the Mongols over control of the Levant. Nevertheless Azzam, bin Laden, and Zawahiri quote Ibn Taymiyyah as if his work were orthodoxy and not opinion.

Azzam then takes a further step toward a destructive interpretation of the significance of Jihad in Islamic orthodoxy. He says, "There is no difference between those who leave prayers when they are capable and those who leave Jihad who are capable." Azzam does not declare outright Jihad to be one of the pillars of Islam (that would be akin to adding a sixth pillar to Islam, when there are only five and Jihad is not one of those five), but he comes ideologically close. (It is by understanding such intricacies that one can expose the manipulation of Islamic Jihadists, who pursue the destruction of Western civilization based on false ideology.) Azzam then takes readers on fantasy journeys based on his own travels with Afghan warriors and his witnessing of the Battle of Jaji (1987). He mythologizes Afghan and Arab fighters. He describes the preservation of the bodies of martyrs who died fighting the Soviets, the calmness of their faces in death (as if in a sound, peaceful sleep), and the sweetness of the smell of their dead bodies. He writes of mythological stories of angels fighting alongside Prophet Muhammad and claims that those same angels were fighting alongside the Arab and Afghan mujahideen.

AZZAM LOBBIES THE SUNNI CLERICAL ESTABLISHMENT
FOR AN ENDORSEMENT OF HIS FATWA

Azzam's other book, *Al-Defaa aan Ardhee al-Muslimeen aham furood al-ayaan* (Defending Muslim Lands Is among the Most Important Individual Obligations), is considered his masterpiece. Unlike bin Laden, who issues edicts of dubious authority, Azzam used his clerical connections to get this fatwa endorsed by leading clerical names in Saudi Arabia and Egypt, in a decade in which such fatwas were seen as anticommunist. Azzam understood that a fatwa is only as good as its author and the prominent, like-minded clerics who endorse it. This is where his decades of cultivating a network of clerical colleagues, some in the senior ranks of the Egyptian, Saudi, Syrian, and Pakistani hierarchies, became vital.

Azzam wrote that this fatwa was part of a larger writ he had authored and put before the Grand Mufti of Saudi Arabia, considered the highest clerical authority at the time of the Soviet war in Afghanistan. Bin Baz endorsed it as correct, thereby giving religious sanction to responding to assaults on Muslim lands like Palestine and Afghanistan as incumbent upon all Muslims until these lands were liberated. This militant and radicalist interpretation of twentieth-century global events and the remedy of violent Jihad would be the hallmark of Azzam.

The Palestinian cleric was savvy in urging Bin Baz to write a preface to his fatwa, something the late senior Saudi cleric never got around to, but the sheikh's public endorsement would cause Azzam's theoretical principles on Jihad and collective obligation to be preached at the Bin Laden Mosque in Jeddah, Saudi Arabia, and the Central Mosque in the Saudi capital, Riyadh. The ideological air within Muslim communities in the eighties would be charged with the proposition that Jihad was no longer *fard kifaya* (an optional or collective obligation) but now *fard ayn,* as Islam came under physical, cultural, and media assault. Although crafted against the backdrop of the Soviet invasion of Afghanistan, Azzam's fatwa would have a corrosive impact upon Islam and energize the Islamist militant movement beyond the decadelong Soviet-Afghan War. Azzam quotes Ibn Taymiyyah but is selective even of him; for instance, Ibn Taymiyyah wrote that if the conflict is one of choice, then it is *fard kifaya,* in which not all Muslims participate.[2] But Militant Islamists quote Ibn Taymiyyah not as opinion but as orthodoxy and declare that the main theme of his writings is that Jihad (as fighting) is the best form of worship.

Azzam could debate with, and get the support of, prominent Saudi and Egyptian clerics, as he held a professorship at King Abdul-Aziz University, teaching Islamist jurisprudence. Here he created a cabal of like-minded clerics, chiefly nine of them who endorsed Azzam's single-handed alteration of Jihad from an individual to a collective duty. This group included Abdullah Alwan, Saeed Hawi, Muhammad al-Uthaimeen (who died in 2001 and was among the top clerics in the Wahhabi establishment, with his own website), and Omar Saif. Azzam's book reveals the methodology by which a fatwa is crafted and more importantly how it is politically endorsed through the Sunni clerical establishment. Azzam's fatwa making Jihad in Afghanistan and Palestine a collective obligation incumbent upon all Muslims was presented before the Markaz Taweeah al-Amaa (the Center for Religious Awareness) during the 1983 pilgrimage season in the Saudi town of Mina, on the outskirts of Mecca. Azzam understood that if he received the endorsement of this group and key clerics, his fatwa could be preached to the global clerical establishment through such mechanisms as the World Muslim League. Azzam opened his speech before an international clerical conference at the center during the *Hajj* (pilgrimage to Mecca) by saying: "The Salafs [early followers of Muhammad, purists] and the Khalafs [caliphs] and the entire *fuquha* [clergy] and commentators [on Islam] in every Islamic generation agree that if one inch of Muslim land is attacked, Jihad becomes a collective duty incumbent upon every Muslim man and woman, therefore a son can leave for war without the permission of his father, and a woman without the permission of her husband."

Azzam used the politically charged invasion of Afghanistan by the Soviets and the Palestinian question to alter centuries of commentary on Islamic warfare, arguments as to who should participate in combat and about just war, to propagate a singular, radical view of Jihad first espoused by Ibn Taymiyyah around 1258. He ended his presentation by declaring, "I bring this writ and declaration from the Commander of the Mujahideen [Abdul Rasul Sayyaf] and after living among the Afghans for three years, as the Jihad in Afghanistan is in need of *rijal* [fighters]. So who among you *Ulama* [clergy] objects, let them object now!" On cue, a cleric in the audience declared, "Brother there is no objection in this matter!" Azzam attended this conference as a known figure, a fighting cleric who had already established his program of bringing in young Arabs to fight the Soviets, among whom was Usama bin Laden.

After this meeting Azzam wrote his book *Defending Muslim Lands,* already mentioned. He had the book endorsed by noted Saudi clerics of the time and also by Sheikh Mutaee (Egypt's chief interpreter of the *Sunna,* or Muhammad's life, and the validity of Islamic rulings, as well as an authority on explaining the different *Madhabs,* the four schools of Sunni Islamic law) and Sheikh Omar Saif, a member of Yemen's Higher *Ulama* Council.

In contrast, Usama bin Laden lacks not only clerical credentials but the clerical connections, cultivated over decades and across countries, to have his fatwas endorsed by important names in the Islamist movement. As a Militant Islamist he has isolated many clerics with Islamist credentials with his anti–Muslim Brotherhood stance.

AZZAM ATTEMPTS TO APPEAL TO THE FOUR
SCHOOLS OF SUNNI ISLAM

Azzam synthesized the most radical elements of the four Sunni schools of Islamic law, leaving out any commentary, historical context, or dissenting views, to justify his interpretation of Jihad. He found an eleventh-century text of Ibn Najeem, who commented on a wide variety of subjects, including the exploration of the validity of Prophetic sayings transmitted two centuries after Prophet Muhammad's death, to argue that when Jihad becomes an individual obligation it becomes as obligatory as fasting or prayer. In the Maliki school of Sunni Islam, prevalent in North Africa, it is understood that Jihad to defend Islamic occupied lands can be undertaken by a slave, woman, or adolescent even if forbidden by their ward or master. Azzam was clever in revealing these few lines and not delving too much into historical context or analysis, in that way tying more and more Sunnis to his view and suggesting that Jihad will set you free, an appealing message in a society in which many are without prospects and for youths desperate to establish themselves as individuals within their tribes, families, or communities. Azzam used the analogy of a drowning person: swimmers do not ask permission to make a rescue. If a parent tells you not to pray or fast and to break God's commandments, do you obey? Azzam simplified Islamic law and history; he did not expose his listeners to the intricacies of Islamic law or the hardships that await those who volunteer to fight the Soviets in Afghanistan. He obscured time, place, and precedent to justify his single-minded goal of redeeming Muslim glory through violence. For instance, he said that at the time of Prophet Muhammad there were no class distinctions for warriors, that people with money like Omar and Uthman fought alongside those less privileged. Azzam did not consider that when these men lived, a pre-Islamic

Arabian male learned how to wield a sword and other weapons before reaching maturity, because tribal society demanded it. In addition, the Meccan oligarchy had threatened Muhammad with annihilation in Medina.

JIHAD IN THE AGE OF AIR TRAVEL, AND OTHER MILITANT INNOVATIONS OF AZZAM

Azzam quoted copiously from Ibn Taymiyyah and applied his own modernist interpretation and innovations. Take Ibn Taymiyyah's quote: "If the enemy enters Islamic lands, the entire Islamic empire and nation are one in repelling the invader, they need no permission to travel to the fringe of the Islamic lands to conduct Jihad." Azzam took this and postulated that the information technology and air travel have compressed the concept of the "fringe of Islamic lands." In the past an Islamic province in the Caucasus would be defended by those living there and neighboring nations; today Muslims from Morocco, Egypt, Saudi Arabia, and Syria can respond. These words were preached as early as 1981 and written as early as 1983, foreshadowing the globalized information network that Usama bin Laden would capitalize on for his own agenda and his organization, al-Qaida. Azzam's view of religion is not a compassionate one; he wrote that all religion was sent to preserve faith, person, honor, thought, and property. The reader is left to ponder how these values are to be preserved, but Azzam made clear that violence is an integral and central part of the method.

Azzam delved into making intelligible and acceptable the murder of Muslims. He wrote that if Muslims are held hostage by infidels, war must be waged even at the expense of their lives. He used verse 9 of the Quranic chapter Hujairat, which ordains that Muslim are to be killed if an accommodation cannot be reached. Azzam again did not discuss the fine details of this verse or the painstaking negotiations and truce making Prophet Muhammad underwent before sanctioning warfare.

"We must focus our efforts on Palestine and Afghanistan, because these are central issues in the Muslim world [of the 1980s]," wrote Azzam. He urged those who could not go to Palestine to instead go to Afghanistan, and he discussed the strategic rationality for considering Afghanistan rather than Palestine the central front for the 1980s Jihad, noting that the Afghan war against the Soviets was in the hands of the mujahideen, whereas Palestine was in the hands of the superpowers. Azzam felt more freedom of operation and maneuver in Afghanistan than in Palestine. The Afghan border, he pointed out, is "3,000 kilometers of open borders, and it has no political nation-state control in large sections of the country." In Palestine, Azzam point out, "the borders are tightly controlled and security is omnipresent."

Azzam argued that a myth had spread that the Afghans were in need of money, not manpower. He appealed that the reverse was true and that the presence of Arabs among the Afghans boosted the fighting spirits of the mujahideen, that the presence of one Arab was better than a million dollars. Afghanistan, he said, was designed by God himself, with its terrain and mountains, ideal for Jihad against major powers. Azzam also shamed Muslims: "The weight of the USSR and international communism stands behind the [communist] Afghan government, while Muslims still discuss what to do!"

IMPORTANT QUESTIONS: A KEY TO UNDERSTANDING
AZZAM'S INSECURITIES

Azzam's book addresses questions he thought might arise, and his answers are revealing, demonstrating the insecurities and ideological holes that he wished to plug in the Jihadist rationale. The section shows how Azzam deals with skeptical minds.

Can we apply these fatwas ordaining individual Jihad today? Azzam answered emphatically that Jihad today is an individual duty, like fasting and prayer. He even stated that *Jihad bil nafs* (personal Jihad, or taking matters into your own hands) is superseded by fasting and prayer. This is Azzam's personal reading of Islamic law; there are clerics who would argue that taking matters into your own hands without consultation would lead to chaos. In addition, a few clerics would argue that as long as Muslims who live in non-Muslim lands are free to practice their faith, those lands are not in the abode of war but the *Dar al-Ahd* (Abode of Truce). Of course, Azzam meant only the Soviet-Afghan War and the Palestinian conflicts; it was bin Laden and Zawahiri who would widen the conflict to include the United States and the world at large. Azzam then used the legalistic Islamic rules of prayer to argue that Jihad supersedes prayer, because the five prayers are abbreviated in times of war or when one travels—even a warrior breaks his fast in Ramadan while on campaign. Therefore war is holier than prayer and fasting. The key to this argument is to convince the Islamic world that in a crisis only collective Jihad is the remedy. He took this rationale a step further, saying one does not need the permission of parents to undertake Jihad. He dismissed the concept of taking the permission of the state, with the rationalization that Islam today is restricted and overburdened by *qawmia* (tribalism and nationalism), that geographic boundaries add further restrictions, as well as international treaties like the Sykes-Picot Agreement.

Can we conduct Jihad without a unifying emir (Muslim leader)? He answered yes, arguing that the Crusaders and Mongols were fought under the banners of many Muslim emirs. No single emir directed or sustained these long wars. In addition, none of the *ulama* (clergy) abrogated or cancelled Jihad for lack of a single, unifying emir. He ended by saying that if an emir, an imam (cleric), or even commander of the faithful (in reference to the caliph) falls in battle this does not excuse the obligation of Jihad.

Should we fight for factional Afghan warlords? Azzam replied yes, Muslims should fight despite divisions among Afghan warlords, as the central objective is the preservation of Islamic land, and each warlord is considered an emir.

Should we fight alone when the rest of the Muslims are apathetic? Jihad is incumbent upon those attacked and then upon Muslims bordering the Islamic region under assault, extending in concentric circles. Azzam argued, however, that changed perceptions of time and distance have made Jihad an obligation upon all Muslims who are able.

Should Muslims fight alongside Muslims of questionable morals? Azzam asked rhetorically: Which is the greater evil, Soviets who suppress the Qur'an and occupy Islamic lands or a *qawm* (Muslim people) who sin? As long as they profess the Islamic creed, they are allies. He then makes an interesting observation, saying that if Muslims had banded together over Palestine, there would be no need for George Habbash, the Christian head of the PFLP or Naif Hawatmeh, head of the Democratic Front for the Liberation of Palestine (DLFP), both Marxist radical Palestinian groups.

Should Muslims consult with infidels? Azzam was pragmatic in his answer, saying that aid from the United States was used to pursue the war in Afghanistan and that help from the Soviets was used to further Palestinian objectives. He argued that one can consult non-Muslims as long as Muslims are in a position of strength, the treachery and intent of the non-Muslim are known, and the needs of the Muslim and non-Muslim are known. Truces cannot be made that undermine the central concept of defending Muslim lands or that give up Muslim lands.

Azzam's *Defending Muslim Lands* synthesizes Azzam's central tenet that Jihad is a collective duty for all Muslims. If one accepts that Muslim society is under siege and that the blame for its ills lies not within but on the West, one can manipulate Islamic texts, take them out of historical context, misquote, and mix modernist reinterpretations of Islamic precedence to sanction Azzam's views. If indeed Azzam can establish that Jihad is a collective duty for all Muslims, he can take readers to the next step, which is equating Jihad to prayer and fasting, even placing Jihad above the five pillars of Islam.

This by no means is an accepted interpretation of Islamic law, and it must be countered—otherwise Azzam will entice youth to participate in Jihad without the permission of parents, guardians, spouses, or even the state. His reinterpretation of Jihad must be exposed as a product of Azzam's own time and thinking, a result of the Soviet invasion of Afghanistan; it has no place in today's world and is of dubious Islamic quality. For instance, the Islamist cleric Yusuf al-Qaradawi, no friend of the United States, writes in his *The Lawful and the Prohibited in Islam* that "pleasing one's parents is considered so important in Islam that the son is forbidden to volunteer for Jihad without his parents' permission, in spite of the fact that fighting in the cause of Allah has great merit in Islam."[3] Qaradawi then cites four *hadiths* of Prophet Muhammad that demonstrate the requirement of parental permission for Jihad. Azzam's theories must be countered by arguing the rational and pragmatic decisions that the Prophet Muhammad and his first four successors took involving negotiation, tolerating other faiths, and attempting to coexist, within the confines of seventh-century Arabian tribal politics.

Azzam's book also reveals the clever and political maneuvering that he undertook to get his fatwa endorsed by some of the most noted clerics of the time. Azzam used his clerical connections to give his ideas a voice and to get them endorsed and thereby preached in local mosques in Saudi Arabia, Gaza, and Egypt of the 1980s. Finally, his book reveals the difference between Azzam and bin Laden, where Azzam was pragmatic in limiting Jihad to Afghanistan and Palestine, while bin Laden globalized it. Where Azzam was pragmatic about acknowledging non-Muslim help in Afghanistan and Palestine, bin Laden credits all success to God, his Arab-Afghans, and his Afghan allies. However, Azzam's ideas on Jihad as a collective duty and his use of key radical texts and Islamic commentaries by the likes of Ibn Taymiyyah all form a part of Usama bin Laden's strategic views.

Today's war will not be fought on the Clausewitzian model; it will be fought by analyzing the fantasy ideology of Islamist militancy and making it unappealing to a greater segment of the Muslim population by staying on message with key Islamic laws, histories, and precedents that discredit Azzam, Ibn Taymiyyah, bin Laden, and Zawahiri. To succeed we must immerse ourselves in the literature and the mind of the adversary, just as our forefathers immersed themselves in Russian books that described Soviet tactics, strategy, and international communist ideology.

AZZAM'S STRATEGIC PROGRAM TO FIGHT THE SOVIETS

Azzam stated that the Soviet-Afghan Jihad began as an Islamic *(harakah)* movement with a few *ulama* (clergy). In the vanguard of this fight against the communists were those who best assumed the discipline and orthodoxy of Islam. Azzam endorsed four Afghan warlords who represented the extreme Salafi Islam discipline and religious acceptability: Rabbani, Sayyaf, Hekmetyar, and Khalis. Azzam openly admitted that they had been raised on Mawdudi, Qutb, and Ibn Taymiyyah and had fought the corrupting influence of Sufi Islam in Afghanistan. Islamist militants and Jihadists immerse themselves in the works of these three ideologues while excluding all other forms of Islamic discourse or alternative thought on Jihad.[4]

This small volume by Azzam is noteworthy, as it describes not only theoretical aspects of Islamist militant Jihad but also an actual program of action:

- Islamic religious institutions throughout the Middle East were to send all students to fight the (Soviet) Jihad and support these students with a regular stipend.
- Islamic centers in the United States and Europe could maintain one fighter for between $6,000–8,000 annually.
- A $27,000 donation opened a madrassa in Pakistan, while $54,000 opened a medical clinic for fifty people.
- There were thousands of needy *muhajiroon* (refugees) from Afghanistan in Peshawar.
- Media were absolutely critical to publicize the plight of the Afghans, increase street outrage, and market the Jihad to those willing to volunteer themselves and donate funds to the cause. For Azzam, media were central to the kind of sub-conventional asymmetric war summed up by this statement from Azzam's

book: "We must mount our own counter-media campaign labels like religious extremists was applied successfully by the Jewish media [Azzam was fiercely anti-Jewish] and is designed to undermine the role and significance of Arab Jihadists in places like Afghanistan."

- Families with the means could open their homes to Arab volunteers; those unable to wage the Jihad physically were to consider donating. It took only $8,000 per year to support an Afghan family. These clinics and schools would grow and cultivate a new generation of committed Muslim fighters to wage war against the enemies of Islam.

Azzam's agenda, then, was not humanitarian. He wanted to alter the ideological landscape of the region and develop new soldiers willing to follow his plan toward resolving Muslim grievances. When one thinks of Hamas's and Hezbollah's humanitarian efforts one cannot be blinded to the basic fact that they are meant to support a system and society organized around hatred of an enemy; the enemies in Azzam's time were the Soviets and Israelis, now the United States and the Israelis.

Azzam wanted to stop the flow of Afghans leaving Afghanistan. He argued in *Jihad Shaab Muslim* that the migration was eroding the ability of guerilla fighters (Jihadists) to blend in within villages and urban areas. An Arab who shared a trench with an Afghan would shame him into remaining in Afghanistan. He wrote that the presence of Arabs among the Afghans energized them, because the Arabs arrived thirsty for battle with the Soviets. He concluded that the Afghan Jihad required people more than money. The psychological and moral presence of Arab Jihadists among the Afghans was significant. Afghans wondered why these Arabs would leave the comfort and riches of their own nations to live in a cave with them. Azzam wrote, "How can we [Muslims] have moral laws that make the feeding of the hungry if capable, yet we sit by and see the Soviets attack the *ird* [honor and dignity] of the Afghans belittling them? Lifting *zulm* [oppression] is an *usul al deen* [requirement of faith]."

AZZAM'S POST-SOVIET AFGHAN VISION

In Azzam's global view, Afghanistan is the preface toward the final chapter in a saga that leads toward the liberation of Palestine. He wrote about a post-Soviet Afghanistan program that included the following objectives:

- The Jihad against the Russians had to be transformed into an international Islamist movement, and then into a war against international communism. Azzam called this "a war between the *Ummahs* [collective peoples of Islam versus communism]."

- *Taaleem al-Mujahideen* (the education of the Afghan generation) was perhaps the most important role Arabs could play in the reconstruction of Afghanistan—filling the void left by a lack of *ulama,* demolished schools, and overcrowded orphanages with Arab (Islamist) volunteer teachers and clergy to shape the young Afghan generation.

- Islamic military, financial, engineering talent, media, and medical talent had to be mobilized against the Soviets at large so as to continue the fight.

- To propagate and export militant Jihad from Afghanistan, differences among Arabs and among the Afghan factions had to be resolved. It is here that Azzam made overtures to Ahmed Shah Masood, whereas bin Laden considered Masood an enemy and infidel. (On September 9, 2001, Masood was assassinated by bin Laden, some argue as a prelude to 9/11.)

Azzam viewed a triad of the psychological and ideological shaping an environment conducive to jihadists. In the post-Soviet Afghanistan the goal was to undermine the Soviet Union and liberate its Islamic republics. The Jihad could not end with the eviction of Soviet forces from Afghanistan but had to encompass Kyrgyzstan, Uzbekistan, Tajikistan, and Turkmenistan. Of course, the tactics learned had to be applied to the eventual liberation of Palestine and the defeat of Israel. In Azzam's mind, the Soviet-Afghan War was a dress rehearsal from which to launch a strategic Jihad in areas ripe for Muslim revolution.

Azzam wrote less about condemning Muslims as apostate—a theme bin Laden engages in—and instead focused on the practicality of mass mobilization for Jihad in the name of Islam. Azzam ended his book by writing that no one can remove love and commitment for Jihad from one's very being; no one can prevent a Muslim from fulfilling this (religious) obligation, just as no one can ever divorce him from the love of God and his Prophet (Muhammad). Azzam is absolute in his righteousness and determination. Although he wished more Muslims would join his movement, he shut out any Muslim leader who opposed him by claiming that his own opinion was orthodoxy. He had no room for the intricacies of Prophet Muhammad's life as a negotiator, tribal leader, leader of a city-state, father, husband, or merchant. In Azzam's world the obsession was with Muhammad the warrior, and nothing else mattered. Azzam scorned those Muslims who argued that Muhammad was first and foremost a preacher, who would have remained in Mecca and not fled to Medina if he had been allowed to preach.

As noted earlier, Azzam believed Afghanistan was the *muqadima* (prologue) to what will come in Palestine. He warned that the Israelis might impose border restrictions for access into Palestine but declared that the Israelis could never erase the memory, desire, and yearning for Palestine, that the international Jihad would not rest until the fight for Palestine was resumed. Azzam, like bin Laden and Zawahiri, viewed any peace agreement or negotiation over the status of Palestine as heresy, if it negotiated away an inch of Muslim land. It was only in February 2007 that Hamas agreed to recognize the legitimacy of the Palestinian-Israeli track toward peace. Hamas leaders share Azzam's views.

However, one can detect insecurities in the Sunni militant Salafi movements like al-Qaida when a Shiite terror group Hezbollah took on the Israeli Defense Forces in 2006. The fight between who will assume the mantle of the Palestinian cause, once the purview of states like Egypt, Jordan, and Syria, and the Palestinian Liberation Organization, has in the twenty-first century been left to terror groups like the Shiite militant group Hezbollah, and Sunni militant groups Hamas, Fatah al Islam, and Asbat al Ansar.

In his final pages Azzam describes his vision of Islam triumphant. The question, then, becomes: Whose Islam? If it is his, it will alienate Shiites, Sufis, and some Sunni groups not to mention significant minorities within the Middle East. He also described the concepts under which bin Laden took to name his own new movement al-Qaida:

This *deen* [religion] will triumph and must burst forth from a *qaida al-sulba* [firm foundation] it is from here [Pakistan, Afghanistan, and the Caucasus] that the Turks and their descendents emerged to rule the Ottoman Empire for five centuries, that Mahamadu Ghaznawi founded the Ghaznavid Dynasty and ruled India for centuries, destroying its pagan idols, and that Ahmed Shah Baba ruled Afghanistan, India and Eastern Iran for decades. Will the triumph over the Soviets be the seeds from where an Islamic empire that will alter world history will emerge?

The final sentence of the book is: "It is not an unattainable objective for God is most merciful."

Azzam's post-Soviet strategy would contradict Zawahiri's, and the two had a massive falling-out over the direction to take the Arab-Afghan movement after the Soviets withdrew. Azzam wished to focus on key conflicts one at a time and in the periphery, not on Arab states. He understood that Arab states and donors would likely support Militant Islamist causes if they involved the victimization of Muslims by non-Muslims in places like Palestine and the Philippines. Zawahiri wanted to send these Arab-Afghan veterans back to their respective countries to energize the Islamist movements around the Arab world. In addition, Azzam was making overtures attempting to unite the Afghan factions and endorsed Ahmed Shah Masood ("the Lion of Panshir") as a leader worthy of following. This upset the Islamist Militant groups led by Gulbuddin Hekmetyar and Usama bin Laden. Azzam's assassination in November 1989 determined the fate of the Arab-Afghan movement. The murder of Azzam made bin Laden the most prominent leader of the Arab fighters in Afghanistan and allowed Zawahiri to proceed with plans to bring the combat experience and motivation learned fighting the Soviets to Egypt.

LESSONS AZZAM CAN OFFER U.S. MILITARY LEADERS AND COUNTERTERRORISM SPECIALISTS

What can one learn from Azzam? The first point is the absolutism of Azzam's cause. Second, although bin Laden was a disciple of Azzam, there are things in which he diverges from Azzam; Azzam never alienated Arab regimes the way bin Laden has. Third, the basic structure of schools, media, and clinics for the Jihad was adopted by bin Laden and applied in Afghanistan and Sudan. Finally, the issue of Jihad being a collective obligation is a core construct in Islamist militant fantasy ideology, yet it can and must be debated, particularly among Muslim scholars who disagree with this view. These scholars, both in the West and in the region, must be given a voice and encouraged to dispel this view using contradictory interpretations of Islam. The West must not define Islam as the enemy, but it must label the ideology of Jihad and *takfir* (declaration of apostasy) as an enemy ideology — a derivative of Islam that has no place in the twenty-first century and that has condemned Muslims and non-Muslims with equal ferocity since its inception.

It is important for readers to look beyond Sheikh Azzam's fantasy ideology and appreciate the strategic, operational, and tactical advice he bequeathed to al-Qaida, Hamas, and many other Islamist militant groups. His beatification began soon after his assassination and took its ultimate expression in the posthumous publication of his collected sermons in 1992, as *Al-Tarbiah al-Jadidah wal Binaa*

(New Self-Discipline and Reconstruction), published first in Peshawar, Pakistan, and made available in the Middle East through a Jerusalem printing house. It is perhaps the best distillation of Azzam's Islamist militant theories. It starts with an attack on Sufism, Baha'i, and Sunni groups who are attempting to rationalize and ideologically attack the one-sided interpretations of Jihad that he and his radical Sunni-Salafist groups espouse. Azzam thought in terms not just of victory against the Soviets but of Islamic generations to come; he was obsessed with leaving a legacy that has been manifested in large measure by Usama bin Laden and al-Qaida. The very name of al-Qaida has its origins in Azzam's concept of a "firm foundation," in which:

- One *manhaj* (Islamic legal system) prevails (there are four major schools of Sunni Islamic law, a multitude of Shiite sects, and various Sufi sects in Islam).
- A single fundamentalist interpretation (as espoused by Azzam) is put into practice.
- A vanguard of self-disciplined fighters defends oppressed Muslims around the globe, going from one conflict to the next.
- Muslims are measured by their *taqwa* (piety).
- Islamist (radical) movements and Militant Islamists mitigate their divisions and come together in a unified cause.
- A single Salafi concept sees a global perspective in regard to benefits Muslims globally and not the day-to-day practices or regional benefits.

In an effort to resolve differences between Islamists and Militant Islamists, Azzam made overtures to the late Afghan fighter Ahmed Shah Masood, going so far as endorsing him. This was in opposition to the agenda of violent Militant Islamists like the Afghan leader Hekmetyar, as well as of bin Laden and Zawahiri. Azzam stumbled upon a fault line, and his killers were likely Militant Islamists. Ahmed Shah Masood, leader of the Northern Alliance, would be an implacable foe of the Taliban and would be assassinated by al-Qaida two days before 9/11. Azzam's sermons, books, and videos are staples of the radicalization process.

sixteen

Usama bin Laden

A Quick Exposé

If inciting people to do that is terrorism, and if killing those who kill our sons
is terrorism, then let history be witness that we are terrorists.

USAMA BIN LADEN, OCTOBER 2001 AL-JAZEERA INTERVIEW

It is impossible to understand Usama bin Laden without comprehending the
family history, in particular that of his father, Muhammad Awad bin Laden, a
true rags-to-riches story. Muhammad bin Laden came from the impoverished
Wadi Doan region of the Hadramaut mountain range. He was so poor that he and
his older brother Abdullah migrated to Somalia and Ethiopia to find their fortunes.
Muhammad bin Laden, not finding success in East Africa, migrated to the seaport
town of Jeddah in the late 1920s or early 1930s; there he worked as a porter and
baggage handler, performing odd jobs in the reconstruction of crumbling homes
made of such rudimentary materials as mud bricks and coral, which required constant maintenance. He and his brother pooled their resources and purchased trucks
and cranes that could be used for the off-loading of cargo and construction projects. By 1967, the year of Muhammad bin Laden's death, his bin Laden Construction Company would be worth $300 million, and he would be a valued partner of
the government of Saudi Arabia.

His first major contract was the construction of a ramp allowing the car of the
ailing, wheelchair-bound King Abdul-Aziz to reach the second floor of his Jeddah
palace. (The king's wheelchair was a gift from President Franklin Roosevelt.) Bin
Laden's second major project was the construction of the palace, in Riyadh, of
Crown Prince Saud, who was so pleased with the work that further government

contracts were sent bin Laden's way. Bin Laden would be integral to the building of roads, schools, and hospitals, and he was given the contracts for the grand mosques of Mecca and Medina. Bin Laden would play a role as a supplicant to the Saudi royal family, never involving himself in their disputes or taking sides. However, in 1963, one crisis could not be avoided: Saud had become king and was spending the country into the ground. His spending had become such a liability that it began to impact on the running of key institutions of government, including the armed forces.

Cleaning up this fiscal mess fell to Crown Prince Faisal. Details are murky, but it is reputed that the Council of Princes decided to confront the king and recommend that he abdicate in favor of Faisal. King Saud took the advice badly and barricaded himself in his Riyadh palace, refusing to talk to any member of the council. The only person the monarch would talk to was the man who had built his palace. Muhammad bin Laden convinced the monarch that this public standoff was damaging the kingdom and that pan-Arabists, Nasser, and leftists were watching for an opportunity to undermine the state. Saudi Arabia and Nasser were locked in a proxy war in Yemen, and the Saudi cities of Najran and Jizan were under aerial threat from Egyptian bombers. King Saud took the advice and abdicated. The new King Faisal ibn Abdul-Aziz attempted to get a loan from the National Commercial Bank, run by another Yemeni-Saudi dynasty, the bin Mahfouzes, but Saudi credit was so bad that the request was refused. Bin Laden is reputed to have financed the government, in part, for a time, allowing the new king to focus on setting the country on the right course.

This made bin Laden indispensable to the Saudi government. One of his company's projects was to build a road, partly military in purpose, to link the city of Najran with the Yemeni border, giving access to royalist Yemeni insurgents to fight Egyptian units and Republican Yemeni forces. Muhammad bin Laden built a winding highway, with tunnels, connecting central Arabia to Mecca through the Sarawat Escarpment, a mountain range that divides Arabia into two unequal parts.

In his own life, Muhammad bin Laden indulged his lust for women by constantly replacing his fourth wife. Some fourth wives were married for a day, others for a year; Muhammad bin Laden would then divorce them and remarry. Usama bin Laden's mother, Alia Ghanem, would be one of those fourth wives; married at the age of fifteen, a little over a year later she was passed off to a Syrian executive of the Bin Laden Construction Company. The only product of their marriage was Usama, the fifteenth of seventeen sons of the fifty-six children known to have been sired by Muhammad bin Laden. Usama bin Laden would admire almost all aspects of his father, except for his practice of polygamy. Islamic law sanctions four wives if you are able to treat all four equally but states that as it is impossible to treat four human beings equally, you are to restrict yourself to one wife. In addition, Prophet Muhammad was monogamous, married to his wife Khadija bint Khuwailid from 595 until her death in 619. So Islam in essence lends itself to monogamy; although Usama bin Laden does not believe in monogamy as such, he does believe that the fourth wife is not a plaything to be discarded on a whim.

Usama was raised primarily by his stepfather and mother in Jeddah, although he had frequent visits with his father. He was not raised an ordinary child, for his stepfather was his biological father's employee; therefore Usama acted as the eldest and surrogate parent to his half-brothers and half-sisters. However, he would suffer ostracism as a son of a divorced mother. As a child Usama enjoyed going on desert outings, raiding horses, and pushing his body by subsisting on dates and water, re-creating in his imagination the desert warriors of the early Islamic conquest. He was inculcated at school with an austere Wahhabism that considered itself the only valid form of Islamic expression and belief. This was reinforced by a layer of politicized Islam and Qutbism in high school and college. He attended King Abdul-Aziz University, from 1974 to 1979; some of his other brothers attended some of the finest universities and preparatory schools in the West. Usama rarely ventured outside Saudi Arabia before 1979, except for, reputedly, traveling to seek medical treatment for his infant son in either the United Kingdom or the United States.

Usama would be given a construction commission to prove his worth to the construction company; he dropped out of the university and totally absorbed himself in the project but failed. This could partly explain why he sought glory in other ways, latching onto Jihad as a new lifestyle. In 1979 and early 1980, he would find a calling in fund-raising and traveling to Pakistan to lavish millions on Afghan refugees and mujahideen fighters. As we have seen, Abdullah Azzam brought Usama into an organization in chaos, which Usama would start to set right in 1983. Azzam was one of many father figures Usama would follow in the world of Militant Islamist theory and practice. However, frustration at Jihadist "tourism" and the treatment of Arab warriors by the Afghans as guests, not worthy fighters, would lead him to establish his own organization of Arabs dedicated to fighting the Soviets as a unit. Such an organization he thought was needed for Arab-Muslim self-esteem. It would be known as Bait al-Ansar (House of the Partisans) and would engage in combat in Jaji; its effectiveness and impact on the Soviet-Afghan War would be mythologized by al-Qaida.

PSYCHIATRIC DIAGNOSIS OF USAMA BIN LADEN

A Dartmouth Medical College clinical psychiatrist, Dr. Peter Olsson, has published a psychiatric assessment of Usama bin Laden. Olsson's study contains historical errors (such as having Muhammad bin Laden getting the commission to rebuild the grand mosques of Mecca and Medina in 1973, when in fact he died in 1967), but it is valuable. *The Cult of Osama* delves into the impact of his father's excessive polygamy, Usama's search for a father figure, his relationship with his mother, and Usama's poetry, as well as issues of shame, humiliation, and disappointment that humanize the al-Qaida leader and drive the reader to the diagnosis of mixed narcissistic, paranoid/persecutory complexes with additional malignant narcissism.[1] Bin Laden has had two wives. His son Omar left him, finding his lifestyle intolerable. In January 2008 Omar appeared with his British wife, saying he wished to become an ambassador of peace between Muslims and the West.[2] His intent needs to be explored to assess to what extent he is willing to denounce his father's worldview and actions publicly.

The process of deconstructing Usama bin Laden personally in the public media will become more commonplace once clerics shift from attacking al-Qaida to attacking bin Laden by name. His malignant narcissism will also elicit a response from his followers, which is exactly what is needed—that is, a setting in which the Islamists respond to *our* media attempts, instead of the other way around.

USAMA BIN LADEN'S COLLEGE YEARS

At King Abdul-Aziz University Usama bin Laden studied commerce and business administration. There he was influenced by the presence of university instructors who were openly affiliated with the Muslim Brotherhood, some having fled Nasser's persecution. Another infusion of Egyptian instructors affiliated with the Muslim Brotherhood entered Saudi Arabia when radical clerics, teachers, and professors were granted amnesty by Sadat in 1971 to serve as counterweights to Nasserists and leftists. Others opted to leave Egypt and seek their fortunes and radicalize the Islamist movement in the friendlier environment of Saudi Arabia. Another current that facilitated the Islamist environment in Saudi Arabia was the assassination of King Faisal ibn Abdul-Aziz in 1975 by Prince Feisal ibn Musaid, a delusional character who blamed Faisal for the death of a radical relative who had been killed while attempting to dismantle Saudi Arabia's first television tower. (The assassin had spent time in the United States, had a history of alcohol and drug addiction, and had been arrested.) The Saudi clergy blamed Western values for King Faisal's assassination and saw them as permeating Saudi life. This led to a government-sanctioned wave of fundamentalism in the kingdom.

Bin Laden's college years were likely dominated by discussions of the Iranian Revolution, the takeover of the Grand Mosque in Mecca by Juhaiman al-Utaybah, and a mixture of Egyptian Islamist militancy and Wahhabism—a potent mix that would stimulate and shape bin Laden. Only an Islamic government, it was argued, could save the kingdom and the Muslim world from the dangers of westernization; these anti-Western values were a useful tool for the Saudi royals of the period, who argued for a traditional conservatism that preserved the monarchy while placating the fundamentalists. However the reaffirmation of the Faustian bargain between clergy and royals of Saudi Arabia would be shattered by the 1990 Iraqi invasion of Kuwait and Operation Desert Storm. King Abdul-Aziz University is where bin Laden came into contact with Azzam ("the Fighting Cleric"), Muhammad Qutb (brother of Jihadist ideologue Sayyid Qutb), and an environment that would foster the movement, born in 1967, known as al-Sahwa (the Islamist reawakening).

POST–SOVIET-AFGHAN WAR AL-QAIDA (1989–1991):
BIN LADEN'S TERRORIST ARCHITECTURE

Bin Laden returned to Saudi Arabia in 1989 feeling abandoned and betrayed by Pakistan. The Arab-Afghan movement (ranging between 12,000 and 25,000 members) had split into three general groups:

- Those who had left Afghanistan and sought political asylum in Europe, mainly Germany, Scandinavia, France, and England.
- Arab-Afghans who had returned to their countries of origin to militarize Islamist parties and groups and foment a violent Islamist revolution.
- People who shared in Azzam's vision of a rapid-response brigade ready to deploy to conflicts involving Muslims, starting with the former Soviet Islamic republics. They remained in Afghanistan, al-Qaida al-Sulba ("the firm foundation"), from which to launch violent Jihad.

Bin Laden would use all three groups of Jihadists in Europe, the Middle East, and Southwest Asia to begin constructing a global terrorist architecture of facilitators, operatives, and technical experts. Bin Laden could train fighters in Afghanistan, rely on contacts in Yemen, and receive access to Western technology and banking through Soviet Jihadist asylum seekers in Europe. Bin Laden's possibilities and options were endless.

The first post-Soviet al-Qaida training camp, claims Abdul-Rahim Ali, in his 2004 *Hilf al-Irhaab,* was established in Yemen in 1990 or 1991.[3] Zawahiri and bin Laden dispatched Muhammad al-Makawi (known as Seif-al-Adl) from Afghanistan to Yemen to set up facilities there. The former Egyptian special-forces field-grade officer established three camps in the Murahqasha Mountains in the Hadramaut region of Yemen, home of the Hashid tribe. The camps were named after two Islamic battles, Badr and Qadisiyah, with the third named after the mountains themselves. The plan was to attract those wishing to carry out Azzam's vision of a rapid-response brigade, collecting Arab-Afghan veterans to train a new generation of recruits. An al-Qaida veteran commander, Abu Ubaydah al-Banshiri, was sent from Afghanistan to Kenya to connect with Somali Islamist groups and seek opportunities for an al-Qaida presence in Kenya and the rest of East Africa. In the Philippines, bin Laden began to turn his attention to Abu Sayyaf.

Zawahiri's central objectives merged into bin Laden's, which was to usher in the "clash of cultures." This was his vision in the early nineties, and it was his vision in 2005 when in a letter to the late Zarqawi he called Iraq the central front. In the nineties he wrote, "We must establish a small presence first from where we can wage war until the caliphate is reestablished."

DETAILS OF BIN LADEN'S SUDAN AND AFRICA CONNECTIONS

In May 1998, Saudi authorities detained Saeedi Taieb, a business associate and relative by marriage of Usama bin Laden. Taieb confessed to managing bin Laden's financial transactions through a web of numerous individuals that held and transferred funds. He had established various front companies with the express purpose of opening bank accounts in Europe and the United States. Investigation of Taieb's financial web revealed a concentrated infusion of funds to Nairobi, Kenya.

This money trail uncovered bin Laden's Sudanese years (1991–1996), when he proved to have been busy not only in planning the embassy bombings in Kenya and Tanzania but with a series of secret meetings and conferences, mainly in 1992 and 1993, to strategize and concentrate the efforts of global Jihad and Arab "rejectionist" groups—that is, Islamist and secular ideological groups opposed to the United States and the global order it imposes—fighting the United States. Conducted under the auspices of Sheikh Hassan al-Turabi and held in Khartoum, these conventions were attended by many representatives of various Islamist radical groups. Their collective agenda was to search for ways to relieve pressure on the Sudanese government fighting the Christians in the south of Sudan by striking the nations supporting the Christians and its Sudan People's Liberation Army. Nations like Uganda, Kenya, and Tanzania were supporting Christian fighters locked in a guerilla campaign against the Sudanese army. Another agenda item was to roll back America's presence in East Africa, and among the proposals was to bomb its embassies. It was in these series of discussions and exchanges in the early nineties that the embassy bombings in Nairobi and Dar-el-Salam were transformed from a concept into an operational mission years later. This strategy would be labeled "the Drops of Blood," meaning that long-term attacks against the United States would be in effect a slow bleeding that would eventually lead to America's withdrawal in the region. A drop of blood would occur in Yemen, another in Somalia to frustrate the United States in the Horn of Africa, and another in the Arabian Peninsula.

The unification of North and (Marxist) South Yemen in 1990 had been mainly stimulated by the finding of petroleum reserves along their common border. The new Yemeni government had to deal with the powerful Islamist Islah Party, whose deputy leader, Shiekh Zindani, was connected to bin Laden and Sheikh Turabi in Sudan. The program to undermine the Yemeni socialists and set the stage to unravel the power-sharing agreement between Yemen's socialists and Arab nationalists led to a civil war in 1994. Bin Laden would finance and export Arab-Afghan veterans to assassinate two dozen Yemen Socialist Party leaders. Explosives and terror experts were brought to training camps in Saada, Yemen, along the Saudi border in 1992. The first "drop of American blood" would be an attack on a hotel in Aden, in Yemen, in December 1992, where American troops were thought to be billeted; the rocket-propelled grenade missed the American troops, who were in a different hotel. Among the most remarkable Jihadist training camps in Yemen was Mina Laas Qurai, a small port not on any map or chart, from which maritime attacks could be staged. It is likely that the attacks on USS *Cole* (DDG 67) and tanker M/V *Limburg*, as well as the attempted attack on USS *The Sullivans* (DDG 68), were developed and tactically trained for there. The Yemen government either turned a blind eye or was too immersed in tribal rebellions and the attempted secession of Yemen's socialists to notice.

Bin Laden, in Sudan, aided that government in building camps for its military and used this as cover to build terrorist training camps on land he owned. Bin Laden looked into providing financial and technical support to Islamists fighting the Ethiopian army in Ogaden. Azzam's dream of aiding Islamist radicalists globally got its conceptual start in Afghanistan but its operational start in East Africa and Yemen.

The question "Why do the Militant Islamists hate us?" is best answered by a strategic view bin Laden postulated during sessions and conferences with other anti-American Islamist rejectionist groups in Sudan. Bin Laden saw the American military operation in Somalia (Restore Hope) as actually a stepping stone to attack and destabilize Sudan. He declared that the United States would never allow an Islamist government or *nahda* (renaissance) to succeed in Sudan—any Islamist gains in territory or through elections would be rolled back by the United States. He advocated that the American presence in Somalia be ended by a series of psychological blows, as a crucial first step to throwing American forces from the toehold they had gained in the Horn of Africa. The Iranian model, with Hezbollah, was seen as the most effective means to this end. In attendance at these Sudanese Jihadist conferences were Iranian intelligence (MOIS) and Ayatollah Yazdi. The tactics for Somalia would be arming the population, galvanizing Somali clerics to sermonize against the infidel/Crusader army, particularly during Friday prayers, and using the Ogaden front as a proving ground for Somali guerilla tactics.

The Jihadist groups in Sudan, including bin Laden, assessed American objectives as establishing logistical access to the Somali interior, imposing a Somali government friendly to the United States, and advancing to southern Sudan, with the objective of creating an autonomous Christian enclave on the Kurdish model.

HASSAN AL-TURABI'S VISION

The vision of the leader of Sudan's National Islamic Front, Sheikh Turabi, was slightly different from bin Laden's. He hoped to set aside Shiite-Sunni differences and create an Islamic Front for the Liberation of Ethiopia that included Lebanese Hezbollah, Egyptian veterans of the Soviet-Afghan War, the Sudanese National Islamic Front, led by Sheikh Turabi, the Somali Islamic Union (Mohamed Farrah Aideed's group), and other Islamists.

If bin Laden had remained in Sudan and had not been evicted by combined Saudi and American pressure, he might have created a three-thousand-fighter force that would operate and train in Kenya, Somalia, and Ethiopia. This force would have had skills in urban warfare and psychological warfare; its main objective would have been eroding the will of Western forces in the Horn of Africa. Bin Laden paid attention to disinformation campaigns to galvanize the Somali population, including false rumors that food aid from the United States was tainted with pork and that Somalis were defending their national sovereignty from the encroachment of foreign invaders.

Allegedly, bin Laden and his associates settled on aspects of Turabi's vision, creating the Vanguard for the Salvation of Somalia, which provided Aideed with trainers, arms, and funds. This vanguard imitated Hezbollah tactics, such as roadside bombs and mines, and its first assault occurred in August 1993. It is claimed that Zawahiri (as bin Laden's deputy) and his protégé Abu Ali al-Banshiri provided Egyptian Islamic Jihad support to Aideed's group, but the extent of the aid is unknown.

Bin Laden's first foray into the Philippines began, as in the Soviet-Afghan War, with an infusion of cash and the opening of bank accounts for funneling donations to such groups as Abu Sayyaf. Reportedly bin Laden sent his brother-in-law Jamal Khalifa under the guise of a Saudi businessman to oversee funds going to the Philippine Islamist insurgency. When questioned in the summer of 1998, Khalifa denied any dealings with Abu Sayyaf. Despite these denials, Ramzi Yussef, the bomber of the World Trade Center, was also operational in the Philippines at this time.

BIN LADEN OPERATIONALIZES QUTB'S STRATEGY: AMERICAN ROLLBACK

Bin Laden uses Qutb's condemnation of all Muslim society of the twentieth and twenty-first centuries as being in a state of *jahiliya* (ignorance) and gives Qutb's overarching theory a tactical application using the writings of Abdullah Azzam.

Bin Laden's theories of rolling back the U.S. presence in the Middle East and the Horn of Africa are based on his selective interpretation of history. He sees the Soviet defeat in Afghanistan, the American withdrawal from Beirut in 1983, the Chechen War (which he saw as a quagmire), the East African American embassy bombings, the Khobar bombings, USS *Cole,* and 9/11 as all part of the momentum of superpower rollback. He uses the imagery and archaic Islamic opinions, developed after Prophet Muhammad's death, of dividing the world into the *Dar al Harb* (Abode of War) and *Dar al Islam* (Abode of Peace). Bin Laden never mentions a scholarly alternative between these two choices, the *Dar al Ahd* (Abode of Truce). He and his clerics suppress this aspect of the complex discussion of concepts of war and peace developed and rationalized during the thirteenth century, a period of the Mongol invasions and the Crusades. These concepts were not inherent in Islamic doctrine until then, a historical point ignored by bin Laden.

The al-Jazeera journalist Muhammad Muwafiq Zaydan published in 2003 an Arabic book detailing a 2000 interview with bin Laden. The book contains nuances not seen in the TV interviews, deep discussions with the al-Qaida leader, and rare insight into his strategic thought. Bin Laden, using metaphor, said that the media transmit the language of the body before the language of speech, meaning that they offer an opportunity to instill raw emotion through imagery before rational thought can be induced through dialogue.[4] Bin Laden's three most important legacies, he recounted to Zaydan, were unity under Islamic *usuls* (traditions); the supersession of divisions, to becoming one (Islamic) community under God; and the resolution of all Islamic protest and disputes by one *manhaj* (methodology or doctrine) of the Salaf.

This vision leaves no compromise for diverse Islamic beliefs, national identity, or tribalism. It conceals the fact that bin Laden or his select clerics will generate what they consider an appropriate re-creation of the *Salaf al-Saliheen* (the pious founders). Bin Laden refuses to comprehend that only a small group of Muslims, even Salafis, appreciate living under his Salafi interpretations. Bin Laden and al-Qaida leaders have many obstacles to overcome; the challenge for the United States and its friends is to increase this friction and obstacles by highlighting the impossibility, naiveté, and pseudo-intellectualism of bin Laden's vision.

WHY THE TALIBAN AND BIN LADEN FAILED IN AFGHANISTAN

The Taliban consistently held themselves to be on the righteous side and everyone else *batil* (spiritually and morally corrupt). This isolated the complex religious and ethnic elements of Afghanistan, the Hazaras and Uzbeks, even members of the Taliban's own ethnic group, who were disenfranchised enough to fall upon the Taliban when they were weakened by U.S. forces in Operation Enduring Freedom. The Taliban had a deficit of intellectuals among their leaders and were ignorant of even the wider Muslim world and its fourteen centuries of history. The world and its history were reduced to a grand conspiracy against them and Islam. The Taliban operate by whim and edict.

In Islam, between actions and intentions that are *haraam* (forbidden) and those that are a *fard* (obligation), are actions and thoughts deemed to be lesser sins or neutral (neither forbidden nor rewarded)—a graduated scale of actions and intentions. For instance divorce, is considered to be a distasteful act that the Prophet Muhammad allowed, known as *makrooh* (disliked but not technically forbidden). Other acts are *mubah* (permitted). In the Taliban world, particularly among low-level functionaries and religious enforcers, an act is either good or evil. This obsession on judging individual acts as good or evil caused the Taliban regime in Afghanistan to neglect the development of the state in favor of attacking music and kite flying, forbidding taxis to transport women, regulating beard length, banning art, and prohibiting tailors from mending women's clothes. It took the Quranic injunction of *amr bil marouf wal nahy an al munkar* (propagating virtue and preventing vice) and created an Ihitisaab (accountability) Ministry that instead of dealing with morality evolved into an internal security service, an internal intelligence arm, and enforcement agency. Religiosity, compassion, and morality was lost in the original Taliban regime; the people of Afghanistan, after initially enjoying the order the Taliban brought, began to abhor the repression of its ignorant rule.

When Zaydan interviewed bin Laden, he asked the al-Qaida leader about his views on Iran. Bin Laden was extremely reserved in his answers, and although his Militant Islamist views are incompatible with Shiism, Zaydan detects some accommodation between elements of the Iranian government and al-Qaida. This accommodation may be as simple as not wanting to cause pressure on al-Qaida leaders detained in Iran. In 2005, two years after the publication of Zaydan's book, Zawahiri admonished the late leader of al-Qaida in Iraq, Abu Musab al-Zarqawi, in a letter for his public beheadings of Shiites in Iraq and reminded him of the hundred senior al-Qaida leaders detained in Iran.[5] Zarqawi was condemned by the Association of Muslim Scholars, a conglomerate of Islamist and Militant Islamist Sunni Iraqi clerics, in September 2005 on the Iraqi Militant Islamist website *al-Ansar:* "We call upon Abu Musab al-Zarqawi to retract these threats since they damage the Jihad and resistance in Iraq and lead to further bloodshed of innocent Iraqis." This statement was posted one day after Zarqawi issued a statement declaring total war on Shiites.[6] Zarqawi could never elevate himself beyond thug and Militant Islamist butcher, never set aside his violent impulses, even to preserve the unity among Sunnis. Soon after, five Iraqi Sunni insurgent groups distanced themselves and condemned Zarqawi: Jaysh Muhammad (Army of Muhammad), the Islamic Army of Iraq, al-Qaqa Brigades, the Army of Mujhideen in Iraq, and the Salah al-Din Brigades.[7] Another voice in the avalanche of criticism from Militant Islamists and Islamists was Sheikh Abu Baseer al-Tartousi, a Syrian Militant Islamist cleric with an Internet following.[8] From the Islamist world the Grand Mufti of Saudi Arabia, Sheikh Abdul-Aziz al-Alshiekh, published a condemnation in *al-Hayat,* a London Arabic newspaper, two days after Zarqawi's declaration.

These condemnations can be stitched together into one or two blocks so as to attain *ijmaa* (consensus from the Islamic community) and isolate Militant Islamist statements and behavior. In the long war against terrorism, Militant Islamist groups and ideology will be a central focus of U.S. policy; it is time that we immerse ourselves in the ideas, words, and vocabulary of the enemy, but with understanding of the nuances and schisms within Militant Islamist groups and between Islamists and Militant Islamists.

Books by Arab authors, like the ones highlighted here, contain plausible histories of bin Laden and al-Qaida, ideological attacks on bin Laden, and a host of other concepts and ideas that can be used as a basis of discussion and debate with our Arab and Muslim allies in helping all understand an intolerant foe. One begins to see that bin Laden, Zawahiri, and Azzam represent men who desperately wish to put the pseudo-intellectual ideas of Qutb into practice. Of course, each makes a unique and deadly contribution, functionally and strategically, to the Islamist militant movement; the art will be to deconstruct their ideas and delegitimate and discredit them in order to compete for the same pool of people in the Muslim world. We cannot possibly argue that bin Laden's interpretation of Islam is no less legitimate than others; this is a path toward surrender, and it is precisely his warped sense of Islamic history, law, modern politics, and international affairs that must be attacked.

The Sudan years show a bin Laden willing to engage in tactical discussions on how to undermine the United States with Islamist groups who do not share his Islamic beliefs, to weave an interesting and systematic plan to roll back U.S. forces from Somalia. The extent al-Qaida played with the forces of Muhammad Farah Aideed is debatable; this was the strategy taught to future al-Qaida leaders. In other words, maybe this is only an al-Qaida legend, but even so this perception and lore is a reality to al-Qaida affiliates and their recruits—we dismiss it at our own peril. Relationships between bin Laden, Sheikh Turabi in Sudan, and Sheikh

Zindani in Yemen are also important reasons to explore Arabic books about bin Laden and al-Qaida.

Finally, these Arabic books contain the basis for designing messages and arguments to counter Islamist militant ideology, using the arguments, scholarship, research, language, and clerical references that the Arab authors do. We should study Arabic books with the zeal with which we studied Soviet books during the Cold War to understand the adversary, entering the adversary's decision cycle and thought process. In addition, the United States must realize that al-Qaida uses religious language and symbols as a weapon; we must begin the long-term process of attacking the destructive interpretations of Islam that bin Laden and Zawahiri represent. Many in the Middle East do not want to adopt bin Laden's Islam or vision but simply admire him for opposing the United States. In a way he is becoming the new Ernesto "Che" Guevara, or the new Fidel Castro, a symbol of resistance, a David to our Goliath. But where Che and Castro sacrificed the Cuban people, bin Laden is sacrificing the religion of Islam on the altar of his insecurities and global vision.

ARAB INTELLECTUAL PERSPECTIVES OF AL-QAIDA'S TWO-DECADE HISTORY

What Arab scholars and commentators are saying about violent Islamist militancy has become an important, if previously neglected, part of the education of American military leaders. U.S. Joint Forces Command has started the process with its three-volume Terrorism Perspectives Project, which provides insight into such al-Qaida thinkers as Abu Musab al-Suri, the "Clausewitz" of al-Qaida networks. The series, published by Naval Institute Press, forms the basis of any serious examination of the narrow ideology of the adversary. Another organization that is conducting serious work in translating and analyzing books by Islamist radicals is the Combating Terrorism Center at the U.S. Military Academy at West Point, New York. CTC West Point was even mentioned by Ayman al-Zawahiri in May 2007, and several times after that. This, in my view, represents a success—that an al-Qaida deputy felt obliged to mention an assessment by a U.S. Army entity.

Post-Soviet Survival of al-Qaida

An Egyptian scholar of Islamist radical movements, Abd al-Raheem Ali, has written the eighth volume of a collection on Islamist radical groups collectively entitled *Tanzeem al-Qaida, Ushrun Ahman, wal-Ghazu Mustamir* (Al-Qaida:

Twenty Years and the Battle Continues). His 498-page book explores al-Qaida—its foundations, its leadership, and its relations to other Islamist radical groups. The series, produced by Dar al-Mahroosa Press in Cairo, offers an Arab perspective of our adversary. The eighth volume describes how, as we saw earlier in this chapter, after Azzam's death and the withdrawal of Soviet forces from Afghanistan, the Arab-Afghans split into three groups. One could add a fourth group, Arabs who remained and settled in Pakistan and Afghanistan, although the leadership and strength that bin Laden would draw upon for al-Qaida would come from the first three groups. Those who remained in Afghanistan and Pakistan were apparently subdued by Afghan warlords and Pakistani security and intelligence personnel.

Operation Desert Storm: Further Erosion of Pan-Arabism

Operation Desert Storm would see another blow to Arab solidarity. The Arab nations were incapable of dealing with Saddam Hussein's invasion of Kuwait. From an Islamist militant perspective this was the death knell of pan-Arabism, already discredited since the 1967 Six-Day War. From a Jihadist theoretical perspective the damage continued with the arrival of U.S. forces in Saudi Arabia. During Operation Desert Storm calls for a worldwide Islamist revolution resonated in backroom mosques, and al-Sahwa clerics of Saudi Arabia, led by Sheikh Safar al-Hawali and Salman al-Awdah, began an Islamist and radical Salafist critique of the Saudi royal family.

Zawahiri and bin Laden Create Vanguards of the Conquest

Usama bin Laden left Saudi Arabia for Sudan, while Zawahiri traveled to several European nations, spending time in Geneva, Switzerland, before joining bin Laden in Sudan. There they would undertake deep strategic analysis, evaluating the situation of the Islamic world after Operation Desert Storm. They discussed the presence of U.S. forces in Saudi Arabia and Somalia and as we have seen, formulated an initial strategy of rolling back American influence in the Middle East, Africa, and Southwest Asia. Zawahiri and bin Laden established al-Qaida training camps in the Sudan, and Zawahiri would call the first trained cadres to emerge from these camps "Talaa al-Fath," the Vanguards of Conquest. (*Fath*, "conquest," symbolically refers to the lightning conquest by Muslim armies from 630 to 711 from Spain to the frontiers of Afghanistan.)

The Arab world would be introduced to Zawahiri's Talaa al-Fath cells when they were rolled up by Egyptian authorities; the subsequent trial was referred to by this name. Zawahiri had associated his Egyptian Islamic Jihad (EIJ) with bin Laden's al-Qaida, giving it the name Tanzeem al-Qaida wal Jihad (The al-Qaida and Jihad Organization), asserting the coequal status Zawahiri and bin Laden had enjoyed in Sudan in the early nineties. Zawahiri began providing bin Laden competent operational commanders, including Muhammad al-Makawi, better known as Saif al-Adl, a cashiered lieutenant colonel in Egyptian Military Intelligence, who would play a key role in establishing communications between bin Laden and Zawahiri in Sudan and Yemeni veterans of the Soviet-Afghan War who settled in Yemen. Through Saif al-Adl's facilitation efforts al-Qaida established base camps under the protection of the Hashid Tribal Confederacy in the Murahqasha Mountains of Yemen. Al-Qaida's main patron in Yemen was Tarek al-Fadly, one of the sons of the last sultans, who had been displaced by the Republic of Yemen as well as by its communist archrival.

Saleh Suleiman, one of the Talaa al-Fath detainees, explained in his trial and to Egyptian investigators that his group trained in psychological warfare, arms, explosives, use of detonators, and urban warfare. Among the graduate of Sudanese camps were a handful of terrorists who would augment Somali insurgents fighting U.S. forces in Mogadishu. In 1992, four hundred members and affiliates of Talaa al-Fath were arrested, exposing operations such as:

- The failed assassination attempt on Egyptian interior minister Hassan al-Alfi
- The failed attempt on the life of Egyptian prime minister Atif Sidqi
- Insurgent pipelines from Yemen, Kenya, to Somalia, and back
- Plans to attack U.S. military personnel in Yemen to strategically draw away military pressure on Somali insurgents
- The 1992 attack on the Golden Mohur Hotel in Aden
- Plans to bring down U.S. military flights taking off and landing from Aden.

Plans to Create an East Africa Network

In 1993, Usama bin Laden, having established a presence in Sudan and Yemen, set his sights on East Africa. Zawahiri visited Nairobi and Mombasa to explore the potential for al-Qaida to establish a new presence in Kenya and infuse East Africa with Jihadists from Afghanistan and Pakistan. Kenya was viewed as a strategic location from which al-Qaida could influence events in Yemen, Somalia, and Sudan. Zawahiri assigned Muhammad Sadek al-Awdah and Ali al-Rashidi (also known as Abu Ubaydah al-Panshiri) to establish cells in East Africa and develop a network.

However, Abu Ubaydah al-Panshiri drowned in a 1996 ferry accident on Lake Victoria, leading to the rise of Muhammed Atef (Abu Hafs al-Masri), who had been introduced to bin Laden and Zawahiri by the late Abu Ubaydah al-Panshiri in the late eighties. Atef would prove to be a competent military trainer of Arabs in Afghanistan, drawing no doubt on his experience as an Egyptian police colonel. He would rise to become al-Qaida's military operations chief and likely played a facilitating and planning role in the 9/11 attacks, dying in a U.S. air strike during Operation Enduring Freedom in 2002. The East Africa embassy bombings occurred under Atef's leadership. He then withdrew the network, anticipating tremendous pressure from African security services; he infiltrated al-Qaida operatives, trainers, and fighters into Somalia, having arranged asylum and protection from Hussein Farah Aideed in return for financial payments to him and his Somali National Alliance. This is an interesting allegation, as Aideed, son of the Somali warlord Muhammad Farah Aideed, was a former U.S. Marine and was recently part of an alliance that ousted the Council of Islamic Courts and has aggressively pursued Islamist militants.

Bin Laden's Vision of a Global Network

Before the East Africa embassy bombings, Usama bin Laden and Zawahiri sought to link their camps and leaders in Sudan, Yemen, and East Africa as well as financial and operational cells in Europe, the Middle East, and North America with other Islamist militant groups into a global network. In 1994 and 1995 they established a union of Islamist militant movements, coordinating a series of conferences and meetings in Cyprus, Teheran, and Khartoum. The Khartoum meeting, in April 1995, was the most important, drawing the late Imad Mughniyah of Hezbollah (killed in 2008), Palestinian Islamic Jihad's Fathi Shikaki, Hamas leader Musa Abu Marzook, Yemen's Abdul-Mejid al-Zindani, Pakistani militant groups, Algerian militant groups, and the Tunisian Islamist militant group al-Nahda. It laid plans for increasing the efficacy and support of Islamist networks fighting in the Balkans, directed donations to Islamist networks in Somalia and Ethiopia, and increased the efficiency of recruitment, financing, and media networks in London and North America.

Vanguards trained in Sudan began planning to kidnap American tourists in Egypt and bomb Egyptian tourist sites in 1995. Perhaps the boldest operation was the assassination attempt against the Egyptian President, Hosni Mubarak, in Addis Ababa, Ethiopia. Egyptian security in combination with Ethiopian officials uncovered a network of 1,600 Jihadists in East Africa, cultivated from 1992 to 1995, with camps training militants in Merka, Bardiera, Jalekieu, Bosasso, Kismayo, and Ogaden.

Zawahiri Versus the Egyptian Government: Messages Sent through Terrorism

Terrorism is not just an act of political violence that sends a message—an abhorrent means of political expression. Zawahiri, in the 1995 bombing of the Egyptian embassy in Pakistan. that Egyptian security officials watching Egyptian Jihadists in Pakistan were unsafe, and that the government of Benazir Bhutto had to cease its cooperation with Egypt and Saudi Arabia in extradition of operatives back to those countries. The first choice for the bombing of a diplomatic mission in Pakistan had been the U.S. embassy, but this was deemed too hard. In November 1995 an Egyptian diplomat, Alaa Nazmi, was murdered in Switzerland. The Egyptians believe that Zawahiri ordered the "hit," because Nazmi had been involved with monitoring him in Switzerland.

While the plans for developing the East Africa network were being laid in 1993, bin Laden visited the Philippines to lay the groundwork for donors, presence, and opportunities in Mindanao and the southern Philippines. Bin Laden's main agent there was his brother-in-law Jamal Khalifa. From the network emerged Operation Bojinka, Ramzi Yussef's plan for the bombing of American airliners and planes bound to the United States and for the assassination of Pope John Paul II.

Reconstitution of al-Qaida under the Taliban

Pressure from the United States, Egypt, and Saudi Arabia on Sudan led to bin Laden's departure in August 1996 for Afghanistan with 125 of his loyal followers. Bin Laden and Zawahiri would have to rebuild. Under the Taliban they established the Farouk camp and within two years had collected 1,400 Arab-Afghans and Jihadists. Bin Laden never abandoned his goal of creating a pan-Islamist global network, and with the aid of the Taliban he hosted fourteen Arab Islamist militant groups, some of which were al-Qaida, the Libyan Islamic Fighting Group, the Islamic Combat Group of Morocco, Zawahiri's Egyptian Islamic Jihad, the Egyptian group Gamaa al-Islamiyah, an Algerian Jihadist cadre, a Tunisian Jihadist cadre made up of Tunisians who had fought in Bosnia, Jordanian and Palestinian cadres led by Abu Musab al-Zarqawi, an Uzbek cadre (the largest non-Afghan group), a Turkestan cadre, and a Turkish cadre, the smallest group, designed to train and return to Turkey to conduct operations and develop cells.

There was also the Khaldan camp, considered the oldest Arab Jihadist camp, set up by Abdullah Azzam; the Abu Khabab Camp, which specialized in explosive training and the use of toxic chemicals; and the Ghurbaa camp, which trained Taliban military leaders in regional tactical, strategic, and doctrinal studies.

THE JULY 2005 ZAWAHIRI LETTER TO ZARQAWI

On October 11, 2005, the Office of the Director for National Intelligence in Washington, D.C., posted on its website (www.dni.gov) its third public release, detailing an extraordinary letter between al-Qaida's ideological leader, Ayman al-Zawahiri, and the late leader of al-Qaida in Iraq, Abu Musab al-Zarqawi. Anyone unconvinced of the importance of Iraq to al-Qaida should note that in it Zawahiri called it the "place for the greatest battle for Islam in the era." Zawahiri outlined a four-stage strategic plan to create a caliphate: to expel Americans from Iraq; to establish an Islamic authority, then develop it into a caliphate; to extend the Jihad to countries neighboring Iraq; and to combine this expansion with a clash with Israel.

He describes a caliphate with two wings, Egypt and Syria, and a heart in Palestine. This is in line with Militant Islamist doctrine, best articulated by Walid Phares in his book *Future Jihad,* which calls for *Tahrir* (liberation), the overthrow of Arab regimes and monarchies; *Tawheed* (unification), the erasure of national borders; and *Khilafa,* a caliphate that incorporates all Islamic lands and includes the oil riches of Arabia and a nuclear Pakistan.[9]

In this letter Zawahiri cited Vietnam to suggest how suddenly the United States withdraws from states and how quickly the void left must be filled. He encouraged Zarqawi to set up a Militant Islamist provisional government in advance: "The Americans will exit soon [from Iraq], God willing, and the establishment of a governing authority . . . does not depend on force alone. . . . It is imperative that in additional to force, there be an appeasement of Muslims and a sharing of governance with them." Zawahiri, writing here as a pragmatist, urged Zarqawi to learn from the mistakes made by the Taliban, "who restricted participation in government to students and the people from Kandahar alone." He points out the need "to complement political action with military action." Zawahiri was concerned that Zarqawi's tactic of public beheadings would alienate Iraqis and—he uses the actual English words—"hearts and minds." Zawahiri reminded Zarqawi that his public aggression against the Shiites could "compel the Iranians to take countermeasures" and of "the one hundred prisoners, many of whom are from the leadership and who are wanted in their countries in the custody of the Iranians." Zawahiri ended, "We need a payment, while new lines are being opened, so if you are capable of sending one hundred thousands [*sic*], we will be very grateful." It seemed that Iraq was not only the central front in their war but the main recipient of donations, necessitating Zawahiri's request for money. Former President George W. Bush quoted extensively from this letter in his weekly radio address, on October 15, 2005, demonstrating its importance.[10]

BIN LADEN'S JANUARY 2006 VIDEO

Al-Jazeera released a video of bin Laden on January 19, 2006. The last tape of Usama bin Laden had appeared on al-Jazeera on December 27, 2004—to this writing, the longest hiatus. Since January 2006 until the present, he has made a video or audio appearance on average every other month. The January 2006 tape was significant compared to previous video and audio statements, especially in combination with statements of Zawahiri and Zarqawi. This allows us to judge al-Qaida's central leadership in terms of what it views as positive and negative developments in the worldwide Militant Islamist movement. (Of course, this is only a snapshot of bin Laden's thinking; four years have elapsed, and the al-Qaida leader does amend his rhetoric to fit what is occurring in the Militant Islamist movement.)

A positive development, in bin Laden's view, was American public opinion; he expressed willingness to make an attempt to reach the American public directly to influence the polls. Bin Laden attempted to show the lack of popular support for U.S. efforts in Iraq, piecing together sound bites from antiwar demonstrations. The pressures on bin Laden leading up to January 2006, included humanitarian aid the United States and other nations provided to victims of the 2005 Pakistan earthquake and the 2004 Indonesian tsunami. (From the Western viewpoint, the problem in 2010 and beyond is consistently reminding the public that the United States and its allies, not Militant Islamist groups, have provided the robust and serious relief needed in natural disasters.)

Zarqawi was still alive at the release of this bin Laden tape. In fact, there was much speculation that Zarqawi was eclipsing Zawahiri, if not bin Laden himself. The tape may have been released to reassert bin Laden's leadership, after thirteen months, over the course of the worldwide Militant Islamist movement and to elevate the morale of Militant Islamist supporters and operatives.

Contrary to media translations, bin Laden did not offer a truce but only pledged to uphold a truce if the United States offered one. This offer, of course, judging from bin Laden's past record of breaking pledges to the likes of Mullah Omar, cannot be taken seriously. Bin Laden may have been concerned about violence against Muslims, or an attempt to distance himself from the violence of Zarqawi, eroding grassroots support for al-Qaida in Iraq. It could also have been a message to leaders that a tactical truce might be the better part of valor. His truce might have reflected frustration with the way aid and development was progressing in Pakistan and Afghanistan, and possibly with his inability to transform al-Qaida into a social movement like Lebanese Hezbollah.

AYMAN AL-ZAWAHIRI: QUTBIST THEORETICIAN AND AL-QAIDA LEADER

Although typically referred to in the West as the al-Qaida deputy, Zawahiri is more properly an integral part of Usama bin Laden's strategic thought process. Studying Zawahiri reveals the numerous strategic, operational, and tactical divisions between Militant Islamists and between Militant Islamists and Islamists. Zawahiri concerns himself with al-Qaida as a legacy, a way of life, and he thinks decades ahead, as evidenced by his book *Knights under the Prophet's Banner*. Born in 1951 and a trained surgeon, Zawahiri has been involved in Islamist politics and later Militant Islamist groups since the age of fifteen. He is a complex jumble of insecurities, one of which is his need to be seen as a serious shaper of the Militant Islamist movement. These insecurities come out vividly in his 2008 answers to questions, as well as such documents as his 2005 letter to Zarqawi. Zawahiri was the main founder of the external wing of the EIJ. Before joining al-Qaida, Zawahiri's attempt at reviving EIJ within Egypt after the Sadat assassination failed, and the Egyptian public had grown outraged at terrorist attacks that had killed innocent Egyptians, especially a young elementary schoolgirl, Shayma Abdel-Halim, killed in 1993 by a bomb intended to kill the prime minister. This failure of EIJ and desperation for funding led Zawahiri to reestablish contact with bin Laden, presumably to colead EIJ and provide funding. Instead Usama co-opted Zawahiri to join al-Qaida and create the World Islamic Front for the Jihad against Crusaders and Jews in 1998. Pressures that drove Zawahiri to a closer merger with bin Laden and the acceptance of an advisory role include:

- The cease-fire brokered between the Egyptian government and Gamaa al-Islamiyah.
- High-profile trials in Egypt of Egyptian Militant Islamists, known by the Egyptian public as the "Returnees from Albania Trials."
- The murder of Shayma.
- Zawahiri's impact on the tourism industry.
- Disagreements between Egyptian Islamic Jihad "external" (Zawahiri's group in Pakistan) and "internal," in Egyptian prisons, over the course of the Militant Islamist movement.

During Zawahiri's own imprisonment, from 1981 to 1983, for his very minor role in the Sadat assassination, he readily betrayed his colleagues, giving up their names under light interrogation. Among those he betrayed was Major Essam al-Qamari, an Egyptian military officer and Militant Islamist, whom Zawahiri considered the ideal warrior in any future Islamist Militant group. Zawahiri's betrayal led to his entrapment and capture. Qamari is reported to have said to Zawahiri words to the effect that Zawahiri could never be a leader.[11]

Zawahiri's personality, idiosyncrasies, and psychology are divisive elements within the Militant Islamist movement. His public alliance with bin Laden in declaring the World Islamic Front, without consultation, led to fiery accusations. The charge that Zawahiri cannot lead is borne out in his alienation of whole swaths of EIJ, the blind cleric Sheikh Omar Abdul-Rahman, and Sheikh Abdullah Azzam (the spiritual founder of al-Qaida). Also alienated are Muntassir al-Zayat, who knew Zawahiri well and shared prison time with him and is now an outspoken critic of Militant Islamists like Zawahiri; Rifai Taha (or Abu Yasir), leader of Gamaa Islamiyah, which undertook the 1997 Luxor massacre; Imam al-Sherief, founding ideologue of EIJ; and Hassan al-Turabi, a Sudanese cleric and leader of the National Islamic Front—this last for Zawahiri's execution of two boys in Sudan who had been entrapped by Egyptian intelligence to spy on and kill Zawahiri. It was considered outrageous by the Sudanese government that al-Qaida would stage a court, trial, and execution within Sudan, as if it were a state within a state. This is by no means an exhaustive list of those within the Militant Islamist world who despise Zawahiri.

seventeen

A Basic Analytic Primer on Shiism

As we have seen, the schism between Sunnis and Shiites began first as a disagreement over Prophet Muhammad's succession; a series of wars fought among Muslims over the issue hardened into differences in practice. It is important for those involved in America's national security to understand these differences, as Shiites make up about one-fourth of 1.3 billion Muslims. Although the minority sect of Islam, Shiites are concentrated in areas of interest to the United States, such as Lebanon, Iran, Iraq, Syria, Bahrain, and northern Afghanistan, as well as forming sizable minorities in Saudi Arabia's Eastern Provinces, home of the bulk of Saudi oil deposits. This chapter will serve as an introduction not only to the differences between Shiite and Sunni Islam but to the nuances within Shiism.

Most Shiites are Twelver Shiites, meaning they believe that from the death of Ali, a series of descendents of Muhammad, culminating with Muhammad al-Mahdi, the Twelfth Imam, went into hiding, to reappear when the world is rife with injustice. Shiites believe these imams are intercessors between humankind and God, that mankind is unworthy to communicate with God directly. Sunnis consider this concept blasphemy, for Sunni Muslims communicate with God directly and believe that the idea of twelve Shiite imams veers toward the veneration of saints, detracting from the worship of God. The ambush site of Hussein (Prophet Muhammad's grandson) in Karbala would become venerated ground, akin to the place of Christ's crucifixion. Shiite epistemology reasons that the venerated imams need to be in hiding because of humankind's lack of preparation and of acceptance.

- *Proper preparation:* Before the Mahdi reappears to establish absolute justice throughout the world, humankind needs to make a certain amount of preparation. There will come a point when all ideologies, doctrines, leaders, and governments fail. It will then become clear that no one is capable of establishing justice in the world except God's vice-regent, the Mahdi. Due to the lack of preparation and mankind's low level of readiness to accept the rules of God, Imam Mahdi has so far been concealed.

■ *Lack of acceptance:* Due to the persecution of believers and, in particular, of the other Shia imams, as well as the prophets, it is clear that people still refuse to accept God's vice-regents. Thus, the Shias believe that just as God concealed the prophets Isa (Jesus), Idris (Enoch), and Ilyas (Elijah), he has also hidden the Mahdi from humankind until suitable circumstances arise.

The tension between Shiites and Sunnis stems in part from the status of these twelve imams. Shiites believe that these imams are *wasi* (legatees) of Prophet Muhammad and were appointed by God as a sign of his *lutf* (grace). Sunnis view this as undermining the legitimacy of *ijmaa* (consensus) in selecting the caliph and detracting from focus on the worship of God and veneration of Prophet Muhammad. One of the labels of Sunnis is *ahl al-Sunnah wal Jamaa* (People of the Prophet's Path and Consensus).

Within Shiism are two doctrines, Usuli and Akhbari. The central distinction between the two is that of what to do while waiting for the arrival of the Twelfth Imam. Akhbaris are quietists, who believe they should patiently await the Imam, interpreting Islamic law on their own or with minimal guidance from clerics. Usulis believe that the clergy acts in lieu of the Hidden Imam and should be followed until the arrival of the Twelfth Imam from occultation. In addition, some Usulis postulate that religious law should be detached from the failing state of the Persian dynasties like the Qajars. Another way to articulate the difference between Usuli and Akhbari Shiites is that Akhbaris feel that the First Imam, Ali, and subsequent imams, along with the Qur'an, contain all that is needed for individual Shiites to live their lives until the arrival of the Hidden Imam. Hence their name "Akhbari," from the Arabic *akhbar,* meaning accounts of a person. Usulis, who represent the majority of Shiites, say that these accounts are of varying degrees of authenticity and that careful study, examining chains of narrations, transmission, and attribution to the Prophet and twelve imams, is necessary to tell authentic versus false accounts. This careful study can only be conducted by a person dedicated to the study of Islam—hence the clerics. The name Usuli comes from the Arabic *usul,* which means "roots" and is linked to the term *usul al-fiqh,* or roots of the law. The schism and debate between these two doctrines flared up in the nineteenth century. (In Sunni Islam, a similar debate on whether to use *aql* [reason] or *naql* [imitation] flared up three hundred years after Muhammad's death, between the Mutazalites and Hanbalis—the Mutazilites wanting to apply rational study of Islamic texts, including the Qur'an, the Hanbalis rejecting this as blasphemy and sticking to literal and fundamental interpretations of texts.)

While most Shiites believe in twelve imams and (and so are known as "Imamis"), there are those who believe the Seventh Imam went into occultation, known as Ismailis, and those who hold that the Fifth Imam was the last, or Hidden Imam—the Zaydis, primarily located in North Yemen. Ismailis, also known as Seveners (for their belief in the Seventh Imam), believe that the Seventh Imam did not go into hiding but is manifested in the person of the Aga Khan, whose descendents run a prosperous global foundation. The Fatimid dynasty (909–1171) in Egypt, North Africa, and the Levant represents the apex of influence of the Sevener Shiites. It was the Fatimids who created the religious rectory of al-Azhar (today the preeminent Sunni school of Islam, having been reconsecrated as a Sunni school by Saladin in the twelfth century). The majority Twelver Shiites deem heretical several Shiite offshoot groups, such as the Alawis of Syria. The Alawis matter simply because they represent the ruling class in Syria, including the current ruling circles, currently led by President Bashar al-Asad. Another, the Druze, although neither Shiite nor Sunni, mixes aspects of ethical monotheism and follows the Letters of Hamza and Daraza, collected in a book known as the *Pearls of Wisdom,* considered by the Druze to be the correct interpretation of Islam but by both Shiites and Sunnis as heretical. The Druze are concentrated in Lebanon and Israel; intense loyalty to the nation is part of their religious obligation. They serve as scouts for the Israeli Defense Forces.

Finally, let us compare some general differences between Sunni and Shiite clergy. Sunni clerics have traditionally been employees of the state, whose salaries depend on the regime in power. They typically move from place to place at the pleasure of the ruling regime, and the expansion of Sunni clerical influence is dependent on negotiations with the state. Shiite clerics' salaries and livelihoods are dependent on tithes given by Shiite followers; this keeps the Shiite cleric in closer touch with his flock than his Sunni counterpart, as good and harsh economic times have a direct bearing on tithing. It is also in Shiite clerics' interest to stand with their flocks against the imposition of government control or downright oppression. Shiite clergy practice *ijitihad* (analytic reasoning) much more read-ily than their Sunni counterparts, meaning that their fatwas are issued to fit the times and the needs of the people. Of course, this trend can be, and has been, abused, but usually fatwas that are unreasonable are debated and, if found lacking, are not endorsed by the wider Shiite clergy, known as *ijmaa* (consensus). Ruhol-lah Khomeini's Iranian state has altered the traditional dependence of the Shiite clergy on the flock and has adopted the Sunni model.

EVOLUTION OF SHIISM IN PERSIA

Persia, modern-day Iran, was once primarily Sunni and remained so until the sixteenth century. Muslims did not enter en masse into Shiism until the Safavid dynasty, established by Shah Ismail in 1501. Before the Safavids, Shiites lived in Nishapur and Qom, with a few minority Shiite clusters in Isfahan, Shiraz, Tabriz, and Khorasan. Iran slowly became a Shiite nation, a fact that had an impact on Iraq, since most of the Shiite holy sites are in Iraq. Over the course of the centu-ries, Iraq would evolve into Shiite Arab majority, dependent upon Persian Shiite clergy. This dynamic could change in the aftermath of Operation Iraqi Freedom, as more and more Arab Shiites take control of their own affairs, a scenario that is being watched and managed by Iran.

One of the main schisms between Sunnis and Shiites is over the concept of *shafaa* (intercession), a general belief on the use of the *sahaba*, Prophet Muham-mad's companions, as intercessors between believers and God. Over the course of early Islamic history, some clerics began to rank-order intercessors based on their closeness to Prophet Muhammad, and the caliphate came to be viewed by some Muslims not in terms of competent or consensus governance in this earth but of a caliph's lineage and so his influence as an intercessor in the hereafter. This formed an essential foundation of what would evolve into the absolute Shiite conviction that Ali must succeed Muhammad, and the evolution of the twelve imams from the *ahl al-bayt*, the family of Prophet Muhammad from Fatima, one of Muhammad's daughters, and Ali, as intercessors. Sunnis reject these notions as blasphemous innovations that detract from the worship of God.[1]

Shah Ismail I publicly disavowed and insulted the first three caliphs (Abu Bakr, Omar, and Uthman), which was uncomfortable for many Muslims of the period as it is today among Sunnis and a few Shiites. These three, Prophet Mu-hammad's closest companions, intermarried and preserved the fledgling Islamic society after Muhammad's death and expanded it. They are a source of many of

Muhammad's sayings, and among Sunnis they are among the ten blessed who went immediately to paradise. Shah Ismail began the campaign to impose Shiism upon Persia, changing the character of Iran and the region. With the increase in Shiite converts, both forced and actual, the significance of Iraq would increase as the spiritual epicenter of Shiism, the place where a significant number of the twelve imams are buried and perhaps the most important imams, Ali and his son Hussein. Shah Ismail would use willingness to insult the three caliphs (whom Shiites believe usurped the caliphate from Ali) as a loyalty test for Persians. If the examiner detected hesitation, the candidate would be killed. Ismail ordered public reading of insults of the three caliphs in markets, mosques, and streets, as a means not only of affirming this new state doctrine but, more importantly, detecting dissenters for liquidation.

It was Shah Ismail who first organized the public mourning rituals commemorating the martyrdom of Hussein, now known as Ashoura, on the tenth day of Muharram. The first Ashoura rituals had been conducted among the Buyyids around 1055, but the practice was thereafter neglected. Shah Ismail revived the practice after five hundred years and added *taziyyah* (passion play) rituals to give it both a somber and carnival atmosphere, as a means of playing upon the emotions of his subjects to convert more Sunnis, Zoroastrians, and Sufis to Shiism. Another innovation of Islamic practice ordered by Shah Ismail was the addition of "Ali is the Friend of God," at the end of the prayer call. This addition remains a matter of debate among Shiites today, and this along with Shah Ismail's other imposed practices, are considered blasphemous innovations by Sunni Muslims.

Shah Ismail died in 1524 at the age of thirty-eight. The new shah, Tahmasap I, only ten years old, held the view that he could not combine the functions of Leader of the Faith and of the Safavid state, so he delegated the former responsibility to the *fuqaha* (clergy). The new shah and his ministers enticed a cleric from Baalbek (in modern-day Lebanon), Sheikh Ali al-Karkhi, to manage the Safavid Empire's religious affairs. The cleric would travel from Baalbek to Qazwain, the first capital of the empire, to meet the shah and his advisers. The shah then issued a *firman* (decree) to be distributed throughout the empire that Sheikh Ali was the deputy to the Hidden Imam and was to be obeyed. Sheikh Ali was not only the first state-sponsored spiritual leader of Shiism but in effect the actual ruler of the Safavid Empire. Sheikh Ali would affirm and make the Twelver version of Shiism and the Shiite Jafari School of Islam the official religion of the empire. He began to enforce morality and organize the clergy, appointing every cleric in every town and village to teach his approved doctrine. There would be dissent against Sheikh Ali's power, not only from Sunnis and members of non-Islamic faiths present in Persia but from Shiites as well. Sheikh Ibrahim Qutaifi, a senior Shiite cleric, argued that any government that did not have the Hidden Imam (referring to Muhammad al-Mahdi, who went into occultation in 869) as its head was an oppressive and imperfect regime. Clergy, he held, have no place in any government. The shah attempted to entice Qutaifi with gifts, which he rejected, and Sheikh Ali chastised him. The reply from Qutaifi was scathing, comparing Sheikh Ali to the Third Imam, Hassan, who accepted bribes from Mua'wiya in return for renouncing the caliphate. Sheikh Ali would marginalize this lone voice among the Shiite clergy, but the argument splits the Shiite clergy to this day. Sheikh Ali reinstated the Friday prayers, long considered by Shiites as optional or not observed, as the prayers were conducted by an oppressive state without the missing imam at its head. He issued propaganda that the shah's government was just and that communal prayers were now mandatory. One of the Safavid Shiite clerics, Sheikh Hussein Abdel-Samad, would settle in Bahrain and introduce the Twelver version of Shiism on the island.

ALI AL-MAJLISI AND THE INSTITUTIONALIZING OF SHIITE ORTHOPRAXY (1616–1698)

Shah Ismail's descendents Abbas I, Ismail, and Suleiman began forced conversions of Sunnis, Sufis, and Zoroastrians. Shah Suleiman would appoint Ali al-Majlisi the highest Shiite cleric in Persia in 1678. For two decades Majlisi would suppress philosophy and Sufism; reestablish clerical authority under his leadership; establish the first *hawza* (clerical hierarchy) in Isfahan, the seat of the Safavid Empire; renew the impetus for conversion from Sunnism to Shiism; and propagate numerous Shia rituals that Iranians regularly practice, such as mourning ceremonies for the fallen imams and pilgrimages to shrines of imams and their families.

It is important to understand that the emergence of Shiism as the uniform religion of Iran is a relatively recent development in Islamic history. The Shiite rituals are considered by Sunnis heretical and detrimental to the worship of God and veneration of Prophet Muhammad. In Sunni Islam Ali is respected but not revered as in Shiism. What makes Majlisi significant is his institutionalization of Shiite rituals in hundreds of writings that comment on proper Shiite ritual to proper Shiite belief.

The *Hawza* (Shiite Clerical Cluster)

Unlike in Sunni Islam, Shiites have a very formal, developed, and rigid clerical hierarchy, located primarily in Qom and Najaf. The premier *hawza* is the seminary in Najaf, centered on the Imam Ali Mosque, where Ali is buried. A person wishing to become a Shiite cleric, having first memorized the Qur'an in its entirety, enters either the Qom or Najaf *hawza* as a *Talib* (seminarian). Najaf always had historical significance, but it was not until 1821, when the Ottoman and Persian empires improved relations, that a wave of Persian Shiite pilgrims began visiting Najaf, some settling for seminary studies. The currently influential Ayatollah Ali Sistani, for instance, is originally from Iran; he completed his studies in Najaf and never left, rising to become the most important cleric in Shiism today, with the rank of *Marja*.

The Shiite clerical hierarchy, from the lowest rank to the highest, is as follows:

- *Talib* (student): A seminarian, who spends four to six years studying Quranic exegesis, oratory, sermon preparation, Greek philosophy, Islamic family law, Islamic divorce law, Islamic inheritance law, mosque administration, management, and collection of tithes and donations. A major research project is required to graduate to the next level, imam.

- *Imam* (prayer leader): Someone trained as a *talib* and allowed to preach a sermon in a mosque and handle the spiritual affairs of a village. An imam with a calling to preach beyond his village and with scholarly attainments, and who has made the pilgrimage to Mecca, can petition the Council of Ayatollah of the *hawza* he graduated from to become a *Hojatoleslam*. Usually one spends several years as imam before being considered for advancement.

- *Hojatoleslam:* A scholar who has published books, articles, and essays on points of Islam and is known in a region for his expertise in Islamic jurisprudence. If the *Hojatoleslam* garners a following and becomes acclaimed throughout the land and desires to become a member of the Council of Ayatollahs, he can petition the *hawza* to advance.

- *Ayatollah:* A cleric and scholar with a large following and a voice in the Council of Ayatollahs of his *hawza*.

- *Marja al-Taqlid* (or *Marja*): In the West, referred to as "Grand Ayatollah," typically the leader of a *hawza* and member of a select circle of ayatollahs who have spent their lifetimes in the service of the Shiite faith. This status is typically granted to a living ayatollah; the term *marja al-taqlid* means "source of emulation." There are an estimated thirty-eight living *Marjas*.

Ayatollah Ali al-Sistani, Ali Khameini, and Muqtada al-Sadr

Let us analyze the positions of Sistani, of Iran's Supreme Leader, and of Muqtada al-Sadr as case studies. Sistani, as noted, is a *marja,* and the most influential single person in Shiism in the twenty-first century. He leads the Najaf *hawza,* the spiritual center of Shiism; millions consider him their imam. Sistani is more influential than Iran's Supreme Leader, Ali Khameini, because of Sistani's longevity, scholarship, reputation, and his perceived autonomy from the taint of politics. Iran's Supreme Leader was elevated by Ayatollah Ruhollah Khomeini from *Hojatoleslam* to ayatollah by political appointment; senior ayatollahs are contemptuous of this sudden elevation without scholarship. Before Khameini's elevation, he was known as an ardent Khomeinist and battlefield clergyman during the Iran-Iraq War. It was believed that Ayatollah Montazeri or the Council of Ayatollahs would select the next Supreme Leader after Khomeini's death.

The issue of whether an ayatollah or *Marja* is working toward individual spiritual development and Islamic spirituality versus accumulating raw power or money is discussed behind closed doors among the Shiite masses. It is questionable if the Iraqi cleric Muqtada al-Sadr has completed his requirements for imam; his pedigree (which, as discussed in the next chapter, places him among the family dynasties that control the Najaf *hawza*) propels him upward within the clerical hierarchy. He does not have a scholarly reputation and will likely advance not in Najaf but in Qom, having alienated a part of the Najaf *hawza* by butchering Ayatollah Khoei in 2003. This incident marked the first time that rivalries between clerical families had turned violent and was viewed within the Najaf *hawza* with great disappointment.

Najaf, the Shiite spiritual and natural center of gravity, has been dominated for centuries by Sunni powers, and only occasionally by the Persians. This has elevated the Qom seminary in Iran. Now that Shiites are free to express themselves religiously in Iraq, Najaf is regaining its natural prominence. This could cause doctrinal stress between Najaf and Qom, and the Iranian senior clergy are likely to attempt to influence the course and development of Najaf, particularly in planning for the eventual passing of Ali Sistani. This point should not be lost to American military planners in Iraq, as the passing of Sistani could have great repercussions.

To understand the influence of the *hawza,* consider the national revolt in Persia against the 1890 Tobacco Concession. The Qajar Persian shah, Nasr al-Din, sold the entire monopoly of tobacco production, packaging, and marketing to

Britain's Imperial Tobacco Company for 15,000 pounds and 25 percent of the profits. Persians called on Marja Mirza Shirazi to free them from this oppression. Shirazi's seat of authority was not in Persia but in Samarra, Iraq, but his fatwa caused a mass boycott of British tobacco products. The boycott was so pervasive that servants refused to prepare water pipes; even the shah's harem is supposed to have observed the ban—demonstrating the power of a respected Marja. It is reputed that this incident led to the Persian constitutional reforms of 1905. Historically, the clerical clusters in Najaf, Karbala, and Qom have debated serious events such as *mashrutiyah* (constitutionalism) versus *isitbdad* (despotism), when both Persia and the Ottomans promulgated constitutions in the first decade of 1900. The point for today: do not underestimate the ability of the senior clergy to influence events on the street in Iraq.

KHOMEINISM: ISLAMIC GOVERNMENT OR KHOMEINI'S INNOVATION?

Ayatollah Khomeini (1902–1989) outlined his vision of an Islamic government in his book *Hukumat Islamiyah* (Islamic Governance). As the concept of what constitutes Islamic government and in particular the actual method of governance is debatable, Khomeini has developed a set of political theories based on his own experience. In Khomeini's view an Islamic government is one in which a *Wilayat al-Faqih* (Supreme Jurisprudent) with the aid of a council of clerics is granted authority to guide the moral course of the state. This sounds eerily like the classic Greek political theoretical text, Plato's *Republic*. Plato argued that philosopher-kings guide the moral course of the hypothetical perfect city-state. In the training of Shiite clergy, Greek philosophy is part of the curriculum, and Khomeini no doubt allocated a significant portion of his studies to Plato. Are we seeing, then, an Islamic government or a Shiite version of Plato's *Republic?*

What is known is that Khomeini's innovations on Islamic government have rocked the foundations of the Shiite clergy. Some argue that since all government has been corrupt since the death of Ali and Hussein in 661 and 680, respectively, the clergy has no place in the running the physical aspects of government. Others argue that the clergy has a place in the judiciary only, but not the legislature or executive branches of government. This debate among the clergy continues, with some ayatollahs concerned that Khomeinism has had a corrupting influence on a new generation of clergy who enter seminary as a means of attaining power and riches, and not to concern themselves with the moral and spiritual development of the people.

Not all Shiite senior clergy agree with Khomeini's concept of *Wilayat al-Faqih*. For instance, Muqtada al-Sadr's uncle, Ayatollah Muhammad Baqir al-Sadr, advocated *Wilayat al-Hawza*, or rule of the clerical hierarchy, in which the clerical cluster guides the moral course of the state. Muqtada's father, Muhammad Sadeq al-Sadr, advocated the concept of *Wilayat al-Umma*, whereby God handed authority from prophets to the people. (As a demonstration of the intellectual chasm between Muqtada and his father, his father wrote a Shiite commentary on the Revolutionary French *Declaration of the Rights of Man and the Citizen*. He also expanded his intellectual diet to include writings from Karl Marx's *Paris Commune*.)[2] Ayatollah Abolqassim Khoi proposed *Wilayat al-Khasa*, which limited clerical authority to matters of personal affairs, such as personal laws, ritual, and morals. The Supreme Ayatollah Muhammad Fadlallah, the highest clerical authority for Hezbollah, advocated using Ayatollah Khoei's limited *wilayat* on personal matters in times of peace and Khomeini's total guide of a single supreme jurisprudent in times of war.[3] Even within the highest level of clerical thinking, then, there are disagreements over the role of the clergy in government.

It is easy to dismiss Khomeini's rhetoric as fiery and radical, which it is, but if one pays close attention to it, a complex combination of democracy, Greek classics, Marxism, and even the German philosopher Friedrich Nietzsche becomes apparent. This depth should come as no surprise, since Khomeini surrounded himself with well-read men of religion. Khomeini even borrowed from anti-shah Iranian political philosophers, who would today probably be imprisoned or worse. One such notable in Iranian political thought was Dr. Ali Shariati, whose writings in the late sixties and late seventies focused on the construction of the Iranian (Shiite) revolutionary self. For the first time, the Shiites' revered Hussein was not treated as simply a martyr. Rather, Dr. Shariati characterized him as a revolutionary who attempted to deal with an unjust order. Hussein-as-revolutionary was exactly the type of message that Khomeini could seize upon. Shariati, who wrote from exile in London and was persecuted by the shah, was looking to create an Iranian-style democracy, but he understood that Shiite Islam could not be divorced from the character of Iran. Shariati sought to revolutionize Iran not through Marxism or military coup but through the natural character of the masses. Being a sociologist, he could not operationalize his vision and instead became the patron saint of the Iranian Islamic revolution, dying before Khomeini's successful toppling of the shah in 1979.

CONCLUSION

Arab media have reported a troubling trend started by Sheikh Yusuf al-Qaradawi, who issued an anti-Shiite fatwa. This has led to a troubling schism, on the Internet and in the media, between those who endorse Qaradawi's views and those who object. Among the interesting development are cyber-assaults on the websites of Shiite ayatollahs and retaliatory attacks on Sunni websites. Is this a fleeting trend or the beginning of further sectarian strife between Sunnis and Shiites? The situation is not helped by remarks by King Abdullah II of Jordan expressing concern over a "Shiite crescent" extending from Iran to Iraq to Lebanon. His remarks were made in the context of the growing influence of Iran. This is balanced by such documents as the 2005 Amman Message, signed by over five hundred Shiites and Sunni leaders from around the world, calling for an end to declaring fellow Muslims, Shiites or Sunnis, apostates.[4] This event was sponsored by the same King Abdullah II of Jordan. Needless to say, increases in sectarian violence between Shiites and Sunnis would not be in the interest of the United States or of stability in the region. However, the Arabic newspaper *al-Sharq al-Awsat* of March 16, 2008, reported a meeting between Iraq's Shiite and Sunni clerics who proposed to establish a *Majlis Ahl al-Hal wal Aqd,* literally a committee of those who loosen and bind, empowered to issue declarations binding on both Sunnis and Shiites, as a way of addressing rising sectarian violence. In addition, Sunni and Shiite political leaders in Iraq are working together to keep their nation from balkanizing. The issues are complex and nuanced, but they must be studied by those who would advise America's senior military leaders and policy makers.

eighteen

Other Major Figures in the Militant Islamist Movement

This chapter introduces the sophisticated nature of our adversary and level of intelligence and outlines the top operational echelons of various Militant Islamist groups. You should not have a stereotyped image of Militant Islamist operatives. In addition, as will be discussed below, in the case of the Shiite radical group Hezbollah (the Party of God), the lines between Islamist and Militant Islamist are blurred.

MAJOR FIGURES

Khalid Sheikh Muhammad

Khalid Sheikh Muhammad, known among as "KSM," is currently in custody at Guantanamo Bay. KSM entered al-Qaida in 2002; before that he was a terrorist for hire, a person who possessed hundreds of ideas for terrorist plots, of which maybe ten would be acted upon—elements of several terrorist plots, to include Operation Bojinka, the plot to cause several airliners to explode and disappear over the Pacific Ocean. There is no question that KSM is creative; he is considered the mastermind of 9/11. He received a degree in agricultural engineering at Chowan College, North Carolina. KSM was comfortable in the United States, asking naturally how the University of North Carolina "Blue Devils" are doing, never giving away that he was an al-Qaida operative. KSM also experiments with numerous covers, one being a "man about town" in Manila, complete with Filipino girlfriend, silk shirts, and even gold chains. He would wear a cross to get through customs and was proficient in creating cover stories wherever he might be operating.

Ramzi Yussef

Ramzi Yussef, the plotter of the 1993 World Trade Center bombing and KSM's nephew, has been in custody since 1995. His motivation for cultivating a unique set of terrorist skills was to become the next "superterrorist," like Carlos the Jackal. He received an electrical engineering degree from Swansea College in Wales and is proficient in several languages. He is capable of transforming digital watches into detonators, constructing bombs, and even making his own home-made plastic explosives and shaped charges. Aside from the 1993 World Trade Center Plot, he participated, created, and tested a bomb that was then planted on a Japanese Airline flight from Manila to Cebu and on to Tokyo. The bomb ripped through the fuselage and killed one Japanese citizen. (This was a test run for Operation Bojinka.) When extradited to the United States in 1995, he was flown by the World Trade Center and shown that the buildings were still standing. He remarked that they would not have been had he had enough money to carry out the job properly.

Imad Mughniyah

Imad Mughniyah is chief of military operations for Hezbollah worldwide and among the most proficient terrorists and unconventional operatives in the Middle East. He was killed in 2008, when his car drove by a vehicle-borne explosive device in Damascus. Mughniyah had made his name by planning the 1983 Marine Barracks Bombing in Beirut, which killed 241 U.S. Marines. Among his numerous plots was the successful bombing of a Jewish center in Buenos Aires. Over the years he created a proficient light-infantry force and had a healthy respect for the military doctrines of his adversaries, chiefly the Israelis. No one has claimed responsibility for Mughniyah's assassination; his techniques and tactics are studied by both Sunni and Shiite Militant Islamist groups. There is speculation that Mughniyah may have met Usama bin Laden during his time in Sudan. This has not been confirmed, but bin Laden might have formed a student-mentor relationship with Mughniyah, however brief.

Abu Ayyub al-Masri

Abu Ayyub al-Masri is the current head of al-Qaida in Iraq, or AQI. It is important not to view AQI as a distinct entity from the al-Qaida senior leadership in Pakistan. Al-Qaida seniors may not directly control AQI, but they do attempt to influence its leaders. This was seen clearly with Zawahiri's 2005 letter to the former AQI leader, Zarqawi, who took Zawahiri's advice under advisement. Abu Ayyub al-Masri is a bomb maker and assumed the leadership of AQI suddenly. It was assumed that after the death of Zarqawi a Jordanian al-Qaida would assign an Iraqi as the leader; instead, Abu Ayyub, an Egyptian, emerged as the true leader. The problem of "Iraqifying" the AQI movement was botched by Abu Umar al-Baghdadi the emir (the figurehead leader). He is little seen and only issues statements via audio, which has called into question his legitimacy among Militant Islamists. A Zawahiri protégé, Abu Ayyub al-Masri likely listens to his mentor's advice in running operations in Iraq.

Abu Musab al-Suri

Al-Suri, in custody since 2005, was born in Syria in 1958 and joined the Syrian Muslim Brotherhood at an early age. He writes in *Mudhkirah al-Suriyah* (Syrian Memoranda) that the "Combatant Vanguard," a militant wing of the Syrian Muslim Brotherhood, was betrayed by the movement, which entered into negotiations with the Syrian regime. These negotiations resulted in the Hama incident of 1982, in which Syrian forces leveled the city of Hama which had been taken over by the Combatant Vanguard. Like al-Qaida deputy Ayman al-Zawahiri, al-Suri hates the Muslim Brotherhood. He blames it for causing him to flee Syria in the aftermath of the Islamist purges conducted by Syria, adding that it was the Brotherhood that made him virtually persona non grata in Saudi Arabia, thwarting his attempts to enroll in Medina Islamic University. By 1984, al-Suri left Saudi Arabia for France and then Spain, marrying a Spanish woman to whom he was devoted. He completed a black belt in judo and found his way to Afghanistan, where he combined his knowledge of mechanical engineering, lessons learned from his observations and experiences in the Militant Islamist movements, martial arts, and combat training in Iraq under Abu Usama al-Misri to become an al-Qaida military instructor from 1988 to 1991. Al-Suri was more than an instructor but also developed courses in politics, strategy, guerilla warfare, and urban tactics. He would lecture and train in the Sada, Zawar Killi, and Farouq training camps in Afghanistan. Some of al-Suri's students included Riduan Issamuddin (also known as Hambali), leader of al-Qaida in Indonesia, and Abu Musab al-Zarqawi, the late leader of al-Qaida in Iraq.

His writings suggest that he is influenced by such militant clerics as Abdullah Azzam, who, al-Suri says, was able to transform violent Jihad from a regional movement into a global one. He is, of course, a disciple of Qutb, Ibn Taymiyah, Dr. Fadl, and the *al-Sahwa* scholars. He is not above recommending the writings of Wahhabi senior clerics like Ibn Baz and Ibn Uthaymeen, after warning listeners of their hypocritical posture toward the Saudi regime. In 1991 he completed his first major book, a two-volume work *Thwarah al Islamiyah al-Jihadiyah fee Suri-yah* (The Islamic Jihad Revolution in Syria), which not only chronicles the history of the Muslim Brotherhood in Syria but draws lessons. Like Zawahiri's *Hisaad al-Murr* (Bitter Harvest), it is a scathing critique of the Muslim Brotherhood and its dealings with secular "apostate" Arab regimes.

Al-Suri's life offers glimpses into the Moroccan, Libyan, Algerian, and Saudi Islamist militant groups, many tied to al-Qaida. Al-Suri's most important book is *A Call to Global Islamic Resistance*, a complex, 1,600-page work that is best remembered for suggesting that the Jihadist cellular structure has become obsolete, that today's al-Qaida sympathizers need to create their own cells and conduct attacks in the name of al-Qaida. There is speculation that al-Suri's writings may have inspired the Madrid train bombing and the London bombings. As an indication that al-Qaida is a learning organization, one that is opportunistic and tactically pragmatic, one of al-Suri's last books was entitled *Fundamentals for Jihadi Warfare in Light of the Condition of Contemporary American Campaigns*. The work is a distillation of American military errors from Vietnam to Iraq. The book was not published before his capture but was reduced to audio-tapes; these tapes have since been transcribed and are available on the Internet.

Abu Jandal

Abu Jandal, bin Laden's bodyguard during Operation Enduring Freedom. While supposedly under house arrest in Yemen, he gave a full interview to the newspaper *al-Quda al-Arabi*. It may cast light on the question of whether Usama bin Laden will be captured dead or alive. Abu Jandal claimed in his interview that among his duties as bin Laden's bodyguard, was to keep a pistol at the ready to shoot bin Laden if coalition forces closed in on him.

Muqtada al-Sadr (Shiite Leader of the Mahdi Army)

Muqtada al-Sadr is the Shiite leader of the Mahdi Army. Muqatda's uncle, Muhammad Baqir al-Sadr, was an ayatollah murdered by Saddam Hussein in 1980. Saddam would also murder Muqtada's father, Muhammad Sadiq al-Sadr, in 1999. A cousin, Musa al-Sadr, is founder of the Lebanese Shiite party Amal; Musa al-Sadr would disappear in Libya under mysterious circumstances. Muqtada's aunt, Amina Sadr bint al-Huda, would also be brutally murdered by Saddam. The family traces its origins to Lebanon; it moved to Iraq in 1785. Muqtada claims descent from the

Prophet Muhammad through the Sixth Imam, Jafar al-Siddiq. These details and martyrs of Muqtada's lineage are important to understanding from where this ill-trained cleric derives his power. His uncle founded the al-Dawa Party, a bold and dangerous move, as it was intended to counter Baathists, Arab nationalists, and leftists. One of the rival clerical families in the Najaf *hawza* (clerical hierarchy) is, as we have seen, the al-Sadrs.[1]

OTHER MOVEMENTS

Hezbollah

Hezbollah in Lebanon is a complex case that straddles the Islamist and Militant Islamist movements. It is a quasi-state in southern Lebanon and areas of Beirut, on one hand, and yet on the other it maintains one of the most sophisticated, asymmetric military formations in the Middle East in terms of tactics, creativity, and military operations. Former deputy secretary of state Richard Armitage calls Hezbollah the "A-Team" of terrorism. There are those who argue that Hezbollah maintains perhaps the best light infantry force in the Arab world. It has crafted this force by carefully studying Israeli tactics and operational procedures. What concerns counterterrorism experts is Hezbollah's constant experimentation with new technology and tactics; operations are videotaped not only for propaganda purposes but also to understand what went right and what went wrong. In 2006, when Hezbollah clashed with the Israeli Defense Forces, its focus shifted from light infantry to rocket forces. Hezbollah kept firing rockets into Israel for the duration of the conflict. Hezbollah is supported by Iran and gets access to Iranian support (estimates range between $100 million and $250 million annually), through Syria. The current leader of Hezbollah is Sheikh Hassan Nasrallah. Should he be killed or die, his designated successor is the chief of the Operations Committee (and Nasrallah's cousin), Hashim Safi-al-Din.[2] This is a recent development, intended to ensure a line of continuation and preparedness in case hostilities with Israel lead to the killing of Nasrallah. The group should be classified as Militant Islamist.

Hamas

Hamas was created in 1987 in Gaza among former Islamists in the Muslim Brotherhood. Hamas is currently part of the Palestinian Authority government, although its failure to compromise has been a consistent problem affecting the effectiveness of that government, which has left the Palestinian people in squalor. Hamas has straddled the Islamist and Militant Islamist divide, using its proficiency in suicide-bomber operations to strike at Israeli targets, yet it is currently in government. What is missed by many is that Hamas won only 44 percent of the electorate and had to assemble a multiparty majority to govern; it has failed in this effort, making its experimentation with Islamist governance a failure. Hamas, although a Sunni radical group, is supported by Iran and Hezbollah.

Front Islamique du Salut (FIS) and Its Offshoots

Those studying the challenges of North Africa must examine Algeria and the Militant Islamist problems of that unfortunate country. Between 1987 and 1992 the Islamic Salvation Front (known by the French acronym FIS) was poised to win in municipal and national elections. These legitimate electoral gains were nullified by a military junta, and a civil war descended upon Algeria between government security forces and Militant Islamists. Many Islamists made the transition to Militant Islamist groups, frustrated by the denial of their gains at the ballot box. However, things may not be that clear-cut, as the FIS had allegedly begun to talk about ridding the Algerian government of such ministries as Justice and Tourism and to send Algerian clerics dressed in Afghan garb and preaching an Islam that is not characteristically Algerian. Deobandi-Wahhabism as espoused by Islamists and Militant Islamists is not compatible with the Sunni Maliki school and Sufism, which are parts of the social fabric of Algeria. The generals, not wanting to see the character of Algeria altered, opted to declare a military junta. It is estimated that 250,000 people were killed in a ferocious, decade-long civil war. The FIS was co-opted into the government, and the more militant elements formed the Groupe Islamique Armé (GIA). The GIA was no longer able to count on public support due to massacres and criminal activities.

From an ideological perspective, it is noteworthy that though Abu Musab al-Suri was involved in promoting the GIA in London, both al-Suri and Usama bin Laden distanced themselves from the GIA, which became a case study of what Militant Islamists should not do. Those GIA members who did not accept amnesty formed the Groupé Salafist pour la Predication et le Combat (GSPC) in 2005. A second offshoot of GIA is the Houmat Daawa Salafia (HDS). It is different from GIA in that it targets security officials only. HDS is critical of the shedding of innocent Muslim blood and recently was critical of al-Qaida in the Land of the Maghreb (AQIM). The GSPC's initial platform was to return to attacking government officials, knowing how unpopular the killing of Muslim civilians was among the Algerian public. The GSPC would be so marginalized that, when its leader Abdel-Razak Para was captured, militant groups within the GSPC morphed AQIM, which formally joined al-Qaida central in 2007. GSPC was an exclusively Algerian creation, but as AQIM it had to work with North and Sahel Africans. (Algerians, Libyans, and Moroccans do not always get along, and North Africans view Sahel Africans with contempt.)

It seems that the pendulum of killing Muslim civilians in Algeria is swinging. The year 2007 saw a series of attacks that killed innocent Muslim civilian bystanders. One attack in December 2007 near a police academy killed over forty people, and a September 2007 attempt on Algerian president Boutiflika missed him and killed innocent civilians instead. Of concern is the introduction of vehicle-borne improvised explosives devices by Algerian Militant Islamists who fought in Iraq and learned terrorist techniques, bringing them back to Algeria. This shedding of Muslim blood by AQIM has drawn criticism from the Islamist cleric Yusuf al-Qaradawi and Algerian Islamist Militant operatives like Muhammad al-Fazzazi, who issued a condemnation from a Moroccan prison. Former Libyan Islamic Fighting Group Leader Noman Benotman wrote an open letter to Zawahiri in November 2007 on the issue of killing innocent Muslims: "Do not delude yourself; what is objectionable is not the tactic of suicide attacks but suicide attacks that kill Muslims that is being debated in Islamist and Militant Islamist websites."

The Taliban

There is a misconception that the Taliban was among the factions that fought the Soviets. That may be true of few of the senior leaders, but the Taliban actually arose among the radicalized Afghan refugees in the camps of Pakistan. The name means "students" or "seminarians"; its leader, Mullah Omar, was a madrassa teacher who encouraged his students to leave the classroom and pick up weapons to fight unjust and abusive warlords who were terrorizing the local populace. The Pakistanis saw in the Taliban a chance to stabilize Afghanistan; the warlords who had raped and murdered, were captured and executed by the Taliban, whose members considered that they were doing God's work. From 1994 to 1996, the Taliban evolved into a movement and captured the majority of Afghanistan; however, its stronghold would always be Kandahar.

From 1995 to 2001, the Taliban granted safe haven to al-Qaida and Usama bin Laden, when the bin Laden was evicted from Sudan. Bin Laden married one of his daughters to Mullah Omar and became an indispensable resource, publicly acknowledging him as *Amir al-Mumineen* (Commander of the Faithful). The title was criticized on grounds that he lacked scholarly credentials, tribal pedigree, or lineage to Prophet Muhammad's family. In addition, all of Afghanistan's *ulema* were supposed to endorse the title, but only 1,200 hard-line Pashtu mullahs did. Bin Laden provided help in Mullah Omar's war against Ahmed Shah Masood and the Northern Alliance.

The Taliban governed Afghanistan with brutality and intimidated the populace by enforcing a Deobandi-Wahhabi mixture of fundamentalist Islam. Under the guise of preventing vice, the Taliban maintained a presence on the streets of Kabul, Kandahar, and Mazar al-Sherief. It massacred Iranian diplomats at Mazar al-Sherief in 1998, which almost led to war with Iran. Usama bin Laden would betray Mullah Omar, promising him not to conduct public interviews and then reneging on his pledge. In 1998, Mullah Omar was irritated by a cruise-missile attack. Bin Laden's conduct of the 9/11 attacks without Mullah Omar's consent, and from Afghanistan, can only be described as the ultimate betrayal. Zawahiri wrote at the time, on a computer drive later captured, about bin Laden, "He has caught the disease of screens, flashes and applause."[3] There are Taliban leaders who consider bin Laden to have caused the loss of the only Islamic emirate then in existence. The former Taliban foreign minister wrote a scathing attack on al-Qaida for abusing the hospitality extended to it by Mullah Omar, in a ninety-eight-page 2005 book.[4]

It is likely that Usama bin Laden is protected not so much by the Taliban as by Mullah Omar personally and his inner circle. The divided Taliban has reconstituted itself into two major blocks. The first is Tehrik e-Taliban Pakistan (TTP), formed in December 2007 out of twenty-seven Taliban factions; its main objective is the "Talibinization" of Pakistan while conducting a defensive Jihad against Pakistani security forces. It has been blamed for the rise in suicide bombings and the murder of former prime minister Benazir Bhutto. Their competitor for Taliban groups is the "Local Taliban Movement," sometimes called the Waziri Alliance, whose platform is fighting International Security Assistance Force, NATO, and American forces in Afghanistan. For the time being, Pakistan is playing the Waziri Alliance against the TTP and its late leader Baitullah Mashud, who, until September 30, 2008, when the media reported his death due to kidney failure, was Pakistan's enemy number one.

Both are antithetical to the interests of the United States, but they must be dealt with piecemeal. Al-Qaida has been able to reconstitute itself in northwest

Pakistan, but not back to the pre-9/11 level. Some of its capabilities focus on training new recruits and replacing midlevel lieutenants who have been wounded, killed, or captured. The problem is that a reconstituted al-Qaida in northwest Pakistan has struck beyond its borders, to Europe and the United States—the 2006 summer airline plot was planned and trained for in Pakistan and put together in Europe, with the objective of striking the American transatlantic air link.

nineteen

Al-Qaida's Wedge Issues for the United States to Consider

This new conflict is not one the United States will be comfortable with, given the religious cloak under which al-Qaida and Militant Islamists cover themselves. However, both Muslims and non-Muslims alike are threatened by Militant Islamists. Amazingly, Abu Yahya al-Libi, a senior al-Qaida leader, himself summed up six strategies for the defeat of al-Qaida, daring the United States and the West to take these measures. It is worth cutting through al-Libi's pomposity for clues as to what really could undermine al-Qaida. He says that to defeat al-Qaida one must:[1]

- Highlight the views of Jihadists who renounce al-Qaida.
- Publicize stories of Jihadist atrocities against Muslims.
- Enlist Muslim religious leaders to denounce Jihadists as heretics.
- Back Islamic movements that emphasize politics over Jihad.
- Discredit and neutralize Jihadist ideologues.
- Play up personal and doctrinal disputes among Jihadists.

The United States and its allies should take him up on parts of his dare. Here are a few pressure points:

Doctrinaire versus Pragmatists. Militant Islamists are split between those wanting to operate clandestinely and others wishing to generate broad social movements. The formation of the Islamic State of Iraq was an attempt by al-Qaida in Iraq to transform themselves from clandestine to broad social movements. They failed, and the attempt has driven wedges between Sunnis wishing to balance pan-Islamist militancy with tribalism and nationalism.

Common Islamic Consensus on al-Qaida. As more and more clerics criticize al-Qaida, we need to attain a collective *ijmaa,* an Islamic position common to Shiite and Sunni clerics on al-Qaida as a movement, ideology, and methodology, a common Islamic condemnation. Condemnations can be practical, theological, or both, but theology-heavy condemnations are better, as al-Qaida is weak there, particularly as a younger generation assumes leadership.

Generational Tensions between Militant Islamist Leaders. Abu Musab al-Suri, al-Qaida's strategic thinker, laments that of the three generations of the Jihadist movement, from the 1960s to the present, none has possessed a good grounding in the language of Islam and Islamic argumentation.

Anonymity of Militant Islamist Leaders. The emir of the Islamic State of Iraq, Abu Umar al-Baghdadi, is known only by audio tapes. The leader of al-Qaida operations in the Levant, Shakir al-Absi, has been barely seen. Mullah Omar has rarely been seen and limits his statements to communiqués and audio statements. The so-called Commander of the Faithful shares the spotlight with another Commander of the Faithful, Abu Umar al-Baghdadi—whereas there can be only one Commander of the Faithful.

Battlefield versus Armchair Militant Islamist Clerics. Battlefield clerics feel that their service in the fight entitles them to issue fatwas, but radical armchair clerics contravene them. This came out clearly in the disagreements between Hamid Ali, a Kuwaiti Islamist Militant cleric, and Abu Yahya al-Libi, who assumes the role of cleric but is of dubious training. Armchair Militant Islamist clerics like Hani Sibai in London, Hamid Ali in Kuwait, and Akram Hijazi in Gaza dominate the Internet.

Al-Qaida Self-Definition. Al-Qaida is split between those wanting to organize the movement into a pragmatic, tactical, guerilla force and those wishing it to morph into a leaderless "brand name." Abu Musab al-Suri attempts to reconcile these differences through his leaderless-Jihad theories.

Arab Muslims as the Hub of Militant Islamist Ideology. It is estimated 90 percent of the Militant Islamist websites are in Arabic, the remainder in Malay, Urdu, and other languages. This trend among Militant Islamist groups can be used to exacerbate the divisive effects of Arab hubris and disdain for non-Arab militants. There are divisions even among Arabs: foreign fighters in Iraq want to dominate Iraqis in their own country, Saudis and Egyptians feel superior to Libyans, and so on. These cultural variations impact the efficacy of Militant Islamist groups.

Zawahiri's Intellectual Insecurity. Zawahiri's 2005 letter to Zarqawi shows him yearning to be taken seriously. In his 2008 answers to questions he mentions CTC West Point being composed of PhDs and appears to be enjoying their intellectual attention.

Al-Qaida as a Dead End. Al-Qaida considers as its enemies the United States, Arab regimes, the West, Israel, Muslims, non-Muslims, laborers in Iraq working on humanitarian projects, the near enemy, the far enemy, Hamas, Hezbollah, Shiites, Iraqi Sunni tribes, the UN, Western NGOs, Western corporations—the list seems endless. Al-Qaida hates too many entities and so can never build a grassroots movement. It is a dead-end ideology. Peter Bergen has written that bin Laden has fastened onto a self-defeating overall strategy which has resulted in the direct opposite of a U.S. withdrawal from the Middle East.[2] Bergen declares that at twenty al-Qaida is losing the war, though its influence will live on. This is all the more reason to begin deconstructing al-Qaida ideology and legacy using Islamic arguments. Militant Islamists, like al-Qaida, reduce Islam to an implausible epic struggle and marginalize the moral or intellectual evolution of Islam itself. Militant Islamists seek civilizational, not theological, change and so cling to ideologues like Qutb and Ibn Taymiyyah, who reinforce their impossible struggle. Ibn Taymiyyah railed against all kinds of *bid'aa* (innovations), demanding that Islam not resemble the practices of non-Muslims. Yet one cannot understand Islam without understanding Judeo-Christianity.

The Loss of Arab TV Support. In 2007 al-Qaida attacked al-Jazeera for airing only sound bites of a bin Laden tape. The Arabic network now airs not only excerpts of bin Laden and Zawahiri tapes but adds critical commentaries. Saudi Arabia's al-Arabiyah TV channel has evolved into an Islamic propaganda arm hostile to al-Qaida. An al-Arabiyah series worth following is *Sunaah al-Mawt* (Manufacturers of Death), which features in-depth discussions on such topics as Iraq's Ansar al-Islam, female suicide bombers in Iraq, who killed Abdullah Azzam, and much more.[3] Many faces now compete on-screen with bin Laden and Zawahiri on Arab networks. In public discourse it is important to emphasize how simply saying one's prayers puts one at risk of murder. The failed attempt on Abdullah Azzam involved a bomb in a mosque, and the deputy governor of Helmand Province was murdered by a detonation inside a crowded mosque.[4] Al-Qaida in Iraq has used mosques as torture chambers and for ammunition storage, which should outrage Muslims more than American forces dirtying the carpet with their boots. This pattern of Militant Islamists defiling mosques with violence can be exploited.

Militant Islamists and Islamists as Competitors. Al-Qaida attempts to preach to Muslim Brotherhood clusters, trying to get them to migrate from the government of technocrats to the government of God. They have very different methodologies, techniques, and views on Muslim society. Al-Qaida views society as corrupt and beyond redemption except through violence; the Muslim Brotherhood works with society and attempts to be part of it.

An example of this is the petition and demonstration against President George W. Bush's visit to Egypt in May 2008. The point is not the demonstration but how Muslim Brotherhood parliamentarians worked with the Tajamu, Nasserist, Wifaq al-Qawmi, and Socialist parties to express their opposition. The Muslim Brotherhood organized a petition and submitted it to the National Democratic Party leader, Fathi Surrur, expressing the desire of the Egyptian parliament to be consulted in President Mubarak's negotiations with President Bush. There is no question that the Muslim Brotherhood is not a friend of the United States, but it use methods that would be impossible for Militant Islamist groups, which cannot compromise. Their xenophobic views prevent them from working with Arab nationalists or socialists, blinded as they are by their labeling of huge portions of twenty-first-century Muslim society as apostate.

A milder example is the weekly column of Saudi Sheikh Ayed al-Qarni in the "Islamic Affairs" section of the newspaper *al-Sharq al-Awsat*. He chastises the obsession with death and argues in Islamic terms the importance of living, rather than dying, for the sake of God.[5] He also discusses such Islamist aspirations in the lack of a truly unified, Islamic twenty-first-century Arab thought; he includes even Ibn Taymiyyah among unifying factors and says that abandoning such philosophies causes Muslim victimization.[6] The trick is to concentrate his anti–Militant Islamist articles and direct them against the real adversary, by interjecting them into Western public discourse.

Another example is the Grand Mufti of Syria, who addressed the European Union Dialogue of Civilization's Conference in Brussels in January 2008. His message was a double-edged sword: on the one hand, condemning those, whether Palestinian, Israeli, or Iraqi, who kill children, declaring that extremism is incompatible with the Islamic world, that there is no holy war, just a sacred peace, but, on the other hand, excusing extremism as a result of the oppression of the rights of Muslims and condemning the Danish cartoons of Prophet Muhammad.[7] The Europeans praised the remarks, but when read carefully these comments are unconstructive, maybe reflecting Syria's complex relationship with terrorism and rejectionist groups.

Tactical Aspects of Undermining al-Qaida. In 2008, Abu Layth al-Libi and Abu Khabab al-Masri were killed, one a senior al-Qaida figure and the other a person who trained many in the arts of bomb-making and experimented with crude chemical and biologic warfare materials. Al-Qaida leaders are being replaced as fast as they are killed or captured. But tribal and Sunni Awakening Council members whom al-Qaida in Iraq has killed have been replaced too, and their replacements have the same tenacity for revenge as al-Qaida. For instance, the Azamiyah Awakening Council suffered the loss of their militia commander Riyad al-Samarrai in December 2007, assassinated by al-Qaida in Iraq operatives. In mid-January, the council named his replacement, a Colonel Abu Abd of the old Iraqi army, who announced a renewed offensive against al-Qaida in Iraq. The ability of Iraq's Awakening Council to achieve gains and recover from setbacks against al-Qaida in Iraq is as important as that of coalition forces.[8]

twenty

Mindsets That Hamper America's Capabilities

When [men] go to war, what they want is to impose on their enemies the victor's will and call it peace.

SAINT AUGUSTINE

DANGERS OF THE ONE-DIMENSIONAL AND CIVILIZATION-CLASH APPROACH

It is important to be aware of one extreme of America's national security debate, which is a one-dimensional view that all Islam is evil. This case can be made if you quote exclusively from militant verses and sayings of Muhammad, as well as offer a steady diet of ideologues without exploring the full breadth of Islamic commentaries. Besides the obvious issue of alienating a billion Muslims, some of whom are needed to combat Militant Islamist groups, this does not lend itself to policy options. The multitude of materials that take this one-dimensional view are short on recommendations; for instance, they argue for a doctrine-based definition of the threat but in the end do not provide that definition or remedies to the problem. Once you paint an entire faith as evil and travel down the road of "civilization clash," you must face the question: What is to be done about it? The only answer to this question in those terms is extreme; it leaves no flexibility. If you believe this long war must be fought multidimensionally, you cannot espouse a one-dimensional view of the threat. You must disaggregate Islam from Islamist, and these two from Militant Islamist, ideology.

Be cognizant of variations in the argument that lead to the "civilizational clash," for instance, a characterization that sharia finance is a new weapon in what is called a "fifth-generational" clash. Fragments of such events as rising oil prices, *jihad bil mal* (Jihad using money), terrorist financing, the investments of the United Arab Emirates in American firms, the central banks of our adversaries like Iran and Syria, *zakat* (poor tax), and *hawala* (informal, unregulated, honor-based banks in the Islamic world) are woven together to suggest that all these are a coordinated new front, that sharia is evil, and sharia finance is the new threat. This is simply another way of missing the nuances needed to isolate those who pose a true threat to America's national security. The sharia is simply not a monolithic bloc; it is subject to interpretation, disagreement, renewal, misuse, and strands of thought inherent in the diversity of 1.3 billion Muslim adherents. Some who advocate this view try to convey certainty that they have the conflict figured out, by embellishing their discourse with Arabic terms and Islamic concepts. Look beyond these sound bites and examine the content of their argument.

On the other end of this spectrum are some Muslim-Americans who, by virtue of being Muslim, feel certain what the problem is and how to solve it, or not solve it. They too interlace their discourse with Arabic terms and Islamic concepts in order to overinflate their status as experts on Islam. The issue is not their arguments, which one can agree or disagree with, but again the certainty with which they express them. Look out for "Islamic experts" who interlace Arabic words to make themselves appear more knowledgeable than they really are and convey an uncompromising certainty. Quasi-preaching and certainty about the evils of one faith or the superiority of another have no place in the realistic world of international affairs. This certainty can be seen in academic and nonacademic sources, which is why positions on this issue need to be assessed based upon the content of the arguments, problems identified, and solutions proposed. Let us not lapse into the epic civilizational struggle our Militant Islamist enemy desires.

PROBLEMATIC MINDSETS

The bulk of this book focused on the adversary and the methodology by which they "hijacking a great religion," to quote the last administration. However the adversary operates within the context of what the United States and its partners do or do not do. The purpose of this volume is to highlight the need to define the threat precisely as Militant Islamist Ideology and disaggregate it from Islamists and Islam. This section focuses on mindsets that interfere with the ability of the United States to counter Militant Islamist Ideology and concepts that Americans do not properly understand.

Confusing psychological operations, information operations (IO), strategic communication, and public diplomacy. Many refer to counter-ideological programs as "IO"; this is unfortunate, as IO connotes shaping the information environment of the battle space and is therefore limited in time and scope. What is needed is an intergenerational program to erode the acceptability of Militant Islamist Ideology and to separate it from Islamist political groups and Islam. The clear difference is the use of violence, combined with the manipulation of philosophy, doctrine, psychology, and anthropology in a way that allows the dead-end Militant Islamist Ideology to delude individuals. Resisting Militant Islamist Ideology involves the identifying of individuals with alternative groups, be they familial, tribal, national, or Islamist. Group associations are as varied as human nature. A narrow emphasis on Islam's past conquests and the deemphasis of its other achievements or aspects of its history serve to marginalize the present. Militant Islamist Ideology and doctrine are designed to isolate the person from the self and the world. That is why Quranic injunctions to explore tribes and nations are selectively discounted by al-Qaida and Militant Islamist ideologues. Because it views tolerance as weakness, this worldview requires the abrogation of whole swaths of the Qur'an. The perversity of Militant Islamist doctrines and the certitude it conveys can be countered by Islamic argument. Only in that way can Militant Islamist theory be deconstructed before it absorbs the person's moral sense and rational thought. These are the complexities that make the IO an insufficient remedy. A former CIA field officer, T. J. Waters, criticizing aspects of the training he received in the CIA as a new recruit, remarks that al-Qaida uses explosives and expression, that bin Laden understands that perception can exact social change more rapidly than military action. Waters fears that our training has not caught up to this nuance and that his training at CIA never addressed it.[1]

The American desire to be loved. Americans want to be popular around the world. This is natural in social interactions but has no place in the harsh world of Militant Islamists. We need to employ techniques that elicit a wide range of emotions—not only love but hate and fear—as a means to protect American interests and deter the adversary.

Drifting off the message. We must continue to stay focused in describing Militant Islamists and identifying them as different from Islamists and from Islam. Al-Qaida stays on message consistently; it has created a mindset of victimization, of which the only remedy is Militant Islamist violent action. Usama bin Laden consistently expresses confidence that the United States will be defeated and that Americans lack the patience to win. We must neutralize bin Laden's and other al-Qaida leaders' methodology and ideology and expose their personal hypocrisies, corruptions, perversions, and atrocities, as well as their other shortcomings, consistently and frequently. The Office of Strategic Influence (OSI), established by former secretary of defense Donald Rumsfeld, quickly criticized and shut down, was America's earliest attempt at addressing one of its weakest pillars of security in the war on terrorism: perception and ideology. Recall Ayman al-Zawahiri's letter to Zarqawi, declaring that half of this battle is fought in the media.

Groups inspired by al-Qaida ideology versus operations it directs. In the realm of counterterrorism it is important to understand whether a terrorist action was directed, tangibly supported, endorsed, or merely inspired by al-Qaida. However, in the realm of strategic communications, even events like the 2004 Madrid bombings, which was only inspired by al-Qaida, need to be constantly linked to al-Qaida ideology. In other words if a cell is inspired by al-Qaida rhetoric to kill innocents, we should never let the public forget that.

"The enemy of my enemy." This conflict will see the ever-increasing utilization of proxies—tribal, Islamist, and nationalist, as examples. The United States has already supported proxies like the Northern Alliance to undermine the Taliban and the Iraqi Sunni tribes to undermine al-Qaida in Iraq. We should at least discuss arming those fighting al-Qaida who may not necessarily like the United States with information damaging to our common enemies. For example, if, hypothetically, al-Qaida in Iraq uses a mosque to torture Muslims, we should not announce this immediately but provide the information to Iraq's Sunni tribes fighting al-Qaida in Iraq, so they can gain an advantage on the ground. The question is not where bin Laden is but which tribe, clan, or subclan is protecting him, within a wider tribal confederation.

The fluidity of Islamist movements and Militant Islamists. Dr. Guilain Denoeux of Colby College in Maine has written a thought-provoking paper entitled "The Forgotten Swamp: Navigating Political Islam." She notes the changing nature of Islamist movements, arguing they are not frozen in time but move from moderate to radical and back again. Denoeux highlights the example of the Egyptian Muslim Brotherhood, which started as a social movement, radicalized, created a militant wing ("The Special Apparatus"), and is now involved in Egypt's political process, renouncing violent political action. This fluidity necessitates the use of such designators as "Islamist" and "Militant Islamist" to label real threats. When Russia invaded Georgia in 2008, one of the notable features of this conflict was Moscow's use of Internet warfare, not only to shutting down anti-Russian websites but offering pro-Russian blogs. This is the wave of the future—the trick is not to shut down a Militant Islamist website outright but make it shift to another service provider or server by saturating it with counterarguments in Islamic language.

The erosion of al-Qaida does not mean the decline of the Militant Islamist movement. Bringing about al-Qaida's decline is attainable, but the overarching decline of Militant Islamist Ideology will require the emergence of alternative ideologies and the solutions of such complex Middle Eastern issues as Palestine, autocratic regimes, and the radicalization of societies.

The movement of Militant Islamist groups from theological to strategic rationalization. More and more Militant Islamist ideologues focus less on theological questions than on strategic issues. "Near enemy" advocates include twenty-first-century Militant Islamist strategists like Abu Bakr al-Naji and Abu Musab al-Suri, and Militant Islamist clerics like Abu Muhammad al-Maqdisi in Jordan and Abu Hamza in London. Abu Hamza has given a popular sermon urging that Mecca be liberated before Palestine. This is an interesting development, as the Muslim popular base concerns itself with theology; many questions posed to Zawahiri were theological, some of which he answered dismissively. The tendency of Militant Islamist theoreticians like Qutb to commingle Marxist, socialist, and revolutionary liberation rhetoric and ultranationalist sound bites with Islamic imagery can be exposed.

Distinguishing between Islam, Islamist, and Militant Islamist. Who is turning from Islamist to Militant Islamist and vice versa? If Militant Islamist, do they target security forces only? How do they assess or treat the killing of innocent Muslims? How fast are Militant Islamists turning in their rivals in Algeria and Iraq? These are all metrics as to the radicalism of a Militant Islamist group. Let us examine the Kashmir model; there, a recent trend has seen Kashmiri groups moving to Pakistan's Federally Administered Tribal Area to be closer to the Taliban and al-Qaida. This has given al-Qaida reach into India and the Kashmiri diaspora in Europe. Kashmiri groups that offer strategic options to al-Qaida and the Taliban cease to be insurgents; their terrorism retards any political settlement of the Kashmir problem, just as every Palestinian suicide bomber sets back the eventuality of a Palestinian state.[2] There have also been many offers from Muslim leaders since the constructive 2005 Amman Message, such as the former president of Indonesia, Abdurrahman Wahid, for a counterstrategy that portrays "a compelling alternative vision of Islam, one that banishes the fanatical ideology of hatred to the darkness from which it emerged." Wahid extends an invitation to the West to help with this endeavor by providing media and marketing expertise.[3] Here is a Muslim who points to fanatic Islamist ideology and understands that only Islamic argument can deconstruct this ideology.

Disaggregating anticolonialism and anti-imperialism from the rejection of all things Western. Hatred of colonialism and the rhetoric of anti-imperialism have been combined in a rejection of all things Western. There is no question that Western ideas and notions have benefited humanity: when a Militant Islamist terrorist wakes up he switches on a light bulb invented by the infidel Thomas Edison, he rides in a car made by infidels, uses a computer made by infidels. His entire existence is touched by technological inventions by the infidel he hates so much. This rejection of all things Western must be revealed for the hypocrisy it is. Militant Islamists have used Islam as an argument for regression, isolation, ignorance, and a culture of death.

In addition, Militant Islamist Ideology has been influenced at a subliminal level by counterproductive ideologies, such as the language of fascism and nationalism. For instance, Abu Ala al-Mawdudi (a key Islamist ideologue) has borrowed heavily from the West: an Islamic state, he writes, would be run by a president, parliament, a judiciary, and a constitution. Mawdudi would influence both Qutb and Khomeini in their conception of Islamic government. Yet Mawdudi reduces Islam to a struggle between Islam and non-Islam, a radical exegesis; however, his ideas are laced with institutions that did not originate in the Islamic world.

The shift from the "far enemy" (the United States) to the "near enemy" (Arab regimes). Is this shift a victory for the United States? This is a deceptive question, as it hides levels of complexity. If it is true and the focus is now on Arab regimes, how does this impact the region? Will Syria shift from tolerating Militant Islamists that do not destabilize the regime? Will Iran have to now deal with Militant Islamist cells that convert from logistical and transit to actual terror operations within Iran?

Militant Islamists as colonizers of Islam. Militant Islamists have no tolerance for diversity in Muslim belief. In their perverse enforcement of morals as a means of instilling societal control through fear and intimidation and their desire to expunge different Muslim beliefs, they must be viewed as colonizers of Islam. Twentieth- and twenty-first-century Militant Islamist Ideology may have been infected by French and British colonial influences of *mission civilisatrice*, whereby European imperialism was merged with Christianity—that is, allowing the modernist Militant Islamist concept of merging the propagation of Islam with global conquest. This also raises the question of the impact of Saudi Islamist Wahhabism, which is colonizing Islam around the world through money and proselytizing. However, the Saudi Wahhabi program is long-term and nonviolent and therefore must be considered Islamist. In addition, one must take into account short-term constructive actions by Wahhabi leaders, like the al-Arabiyah TV network, which has become an anti–Militant Islamist network. King Abdullah's remarks to the opening session of the Shura Council in 2008 attacked terrorism, praised Saudi security forces in breaking cells, and exposed the realities of their ideology.[4] However, the spread of Wahhabism in a way that changes the character of Muslim nations such as Indonesia or Morocco, marginalizing Sufism or the Maliki school of Sunni Islam in North Africa, is not in the long-term interest of the United States or other nations.

Exploiting differences in definition. Perhaps no word more deserves to be challenged in the public sphere than "Jihad." Jihad is marketed as "fighting" by Militant Islamist clerics like Azzam. However, the *ijmaa* (consensus) on Jihad is that *as* warfare it should be undertaken by a ruler of the era, whatever his morals may be, that Jihad derives its credibility from the law and is validated by communal consensus, not by the ruler.[5] This validity of Jihad (as war) is central to the weakness of al-Qaida's ideological rationalization of total warfare. There are many fine points that can be brought out to challenge the pseudo-intellectualism of Militant Islamist Ideology.

Unintended consequences of criticism of al-Qaida. If al-Qaida faces marginalization and criticism for the killing of innocents, will this lead or drive it toward a more coordinated global strategy? Currently Zawahiri and other al-Qaida seniors recommend abstract zones of conflict, and regional as well as self-motivated Militant Islamist cells answer their call. This approach is disjointed and erratic and emphasizes the discretion of the regional Militant Islamist groups, which in turn lends itself to the killing of innocent Muslims. Today al-Qaida is not as coordinated as it was immediately post-9/11.

The center of gravity. Dr. Max Gross, the former dean of intelligence studies at the National Defense Intelligence College, has written, "I think the real strategic center of gravity of the Jihadists may lie among those of us who convince ourselves that they represent the true face of Islam. We must work with our millions of other Muslim allies in the Islamic world to demonstrate and to convince ourselves they do not."[6] The chief center of gravity is in fact Militant Islamist Ideology, which incites violence. But he is correct that we should take care not to convince ourselves that this is a bipolar struggle of the West versus Islam, or Islamists; this is a war against Militant Islamist groups. We cannot derive effective policy from the view that Islamic law and tradition justifies the Militant Islamist Ideology; this line of rationalization leads down the path of "civilization clash." That would be an outcome that our adversary (Militant Islamists) would welcome, as it is they who define Islam as an epic struggle.

The role of U.S. war colleges. American service colleges must seriously engage Islam, then Islamist politics, and finally Militant Islamist Ideology. Today, most Islamic subjects in our war colleges are taught as elective and not required courses. Such courses cannot, it is argued, be made to fit into the joint doctrine framework. It is vital to our national security that America's future military leaders be immersed in the nuances and differences inherent in Islam, among Islamists and Militant Islamists.

The need for innovative thinking. One valuable source of innovation in this area is the Minerva Research Initiative (MRI), a Defense Department program of social-science research grants available for work on topics of interest to American national security. The 2009 MRI competition was for research related to five listed topics, of which two dealt with Islamic, Islamist, and Militant Islamist issues: "Studies of the Strategic Impact of Religious and Cultural Changes within the Islamic World" and "Studies of Terrorist Organization and Ideologies."[7]

This program encourages the game-theory and effects-based studies that provide historical perspectives to potential conflicts and, more importantly, bring much-needed nuance to American national security policy formulation. Of course, the organizers of MRI must take care to get unbiased research, not findings tailored to please Defense Department funders. Maria Glod of the *Washington Post* has written usefully regarding self-fulfilling prophecies, ethical anthropology, and advocacy of a Pentagon worldview.[8] The benefits of bringing university minds to think about national security outweigh the concerns. Currently, there appears to be a disconnect between American college campuses and the military. Perhaps increased funding from the Defense Department on research issues of importance to national security will benefit both.

A new functional combatant command. In 1962 the United States included four thousand American military advisers in Vietnam on a counterinsurgency council.[9] Should the United States now consider a new functional command for counterinsurgency? A counterinsurgency command would concentrate on the ideological, military, advisory, and tribal affairs, and weapon sales, as well as gauge whether an advisory role should mutate into a troop commitment. The early stages of the Vietnam conflict would have been different had we understood that the Buddhists initially had no more liking for the communists than for the South Vietnamese president, Ngo Dihn Diem. Short of a functional command, counterinsurgency advisory elements might manage training and weapons integration in selected nations.

Militant Islamist Groups as an irregular force multiplier. In Yemen in the 1990s, Somalian, Sudanese, and Afghani, al-Qaida affiliates offered local warlords and leaders of lawless regions ways to counter their enemies. In Yemen in the 1994 war of secession, Militant Islamist groups purged the Yemen Socialist Party.[10] What this means is that reports of al-Qaida shifting its focus from Iraq to Afghanistan may be premature; the real indicator of success would be that al-Qaida in Iraq has been so marginalized that Iraqi security forces can handle the threat. Abu Ayyub al-Masri, the al-Qaida in Iraq leader, may have fled to Afghanistan or have even been deposed.[11] This is not the end of al-Masri, but trumpeting his retreat should be part of any systemic information campaign designed to articulate the phased withdrawal of U.S. forces in Iraq by 2011.

Once Militant Islamists have triumphed over a regional threat, they set up an Islamic government in their image. Such a government will eventually have no room for national, tribal, or religious differences, and it will misuse Islam to submerge these differences. There may be a short-term triumph over a tribal rival, but this will be short-lived; Egyptians, Saudis, and Algerians within the Militant Islamist movement will have more and more say in the affairs of the tribe protecting them. This inevitable schism needs to be explored and if possible amplified to induce tribes protecting these elements to purge them from their ranks, to avoid being marginalized by tribal rivals.

twenty-one

Conclusion and Further Reading

If you want a war, nourish a doctrine. Doctrines are the most frightful tyrants to which men are ever subject, because doctrines get inside a man's reason and betray him against himself. Civilized men have done their fiercest fighting for doctrines.

WILLIAM GRAHAM SUMNER, YALE ACADEMIC (D. 1910)

The best books stimulate thought and discussion and leave the reader wanting to explore the topic further. Michael Howard has written, "It was the inadequacy of the sociopolitical analysis of the societies with which we were dealing that lay at the root of the failure of the Western powers to cope more effectively with the revolutionary and insurgency movements that characterized the post-war era, from China in the 1940s to Vietnam in the 1960s."[1] I do not want the United States and its allies to suffer from such an inadequacy in addressing what is essentially a pseudo-intellectual movement (Militant Islamist Ideology) that has defamed, maimed, and killed Muslims and non-Muslims alike. It is my earnest hope that this book introduced the need to disaggregate Militant Islamists from Islamist political groups, and these two from Islam itself. From a military perspective we have passed through the phase of overreliance on technology and slowly are beginning to turn our awesome capabilities toward the societal implications of military intervention. The late influential professor of international relations Hans Morgenthau (d. 1980), a prominent advocate of the realist school, wrote in *Politics among Nations* four fundamental rules that prevail in foreign affairs: diplomacy must be divested of any crusading spirit; objectives of foreign policy must be defined in terms of national interest; diplomacy must look at the political scene from the point of view of other nations; and nations must be willing to compromise on all issues that are not vital to them.[2]

The chief of the World War II Office of Strategic Services, Gen. William J. "Wild Bill" Donovan, crafted an integrated, combined-arms approach to shadow-war techniques. Donovan equated persuasion, penetration, and intimidation with the sapping and mining of siege warfare.[3] His ideas have application in today's world, requiring persuasion and counterideological programs, penetration of terror networks (through the Internet and physically), and finally intimidation—that is, deterring terror groups by threatening retaliation and making examples of proxies, not just nation-states but tribes that harbor violent Militant Islamist groups.

If you wish to begin your own journey exploring the nuances between Islamic, Islamist, and Militant Islamist ideologies, let me suggest the following books, in this order. Start with a holistic view of Islam, a broad view covering what is not taught by Militant Islamists. Read Karen Armstrong's *Islam: A Short History* and her biography of Muhammad. After reading these works immerse yourself in the world and ideas of Islamist Militant politics and the narrow militant Qutbist theory by reading Lawrence Wright's *The Looming Tower* and Mary Haybeck's *Knowing the Enemy*. For a deep probing of Islamist politics as a solution to the decline of Muslim civilization, Bernard Lewis's *What Went Wrong* is highly recommended. There is much misinformation and mythologizing about Usama bin Laden, which is not helpful for the serious student of al-Qaida; such misinformation ranges from exaggerations of his net worth to assertions that he discovered Militant Islamist Ideology in the fleshpots of Beirut and London. For a realistic look at bin Laden and al-Qaida read Peter Bergin's *The Osama bin Laden I Know* and Michael Scheurer's *Through Our Enemies' Eyes*.[4]

If this book has only piqued your interest and instilled a healthy skepticism of speakers mixing Islam, Islamism, and Militant Islamism, then it has been successful. But beyond that, after reading generally about Islamic history and theology, you may wish to shift toward political Islam or the evolution of Islamist groups like the Egyptian Muslim Brotherhood. Finally turn your attention to Militant Islamist Ideology, figures, and groups. At that point, make it a habit to read the products of the Combating Terrorism Center at West Point. This organization has done much to provide American military personnel with excellent translations of Militant Islamist manuals and manifestos, as well as essays on this phenomenon.

Perhaps the best advertising for CTC West Point is that, as we have noted, Ayman al-Zawahiri, the al-Qaida deputy, has mentioned this organization more than once in his remarks, videos, and audios.

It is appropriate to end with a quotation from Angelo Codevilla and Paul Seabury's classic *War: Ends and Means:* "In the end labeling Islamic all that strikes at the enemy and infidel all that does not, reduces a complex, transcendental faith (Islam) to a simple propellant for war."[5] This is a cogent thought for America's future military and political leaders as they ponder how Militant Islamists have hijacked Islam.

NOTES

Introduction

1. Michael Dobbs, *One Minute to Midnight* (New York: Knopf, 2008).

Chapter 1. Precise Definitions of the Threat

1. Bill Gertz, "Report Says Terms 'Jihad,' 'Islamist,' Needed: Military Team See Reason to Soften Word," *Washington Times,* October 20, 2008, 1.
2. Bahrain TV, memritv.org, 2005.
3. Michael A. Palmer, *Last Crusade: Americanism and the Islamic Reformation* (Dulles, Va.: Potomac Books, 2008), 11.
4. Masso Anna Iivni, "Interview with Daniel Pipes," *Tundra Tabloids* (Helsinki), June 22, 2008, http://tundratabloidsextra.blogspot.com/2008/07/interview-with-daniel-pipes.html.
5. Gamal Abdel-Rahim, *Abu Musab al-Zarqawi, Shaykh al-Qaida fee Bilad al-Rafidayn* [Abu Musab al-Zarqawi, Sheikh of al-Qaida in the Land of the Two Rivers] (Cairo: Arabiyah, 2005), 27–32.
6. Available at http://www.whitehouse.gov/news/releases/2005/10/2005100 6-3.html.
7. U.S. Defense Department, *Measuring Stability in Iraq* (Washington, D.C.: February 2006), 23, refers to the threat as "extremist Islamist ideology."

Chapter 2. A Hidden Center of Gravity: Militant Islamists Cloaking Themselves in Islam

1. Muhammad Kamal Hattah, *Al Qiyam al Deeniyah wal Mujatama* [Islamic Values and Society] (Beirut: n.p.), 218.

2. A useful search engine of the Qur'an was designed by the University of Southern California Muslim Student Association; it is available at www.usc.edu/dept/msa/quran. There are Islamist articles in this website, and any website should be treated with a degree of skepticism. However, this one provides several translations of single verses. Another useful tool for deploying military personnel is the History Channel™ DVD *Decoding the Past: Secrets of the Qur'an* (A&E TV, 2006).

Chapter 3. What Is *Not* Being Taught in Politicized Madrassas: Beginning to Understand Militant Islamist Ideology

1. W. B. Fisher, *The Middle East: A Physical, Social and Regional Geography,* 7th ed. (London: W. B. Meuthen, 1978), 113–15.
2. Michael Hamilton Morgan, *Lost History: The Enduring Legacy of Muslim Scientists, Thinkers, and Artists* (Washington, D.C.: National Geographic, 2007), 9. Morgan's work was translated into Arabic in 2008 and is an example of constructive works that form a basis for effective interfaith dialog and cultural exchange.
3. Muhammad Haykal, *Life of Muhammad PBUH* (New York: Islamic Book Trust, 1976, 2003 reprint edition), 55.
4. Ibid., 99.
5. Available at http://muslimmatters.org/2007/09/18/shaykh-salman-al-oudahs-ramadan-letter-to-osama-bin-laden-on-nbc/ (accessed June 19, 2008).
6. David Bulkay, *From Muhammad to bin Laden: Religious and Ideological Sources of the Homicide Bombers Phenomenon* (New Brunswick, Me.: Transaction, 2008), 10–11.
7. Ali Andijani and Nehad Andijani, "Saudis Warn of Scams to Urge Citizens to Engage in Dawa to Build Mosques: Internal Security Expert Says the Arbitrary Collection of Donations Will Result in Penalties," *al-Sharq al-Awsat,* 15 March 2008, Business, 1.

Chapter 4. The Qur'an: How Do Militant Islamists Abuse Verses?

1. Michael Sell, *Approaching the Quran: The Early Revelations* (Ashland, Ore.: White Cloud, 2006).
2. Karen Armstrong, *Islam: A Short History* (New York: Modern Library, 2003), 15–16.
3. *National Geographic,* "Inside the Quran," National Geographic Channel, August 5, 2008.

4. "U.S. Soldier Uses Quran for Target Practice; Military Apologizes," http://www.cnn.com/2008/WORLD/meast/05/17/iraq.quran/index.html, May 18, 2008 (accessed January 13, 2009).

5. Abdul-Hamid Abu Sulayman, *Islamic Theory of International Relations: New Direction for Islamic Methodology and Thought* (Herndon, Va.: International Institute for Islamic Thought, translated in 1993), 36.

6. Abu Libaba Hussein, *Al-Islam wal Harb* [Islam and Warfare] (Riyadh: n.p.), 41.

Chapter 5. The Term *Jihad*: Various Interpretations

1. Saaleh al-Saadlaan, *Fiqh Made Easy,* trans. Jamal-al-Din Zarabozo (Boulder, Colo.: al-Bahseer, 1999), 117–18.

2. Ibid.

3. Christon Archer et al., *World History of Warfare* (Lincoln, Neb.: Bison Books, 2008), 161.

4. See David Levering Lewis, *God's Crucible: Islam and the Making of Modern Europe, 570–1215* (New York: Norton, 2008), reviewed by this author in *Marine Corps Gazette*, July 2008, 59.

5. Hugh Kennedy, *The Arab Conquests: How the Spread of Islam Changed the World We Live In* (Cambridge, Mass.: DaCapo, 2007). This excellent work brings to life Islamic chroniclers like the ninth-century Islamic scholar Ahmed ibn Yahya al-Baladhuri, whose *Kitab Futuh al-Buldan* (Book of Conquests) is among a handful of important works that explain, realistically if only in part, how Muslims achieved their empire in so short a period. Another vital work of classical Arabic was al-Tabari's multivolume *History of Prophets and Kings,* which offers glimpses of the tactics, military organization, logistics, and leadership that led to the Muslim victory over the Byzantine Empire at Yarmuk and the Persian Empire at Qadisiyah. The leadership of al-Qaida evokes images of the sixth through the fourteenth centuries; American leaders must immerse themselves in those images to counter its manipulations.

Chapter 6. Muhammad and the Succession Crisis

1. Barnaby Rogerson, *Heirs of Prophet Muhammad: Islam's First Century and the Origins of the Sunni-Shia Split* (New York: Overlook, 2007), 311. This is a book I have recommended in my lectures to deploying units. It is perhaps one of the finest historical narratives of early Islamic history after the death of Prophet Muhammad and the first four caliphs.

2. Ibid., 75.

3. Ibid., 164.

4. Ibid., 282–311.

5. Ibid., 94.

6. Ibid., 95–103.

7. One of the best books in English on the social, political, and personal realities of the first four caliphs is Barnaby Roberson, *The Heirs of Muhammad: Islam's First Century and the Origins of the Sunni-Shia Split* (New York: Overlook, 2007).

8. Ibid., 315.

9. Abdu Zaina, "Brotherhoods Programs Marginalizes the Slogan 'Islam Is the Solution,'" *al-Sharq al-Awsat,* March 9, 2008.

10. Robert Baer, *The Devil We Know: Dealing with the New Iranian Superpower* (New York: Crown, 2008), 170–71.

11. "Mufti Majlis of Lebanon Calls for the Election of a President and the Re-opening of Parliament," *al-Sharq al-Awsat,* March 3, 2008, 8.

Chapter 7. Islamic Government: A Highly Debatable Concept among Muslims

1. Fouad Ajami, *The Foreigner's Gift: The Americans, the Arabs and the Iraqis in Iraq* (New York: Free Press, 2006).

2. *President's Address to the Nation,* http://www.whitehouse.gov/news/releases/2007/01/20070110-7.html (accessed January 27, 2007).

Chapter 8. The 1925 Caliphate Debates

1. Ali Abdul-Razak, *Al-Islam wa Usul al-Hukm* (Cairo: n.p.), book 1, chap. 3, 34–38.

2. Taqi al-Din ibn Taymiyyah, *Manhaj al-Sunnah* (Cairo: reprint 1962), vol. 1, 70–72.

3. Feisal Abdul-Rauf, *Islam—A Sacred Law: What Every Muslim Should Know about the Shariah* (Watsonville, Calif.: Qiblah Books, 2000), 7–8.

4. Abdul Hakim Murad, *Understanding the Four Madhabs* (Wembley, U.K.: Wise Muslim, 1995), 15.

5. Milton Viorst, interviews with Hassan al-Turabi, and his *In the Shadow of the Prophet: The Struggle for the Soul of Islam* (New York: Basic Books, 2001).

6. Yusuf Qaradawi, *The Lawful and Prohibited in Islam* (Indianapolis, Ind.: American Trust Company, n.d.), available at http://irn.no/old/halal/lawfull.pdf, 8.

7. Patricia Crone, *God's Rule—Government and Islam: Six Centuries of Medieval Islamic Political Thought* (New York: Columbia University Press, 2004), 18.

8. Haykal, *Life of Muhammad,* 176.

9. Ibid., 189–90.

10. Ahmed ibn Rini al-Dhalan, *Iktifaa al-Qunua* (n.p.: n.d.), "al-Sira al-Nabawiyah."

Chapter 9. Countering Militant Islamist Rhetoric Using Islam

1. Abdul Wahid Ali, "The Ethics of Disagreement in Islam," *University of Southern California Muslim Student Association,* http://www.usc.edu/dept/MSA/humanrelations/alalwani_disagreement/. There are elements of this website that one could disagree with; however, it does have a useful search engine for Quranic verses with various translations for the same Arabic verses.

2. Rhonda Schwartz, *American al Qaeda Resurfaces in New Tape after Nearly 7 Months of Silence: Adam Gadahn Addresses U.S. Financial Crisis,* Web video, http://www.abcnews.go.com/Blotter/story?id=5954587&page=1 (accessed October 4, 2008).

3. Richard Antoun, *Muslim Preacher in the Modern World: A Jordanian Case Study in Comparative Perspective* (Princeton, N.J.: Princeton University Press, 1989).

4. Ibid., 90–91.

5. Robert Pape, *Dying to Win: The Strategic Logic of Suicide Terrorism* (New York: Random House, 2005).

6. Ali al-Wardi, *Social Aspects of Modern Iraqi History* (in Arabic), 2nd ed. (London: al-Warrak Books, 2007), vol. 1, 106–13.

Chapter 10. Marginalizing al-Qaida: Utilizing al-Qaida Rhetoric and Actions

1. Al-Wardi, *Social Aspects of Modern Iraqi History,* 106–13.

2. From Lawrence Wright website, http://www.lawrencewright.com/art-zawahiri.html, from his article in *New Yorker* (September 16, 2002).

3. We need not only to publicize such events once but stay on message and remind people time and again of the many counterarguments to Militant Islamist diatribe. See www.ammanmessage.com/.

4. King Abdullah II of Jordan, preface to *Lost History: The Enduring Legacy of Muslim Scientists, Thinkers, and Artists,* by Michael H. Morgan (Washington, D.C.: National Geographic, 2007). In March 2008 it was translated into

Arabic and published in the Arab world. This book needs to be highlighted more in public diplomacy discourse. The website www.islamdenouncesterro rism.com lists public condemnations of Militant Islamist violence and can be used to stay on message to remind the world of the unacceptability of Militant Islamist ideology. Finally, see www.dni.gov.

5. Jay Tolson, "Egypt's Grand Mufti Counters the Tide of Islamic Extremism," *US News and World Report*, March 6, 2008, www.usnews.com/articles/news/world/2008/03/06/.

6. Morgan, *Lost History,* 47–49.

7. *Terrorism Focus* 5, issue 12 (March 25, 2008).

8. *Al-Sharq al-Awsat,* March 15, 2008, 4.

9. *Al-Sharq al-Awsat,* March 16, 2008, 4.

10. Associated Press, March 9, 2008.

11. Mohamed Sifaoui, "I Consider Islamism to Be Fascism," *Middle East Quarterly* (Spring 2008): 13–17.

12. "Al-Qaeda's Star Falling in Iraq but Rising in the Mahgreb," *Economist,* July 18, 2008.

13. Colin S. Gray, *Maintaining Effective Deterrence* (Carlisle, Pa.: Army War College Strategic Studies Institute, 2003), 33–34.

Chapter 11. Ibn Taymiyyah: Unlocking the Origins of Current Militant Islamist Ideology (1263–1327)

1. Available at www.islamword.net/advice_jihad.html (accessed March 17, 2008).

Chapter 12. Ibn Abdul Wahhab (1703–1792): The Founder of Wahhabism

1. Al-Wardi, *Social Aspects of Iraqi Modern History*, vol. 4, 161–63.

2. Youssef Choueiri, *Islamic Fundamentalism* (London: Continuum, 2002).

3. Michael Oren, *Power, Faith, and Fantasy: America in the Middle East, 1776 to the Present* (New York: W. W. Norton, 2007), 27–28.

Chapter 13. Hassan al-Banna and the Egyptian Muslim Brotherhood: The First Islamist Political Party

1. Some of the best books on the Muslim Brotherhood and Hassan al-Banna in English are Brynjar Lia, *The Society of the Muslim Brothers in Egypt: The Rise of an Islamic Mass Movement* (Reading, U.K.: Garnet, 1998); Richard

P. Mitchell's dated *The Society of the Muslim Brothers* (London: Oxford University Press, 1969); and Lawrence Wright's excellent *The Looming Tower: Al-Qaeda and the Road to 9/11* (New York: Knopf, 2006).

Chapter 14. Sayyid Qutb: Twentieth-Century Theoretician of Militant Islamist Ideology (1906–1966)

1. Ibrahim Abu-Rabi, *Intellectual Origins of Islamic Resurgence in the Modern Arab World* (Albany: State University of New York), 209. This is an excellent volume for a deeper understanding and evolution of the ideological narrative developed by Sayyid Qutb and Hassan al-Banna.

2. See Alexis Carrel, *Man: The Unknown* (New York: Harper and Brothers, 1935), and Abu-Rabi, *Intellectual Origins,* 157.

3. Ibid., 160.

4. Sayyid Qutb, "Jihad in the Cause of Allah," in *Milestones,* trans. S. Badrul Hasan, 2nd ed. (Karachi: International Islamic, 1988), 107–42.

5. John W. Livingston, "Ibn Qayyim al-Jawziyyah: A Fourteenth Century Defense against Astrological Divination and Alchemical Transmutation," *Journal of the American Oriental Society* 91, no. 1 (1971): 99.

6. Muntasser al-Zayat, *Al-Gamaat al-Islamiyah Ruaa min al-Dakhil* [Islamist Groups Observations from the Inside] (Cairo: Dar al-Marousa, 2005), 48. Al-Zayat knew Zawahiri and served as a lawyer for Islamist groups, but he has developed into a critic of Zawahiri and al-Qaida. This is an example of Militant Islamist ideology being attacked by Islamist arguments.

7. *Muslim Brotherhood Supreme Guide: Bin Laden Is a Jihad Fighter,* MEMRI Special Dispatch 2001, 25 July 2008.

8. *Al-Hayat,* April 5, 1998, 6.

9. The 1916 Sykes-Picot Agreement between France, England, Italy, and Russia divided the Ottoman Empire and the Middle East into spheres of influence. It was leaked by the communist leader V. I. Lenin to embarrass the Western powers.

10. Jim Lacey, *A Terrorist Call to Global Jihad: Deciphering Abu-Musab al-Suri's Jihad Manifesto* (Annapolis, Md.: Naval Institute Press, 2008), 10–11.

Chapter 15. Inside the Soviet-Afghan War (1979–1989): A Militant Islamist Perspective

1. Bernard Rougier, *Everyday Jihad* (Cambridge, Mass.: Harvard University Press, 2008), 71–72.

2. Ibn Taymiyyah, *Al-Siyasa al-Shairyah* [The Perfect Polity] (Beirut: Islamic, n.d.), 149.

3. Yusuf al-Qaradawi, *The Lawful and the Prohibited in Islam* (Indianapolis, Ind.: American Trust, n.d.).

4. For more information on Qutb and Ibn Taymiyyah, see Mary Habeck, *Knowing the Enemy* (New York: Columbia University Press, 2006), and Wright, *Looming Tower.*

Chapter 16. Usama bin Laden: A Quick Exposé

1. Peter Olsson, *The Cult of Osama* (Westport, Conn.: Praeger Security International, 2008), 102–7.

2. *Al-Sharq al-Awsat,* January 18, 2008, 4.

3. This discussion is largely based upon Abdul-Rahim Ali, *Hilf al-Irhaab, Tanzeem al-Qaida min Abdullah Azzam ils Ayman al-Zawahiri 1994–2003* [Alliance of Terrorism: The al-Qaida Organization from Abdullah Azzam to Ayman al-Zawahiri 1994–2003] (Cairo: Markaz al-Mahroosa, 2004).

4. See Youssef Aboul-Enein, "Al-Jazeera Correspondent Reveals Details from bin Laden's Interview," *Infantry* (September–October 2007), 24.

5. Ibid., 21.

6. Available at www.irhaab.com/ansarnet/showthread.php?t=3970.

7. Available at www.islamonline.net/Arabic/news/2005-09/18/article.shtml.

8. Available at www.irhaab.com/ansarnet/showthread.php?t=431880.

9. Walid Phares, *Future Jihad* (New York: Palgrave, 2005), 59–61.

10. Available at www.whitehouse.gov/news/releases/2005/10/20051015.html.

11. Wright, *Looming Tower,* 49.

Chapter 17. A Basic Analytic Primer on Shiism

1. The Naval Institute Press has published a two-hundred-page English translation of *A Call to Global Islamic Resistance* that distills the most important aspects and ideas. The best book on the evolution of Shiism in Mesopotamia and Persia is al-Wardi, *Social Aspects of Iraqi Modern History.* Muqtada al-Sadr is discussed at length in the present book in chapter 17. The best biography of him is Patrick Cockburn's *Muqtada.*

2. Nicholas Pelham, *A New Muslim Order: The Shia and the Middle East Sectarian Crisis* (New York: I. B. Tauris, 2008), 15, 147.

3. Ibid., 15, 94–95.

4. See http://www.ammanmessage.com/.

Chapter 18. Other Major Figures in the Militant Islamist Movement

1. See Patrick Cockburn, *Muqtada: Muqtada al-Sadr, the Shia Revival, and the Struggle for Iraq* (New York: Scribner's, 2008).
2. Available at http://www.alarabiya.tv/articles/2008/10/13/58179.html.
3. Lawrence Freedman, *A Choice of Enemies: America Confronts the Middle East* (New York: PublicAffairs), 365.
4. *Karachi Ummat,* September 4, 2005, 2–8.
5. Rachel Ehrenfeld and Alyssa A. Lappen, "The Fifth Generation Warfare," FrontpageMagazine.com, June 20, 2008.

Chapter 19. Al-Qaida's Wedge Issues for the United States to Consider

1. "How to Win the War within Islam," *Economist,* July 19, 2008, 16–17.
2. Peter Bergen, "Al-Qaida at 20: Dead or Alive," *Washington Post,* August 17, 2008, B1.
3. Available at http://www.alarabiya.tv/archive.php?content_type=Programs& category_code=progs_death. This is an archive of Arabic transcripts of the weekly program *Manufacturers of Death,* featured on al-Arabiyah TV. As we attempt to explain the phenomenon of Militant Islamists, we ought to consider translating shows that appear on Arab TV about Militant Islamists and feature them on such channels as PBS.
4. *Al-Sharq al-Awsat,* February 1, 2008, 7.
5. Ibid., January 31, 2008, 15.
6. Ibid., January 24, 2008, 15.
7. Ibid., January 16, 2008, 1.
8. Ibid., January 16, 2008, 7.

Chapter 20. Mindsets That Hamper America's Capabilities

1. T. J. Waters, *Class 11: Inside the CIA's First Post-9/11 Spy Class* (New York: Tantor Media, 2006), audiobook disk 5 of 9.
2. Mike Allen and Glenn Kessler, "Bush Goal: Palestinian State by 2009," *Washington Post,* November 13, 2004, A01.
3. "Right Islam vs. Wrong Islam," *Wall Street Journal,* December 30, 2005.
4. "Shura Council Address Calls Upon Those Who Love the Nation to Reject the Jahili [Ignorant] Voices," *al-Sharq al-Awsat,* March 16, 2008, 5.
5. Musannaf Abdul-Razak (d. 862), *Al-Musannaf of Abdul Razak al-Sanani,* v, nos. 9610–9613. This work has been published in eleven volumes, containing 11,033 *hadiths* (sayings and actions of Prophet Muhammad).

6. *Global War on Terrorism: Analyzing the Strategic Threat*, Discussion Paper 13 (Washington, D.C.: Joint Military Intelligence College, November 2004), xi.

7. Available at http://blog.historians.org/news/537/department-of-defense-minerva-research-initiative-grants.

8. "Military Social Science Grant Raises Alarm," *Washington Post,* August 3, 2008, A5.

9. Michael MacLear, *Vietnam: The Ten Thousand Day War* (London: Thomas Methuen, 1981), 51.

10. See Youssef Aboul-Enein, "Islamist Militancy and Yemen's Internal Struggles: A Look at the Writings of Yemeni Colonel Abd al-Wali al-Shumairy," *Infantry* (January–February 2008), 49.

11. Amit R. Paley, "Al-Qaeda in Iraq Leader May Be in Afghanistan," *Washington Post,* July 31, 2008, A01.

Chapter 21. Conclusion and Further Reading

1. Michael Howard, *The Causes of War and Other Essays* (Cambridge, Mass.: Harvard University Press, 1983), 108.

2. See Hans Morgenthau, *Politics among Nations: The Struggle for Power and Peace* (New York: Knopf, 1948), 540–44.

3. Patrick K. O'Donnell, *The Brenner Assignment: The Untold Story of the Most Daring Spy Mission of World War II* (New York: DaCapo, 2008), 6–7.

4. You can immerse yourself in the schisms within al-Qaida by listening to programs on the Internet like British correspondent Frank Gardner's excellent 2008 discussion of the war of ideas; it can be downloaded at http://www.bbc.co.uk/worldservice/documentaries/2008/08/080826_alqaeda.shtml.

5. Angelo Codevilla et al., *War: Means and Ends,* 2nd ed. (Dulles, Va.: Potomac Books, 2006), 192.

GLOSSARY

A'alia Ghanem (Usama bin Laden's Mother) came from a Sunni Syrian family. She married Mohammed Awad bin Laden in Latakia in 1956. She was his tenth wife. She moved to Saudi Arabia with her husband and had her only child with Muhammad bin Laden, Usama bin Laden. She divorced Muhammad bin Laden soon after Usama was born and remarried Muhammad al-Attasi in 1958.

Abbasid is the dynastic name generally given to the caliph of Baghdad, the second of the two great Muslim caliphates of the Arab Empire, who overthrew the Umayyad caliphs from all but al-Andalus. The Abbasid caliphs officially based their claims to the caliphate on their descent from Abbas ibn Abd al-Muttalib, 566 to 662, one of the youngest uncles of Muhammad, by virtue of which descent they regarded themselves, as opposed to the Umayyads, as the rightful heirs of Muhammad, The Umayyads, descended from Umayya, were a clan separate from Muhammad's in the Quraysh tribe. The Abbasids also distinguished themselves from the Umayyads by attacking their moral character and administration in general. According to Ira Lapidus, "The Abbasid revolt was supported largely by Arabs, mainly the aggrieved settlers of Marw with the addition of the Yemeni faction and their Malawi." The Abbasids also appealed to non-Arab Muslims, known as *malawi,* who remained outside the kinship-based society of Arab culture and were perceived as a lower class within the Umayyad empire. Muhammad ibn Ali, a great-grandson of Abbas, began to campaign for the return to power of the family of Muhammad, the Hashimites, in Persia during the reign of Umar II, Muhammad ibn Ali.

Abdullah Yusuf *Azzam* (1941–1989) was a highly influential Palestinian Sunni Islamic scholar and theologian, a central figure in preaching for defensive

Jihad by Muslims to help the Afghan mujahideen against the Soviet invaders. He raised funds, recruited and organized the international Islamic volunteer effort of Afghan Arabs through the 1980s, and advocated the political ascension of Islamism. He is also famous as a teacher and mentor of Usama bin Laden, the man who persuaded bin Laden to come to Afghanistan and help the Jihad, although the two differed as to where the next front in global Jihad should be after the withdrawal of the Soviets. He was assassinated by a bomb blast in November 1989.

Abu Bakr, also called "the Upright," or "al-Siddiq" in Arabic, was born in 573 and died in 634. Muhammad's closest companion and adviser, he succeeded to the Prophet's political and administrative functions, thereby initiating the office of the caliphate.

Abu Jandal was a member of al-Qaida and former chief bodyguard to Usama bin Laden. He is a Saudi citizen of Yemeni descent. Abu Jandal was arrested by Yemeni authorities in connection with the USS *Cole* bombing in October 2000. He is currently free from custody and lives in Yemen.

Sakhr ibn Harb, more commonly known as *Abu Sufiyan*, was born in 560 as a son of Harb ibn Umayya. Abu Sufyan's grandfather was Umayya, after whom the Umayyad dynasty was named. Abu Sufyan was the chieftain of the Banu Abd-Shams clan of the Quraysh tribe, a fact that made him one of the most powerful and respected men in Mecca. Abu Sufyan viewed Muhammad as a threat to Mecca's social order, a man aiming for political power and a blasphemer of the Quraysh gods.

Ali ibn *Abi Talib* was born in Mecca, Arabia (now Saudi Arabia), in 600 and died in Kufah (what is now Iraq) in 661. He was a cousin and son-in-law of the Prophet Muhammad and the fourth of the "rightly guided," or *rashidun* in Arabic, caliphs, as the first four successors of Muhammad are called. Reigning from 656 to 661, he was the first leader, or imam, of Shiism in all its forms.

At the request of Caliph Omar ibn al-Khattab, *Abu Ubayda* al-Jarrah took command of the Muslim army that was besieging Bayt al-Maqdis. Abu Ubayda organized Muslim commanders under him and provided each with an army of thousands.

Al-Ansar wal-Sunnah, the "Protectors of the Faith," is a militant group in Iraq fighting the U.S.-led occupation and the elected government led by Nouri al-Maliki.

Ghadir Khumm, or the Pond of Khumm, was a pond or marsh formed by a spring east of the road between Medina and Mecca, approximately 180 kilometers from each and four to six kilometers from al-Johfa (modern-day Wadi Rabigh). It was situated on the Incense Route between Syria and Yemen, and there travelers could replenish their water in the most arid part of Arabia.

Hussein ibn *Ali* ibn Abi Ṭalib was born in 625 in Medina and died in 680 in Karbala. He was the grandson of Prophet Muhammad and the son of Ali, the first imam and the fourth caliph, and Muhammad's daughter Fatima Zahra. Hussein ibn Ali is revered as a martyr who fought tyranny, as the third imam by most Shia Muslims, and as the second imam by the majority of Ismaili Shia Muslims. He refused to pledge allegiance to Yazid I, the Umayyad caliph. As a consequence, he was assassinated by Yazid's army in the Battle of Karbala in 680. The anniversary of his martyrdom is called Ashura, and it is a day of mourning and religious observance for Shia Muslims. Revenge for Husayn's death was turned into a rallying cry that helped undermine the Umayyad caliphate and gave impetus to the rise of a powerful Shia movement.

Ali Abdul-Razik (1888–1966) was an Egyptian Islamic scholar, sharia (Islamic religious law) judge, and liberal activist. He can be regarded as the intellectual father of Islamic separation of the caliphate and religion. His main work, *Islam and the Foundations of Government,* maintained controversial views regarding the necessity of the caliphate and religious government and triggered an intellectual and political battle in Egypt.

Ali ibn Hussein (1879–1935) was king of Hejaz and grand sharif of Mecca from October 1924 until December 1925. He was the eldest son of Sharif Hussein bin Ali, the first modern king of Hejaz, and a scion of the Hashemite family.

Muhammad *Ali Pasha* al-Mas'ud ibn Agha (1769–1849), of Albanian parents, was *wali* (viceroy or governor) of Egypt and Sudan. He is regarded as the founder of modern Egypt. The dynasty he established would rule Egypt and Sudan until the Egyptian Revolution of 1952.

Amr ibn al-A'as, born about 583 and died in 664, was an Arab military commander, most noted for leading the Islamic invasion of Egypt in 640. A contemporary of Muhammad, he rose quickly through the Muslim hierarchy following his conversion to Islam in 629. He founded the Egyptian capital of Fustat and built the mosque of Amr ibn al-A'as at its center—the first mosque on the continent of Africa.

One who formally abandons or renounces one's religion, especially if the motive is deemed unworthy, is called an *apostate.*

Dr. *Ayman* Muhammad Rabaie *al-Zawahiri* (1951–2008) formally merged the

Egyptian Islamic Jihad into al-Qaida in 1998. According to reports by a former al-Qaida member, he worked in the organization from its inception and was a senior member of the group's *shura* (consultation) council. He was often described as a "lieutenant" to Usama bin Laden.

Abu *Ayyub al-Masri,* also known as Abu Hamza al-Mujahir, born in 1967 in Egypt, was announced as the de facto new leader of al-Qaida in Iraq on June 12, 2006, following the death of the former leader Abu Musab al-Zarqawi, who was killed in a U.S. airstrike. A former member of the Muslim Brotherhood, he joined the Egyptian Islamic Jihad in 1982. In 1999, he went to Afghanistan, where he became an explosives expert.

The Arab Socialist *Baath Party*, the original secular Arab nationalist movement, was founded in Damascus in the 1940s to combat Western colonial rule. In Arabic, *baath* means renaissance or resurrection. It functioned as a pan-Arab party, with branches in different Arab countries, but was strongest in Syria and Iraq, coming to power in both countries in 1963. Baathist beliefs combine Arab socialism, nationalism, and pan-Arabism. Its mostly secular ideology often contrasts with that of other Arab governments in the Middle East, which tend to have leanings toward Islamism and theocracy.

A *backwater* is an isolated, unpopular, or unimportant place.

The *Banu Qurayza* was a Jewish tribe whose members lived in northern Arabia during the seventh century at the oasis of Yathrib (now known as Medina). In 627 the tribe was charged with treachery during the Battle of the Ditch (also known as the Battle of the Trench) and besieged by Muslims commanded by Muhammad. The Muslims took the Qurayza captive, beheaded all the men, apart from a few who converted to Islam, and enslaved all the women.

The *Battle of Badr* in 624 was the first military victory of Prophet Muhammad. It seriously damaged Meccan prestige while strengthening the political position of Muslims in Medina and establishing Islam as a viable force in the Arabian Peninsula.

The *Battle of Nahrawan* was a battle between Ali ibn Abi Talib (the fourth Sunni caliph and the first Shia imam) and the Kharijites.

After the unsatisfactory conclusion at the *Battle of Siffin,* Imam Ali ibn Abi Talib returned with his army to Kufa. During the march, a group of 12,000 men kept themselves at a distance from the main part of the army. This group was composed of the Kharijites, who were furious at how the Battle of Siffin had ended.

The *Battle of the Ditch,* or *al-Khandaq* (also meaning trench), began on March 31, 627, and was an early Muslim victory that ultimately forced the Meccans to recognize the political and religious strength of the Muslim community in Medina.

In the *Battle of Uhud,* in 625 (as generally accepted), an army of three thousand men under the leader of Mecca, Abu Sufyan, opposed the Muslims under Muhammad. Muhammad led his forces down from the arid Hejaz mountain range, which encloses Medina. (The highest of these hills is called Mount Uhud, which rises to more than two thousand feet above the oasis.) Battle ensued and the Muslims were forced to withdraw, but not before fighting the Meccans to a draw.

Bay'aa (literally "to sell" in Islamic terminology) is an oath of allegiance, sometimes under a written pact, given on behalf of followers by leading members of a tribe with the understanding that as long as the leader abides by certain requirements toward his people, they are to maintain their allegiance to him. *Bay'aa* is still practiced in such countries as Saudi Arabia and Sudan.

The *Bin Laden Construction Company,* formally known as the Saudi Binladen Group, is a global construction and equity management conglomerate grossing $5 billion U.S. dollars annually. It is one of the largest construction firms in the Islamic world, with offices in London and Geneva.

The *Black Stone,* or *al-Hajar al-Aswad* in Arabic, is a Muslim object of veneration built into the eastern wall of the Kaaba. It probably dates from the pre-Islamic religion of the Arabs. It now consists of three large pieces and some fragments, surrounded by a stone ring and held together with a silver band. In 930 it was carried away by the fanatics of the Qarmatian sect and held for ransom for about twenty years.

Ilich Ramírez Sánchez, born in 1949 in Venezuela, is a self-proclaimed leftist revolutionary who is nicknamed *"Carlos the Jackal."* After several bungled bombings, Ramírez Sánchez achieved notoriety for a 1975 raid on the Organization of the Petroleum Exporting Countries (OPEC) headquarters in Vienna, resulting in the deaths of three people. For many years he was among the most wanted international fugitives. He is now serving a life sentence in Clairvaux Prison in northeast France. He was given the nom de guerre "Carlos" when he became a member of the leftist Popular Front for Liberation of Palestine (PFLP). Carlos was given the "Jackal" moniker by the press *(The Guard-*

ian) when the Frederick Forsyth novel *The Day of the Jackal* was reportedly found among his belongings. Although the book actually belonged to someone else, the nickname stuck.

The *Deobandi* is a Sunni Sufi Islamic revivalist movement that started in India and has more recently spread to other countries, such as Afghanistan, South Africa, and the United Kingdom. The name derives from Deoband, India, where the school Daral-Uloom Deoband is situated. Deobandis follow the school of law *(fiqh)* of Abu Hanifa and Abu Mansur Maturidi, who thought in terms of Aqidah (systems of Islamic belief) and Kalam (Islamic philosophic discourse). The Taliban have abandoned Islamic philosophic discourse that originally came with the introduction of Deobandi Salafism, in favor of a more reductionist interpretation in the twentieth century.

In the 1948 Arab-Israeli War, the Israelis repeatedly attacked an Arab position as the *"Fallujah pocket."* While these succeeded in nibbling away at the Egyptian position, the infantry defenders, led by Lieutenant Colonel Gamal Abdel Nasser, clung to their fortifications, fighting incredibly hard.

Fatah is a reverse acronym of the Arabic *Harakat al-Tahrir al-Watani al-Filastini,* meaning "Palestinian National Liberation Movement." Fatah is a major Palestinian political party and the largest faction of the Palestine Liberation Organization (PLO), a multiparty confederation. In Palestinian politics, it is on the center-left of the spectrum. It is mainly nationalist, although not predominantly socialist. Fatah has maintained a number of militant groups since its founding. Its mainstream military branch is al-Assifa. Unlike its rival Islamist faction Hamas, Fatah is not considered a terrorist organization by any government. In the January 25, 2006, parliamentary election, the party lost its majority in the Palestinian parliament to Hamas and resigned all cabinet positions, assuming the role of the main opposition party.

Fedayeen, meaning "freedom fighters" or "self-sacrificers" in Arabic, describes several distinct, primarily Arab, militant groups and individuals at different times in history. In Egypt, the clandestine revolutionary *Free Officers Movement* was composed of young junior army officers committed to unseating the Egyptian monarchy and its British advisers. It was founded by Colonel Gamal Abdel Nasser in response to Egypt's sense of national disgrace in the aftermath of the war of 1948.

Fouad I, born Ahmed Fouad in 1868 (d. 1936), was the sultan and later king of Egypt and Sudan, and sovereign of Nubia, Kordofan, and Darfur. The ninth ruler of Egypt and Sudan from the Muhammad Ali dynasty, he became sultan of Egypt and Sudan in 1917, succeeding his elder brother Sultan Hussein Kamil. He substituted the title of king for sultan when the United Kingdom formally recognized Egyptian independence in 1922. He struggled with the Wafd party throughout his reign.

The title of *Grand Mufti* is conferred upon the highest official of religious law in a Sunni Muslim country. The Grand Mufti issues legal opinions and edicts, fatwa, on interpretations of Islamic law for private clients or to assist judges in deciding cases.

The organization named in French as the "Groupe Salafiste pour la Prédication et le Combat" *(GSPC)* was founded by Hassan Hattab, a former Armed Islamic Group (GIA) regional commander who broke with the GIA in 1998 in protest over the GIA's slaughter of civilians. This organization is now known as the al-Qaida Organization in the Islamic Maghreb (AQIM). It is a neo-Khawarij Takfiri Islamist militia that aims to overthrow the Algerian government and institute an Islamic state. To that end, it is currently engaged in an insurgent campaign.

Hamas is an acronym for Harakat al-Muqawama al-Islamiyya, the Islamic Resistance Movement. It is a Palestinian Sunni Islamist militant organization and political party, created in 1987 by Sheikh Ahmed Yassin of the Gaza wing of the Muslim Brotherhood, which currently holds a majority of seats in the elected legislative council of the Palestinian Authority. It is best known for numerous suicide bombings and other attacks directed against Israeli civilians and security forces.

The *Hanafi* school is the oldest of the four schools of thought or religious jurisprudence within Sunni Islam; the other three are the Shafi, Maliki, and Hanbali. The Hanafi school of thought is named after its founder, Abu Hanifa an-Nu'man ibn Thabit, but its doctrine derives primarily from his two most important disciples, Abu Yusuf and Muhammad al-Shaybani.

The *Hanbali* school is one of the four schools of thought *(madhabs)* or religious jurisprudence *(fiqh)* within Sunni Islam; the other three are Shafi, Maliki, and Hanafi. It is also claimed to be a school of *aqeedah* (creed) in Sunni

Islam according to the Wahhabi and Salafi sects, but Sunni scholars reject this position. The Salafis have also referred to this as the Athari (Textualist) school. This religious jurisprudence school was started by the students and disciples of Imam Ahmad bin Hanbal (d. 855) founder of the Hanbali School of Islam.

Hanif is an Arabic term that refers to pre-Islamic non-Jewish or non-Christian Arabian monotheists. More specifically, in Islamic thought it refers to the Arabs during the pre-Islamic period known as the *Jahiliya,* who were seen as having rejected polytheism and retained some or all of the true tenets of the monotheist religion of Ibrahim (Abraham) that, according to Islamic view, preceded Judaism and Christianity. Hanif also means "hermits," and it refers to pre-Islamic Christians in Arabia who continued to debate the nature of Christ when it was prohibited in Byzantium, and to proselytize.

Hasafiya is a sharia-minded Sufi order that strictly observes scripture in rituals and ceremonies. The Hasafiya forbid men to wear gold, encourage women to dress modestly, and restrict conduct at tomb visits to acts and words sanctioned by scripture. Hassan al-Banna joined this order when he was thirteen years old. He also served as secretary for the order's charitable society, which strove to reform public morality and combat the influence that Christian missionaries attained by assisting orphans.

Hassan al-Banna was born in Mahmudiyya, Egypt, in 1906. When Hassan al-Banna was thirteen years old, he became involved in the Hasafiya Sufi order, becoming a fully initiated member in 1922. At thirteen he participated in demonstrations during the revolution of 1919 against British rule. In 1923, at the age of sixteen, al-Banna moved to Cairo to enter the Dar al-Ulum college. In his last year at Dar al-Ulum, he wrote that he had decided to dedicate himself to becoming "a counselor and a teacher" of adults and children, in order to teach them "the objectives of religion and the sources of their well-being and happiness in life." He graduated in 1927 and was given a position as an Arabic language teacher in a state primary school in Isma'iliyya, a provincial town located in the Suez Canal Zone. To spread his message al-Banna launched the Society of the Muslim Brothers in March 1928.

Dr. Hassan 'Abd Allah al-Turabi, commonly called *Hassan al-Turabi,* born in 1932, is a religious and Islamist political leader in Sudan who may have been instrumental in institutionalizing sharia (Islamic religious law) in the northern part of the country. Turabi was imprisoned in the Kobar (Cooper) prison in Khartoum on the orders of his one-time ally, President Omar al-Bashir, in 2004. He was released in 2005.

The *Hazara* are a Persian-speaking Asiatic people residing in the central region of Afghanistan and northwestern Pakistan. The Hazara are predominantly Shia Muslims and are the third-largest ethnic group in Afghanistan. Hazaras can also be found in large numbers in neighboring Iran and Pakistan, primarily as refugees, and in diaspora around the world. Their native homeland is referred to as Hazarajat.

Hezbollah, meaning "Party of God," is a Shia Islamic political and paramilitary organization based in Lebanon. Hezbollah first emerged as a militia in response to the Israeli invasion of Lebanon in 1982, set on resisting the Israeli occupation. Its leaders were inspired by Ayatollah Khomeini, and its forces were trained and organized by a contingent of Iranian Revolutionary Guards. Since 1992, the organization has been headed by Hassan Nasrallah, its secretary-general.

Taqi ad-Din Ahmad *ibn Taymiyyah* (1263–1328) was a Sunni Islamic scholar born in Harran, in what is now Turkey, close to the Syrian border. As a member of the madrassa founded by Ibn Hanbal, he sought to return Islam to its sources, the Qur'an and the *sunnah.*

Ibrahim Pasha (1789–1848), born in Macedonia, was a nineteenth-century general of Egypt. He is better known as the (adopted) son of Muhammad Ali of Egypt (Muhammad Ali Pasha al-Mas'ud ibn Agha), who served as regent during his father's illness from March 1848 to November 1848.

Ilm (Knowledge), a single Qur'anic sound bite that stimulated the preservation of Greek and Roman classics by Muslim scholars of ninth-century Baghdad and twelfth-century Spain. The word appears more than *Jihad* in the Qur'an.

Imad Fayez *Mughniyah* (1962–2008), alias Hajj Radwan, was a senior member of the Hezbollah organization. Mughniyah was associated with the Beirut barracks and U.S. embassy bombings in 1983 and the kidnapping of dozens of foreigners in Lebanon in the 1980s. He was indicted in Argentina for his role in the 1992 Israeli embassy attack in Buenos Aires. Imad Mughniyah was killed on February 12, 2008, by a car-bomb blast in Damascus, Syria.

Jahiliya refers to the period preceding the revelation of the Qur'an to the Prophet Muhammad. In Arabic, the word means "ignorance," or "barbarism," and it indicates a negative Muslim evaluation of pre-Islamic life and culture in Arabia, as compared to the teachings and practices of Islam. More recently, its meaning has been expanded to mean Western non-Muslims.

Jamal al-Din al-Afghani was a Muslim political activist in Iran, Afghanistan, Egypt, and the Ottoman Empire during the nineteenth century. One of the founders of Islamic modernism and an advocate of pan-Islamic unity, he was "less interested in theology than he was in organizing a Muslim response to Western pressure."

The three *Jewish tribes* present in Medina at this time of Muhammad's Prophethood were the Banu Qaynuqa, Banu Nadir, and Banu Qurayza.

Jihad can have the narrow meaning of offensive warfare or the wider meaning of personal struggle to fulfill prayers and live a moral life in addition to warfare both defensive and offensive.

The *Kaaba*, also transliterated as Ka'bah, is the holiest site in Islam. It is a large cuboid building in the center of the al-Masjid al-Haram Mosque, or Great Mosque, in Mecca. Muslims orient themselves toward this shrine during their five daily prayers, bury their dead facing its meridian, and cherish the ambition of visiting it on pilgrimage, or *hajj,* in accordance with the Qur'an.

Mustafa *Kemal Atatürk* (1881–1938) was an army officer, revolutionary statesman, and founder of the Republic of Turkey as well as its first president. Mustafa Kemal established himself as an intelligent and extremely capable military commander. His successful military campaigns in the Turkish War of Independence led to the liberation of the country.

Khadijah was the first wife of the Prophet Muhammad, whom she met when she was the widow of a wealthy merchant and had become prosperous in the management of her own commercial dealings. She died in Mecca, Arabia (now Saudi Arabia), in 619.

Major General *Khalid Nezzar,* born in 1937, is an Algerian general and former member of the High Council of State. He became minister of defense in 1990. Unusually for an Algerian general, in 1999 he published memoirs, in which he recounts his hostility during this period to the interim prime minister, Mouloud Hamrouche, and president Chadli Banjedid, whom he accuses of effectively "conniving" with the Islamic Salvation Front for the sake of increasing their power.

Khalid Sheikh Muhammad, born in 1964 or 1965 and known by at least fifty aliases, has been a prisoner in U.S. custody since 2003 for alleged acts of terrorism, including mass murder of civilians. He was charged on February 11, 2008, with war crimes and murder by a controversial extra-judicial U.S. military commission and faces the death penalty if convicted.

Kharijites, literally "Those Who Went Out," is a general term embracing various Muslims who, initially supporting Caliph Ali ibn Abi Talib, later rejected him. They first emerged in the late seventh century, concentrated in today's southern Iraq, and are distinct from the Sunnis and Shiites. The Kharijites insist that any pious and able Muslim can be a leader (imam) of the Muslim community.

Kufa, also transliterated as al-Kufah, was the final capital of Imam Ali ibn Abu Talib and is now one of four Iraqi cities of great importance to Shia Muslims. Kufa exists today about 170 kilometers south of Baghdad and ten kilometers northeast of Najaf, on the banks of the Euphrates River.

The term *Levant* is derived from the French word *"lever,"* which means "to rise," as in sunrise, thus metaphorically indicating the East. Historically, it has referred to the countries along the eastern Mediterranean coast. The name "Levant States" was given to the French mandate of Syria and Lebanon after World War I, and the term is sometimes still used for those two countries, which became independent in 1946.

A *madrassa,* also transliterated as madrasah, is a Muslim institution of higher education. Until the twentieth century, the madrassa functioned as a theological seminary and law school, with a curriculum centered on the Qur'an. In addition to Islamic theology and law, Arabic grammar and literature, mathematics, logic, and, in some cases, natural science were studied in madrassas.

The *Maliki* school is the third-largest of the four schools of thought *(madhabs)* or religious jurisprudence *(fiqh)* within Sunni Islam; the other three are Shafi, Hanafi, and Hanbali. The Maliki school derives from the work of Imam Malik. It differs from the three other schools of law most notably in the sources of its rulings. All four schools use the Qur'an as primary source, followed by the *sunnah* of Muhammad, transmitted as *hadith* (sayings), *ijma* (consensus of the scholars), and *qiyas* (analogy). The Maliki school, in addition, uses the practice of the people of Medina as a source.

A *mameluk,* meaning "owned" in Arabic, was a slave soldier who converted to Islam and served the Muslim caliphs and the Ayyubid sultans during the

Middle Ages. Over time, they became a powerful military caste, repeatedly defeating the Crusaders and, on more than one occasion, seizing power for themselves—for example ruling Egypt in the Mameluk Sultanate from 1250 to 1517.

The *Medinese Compact,* or Dastur al-Medina in Arabic, is a document from early Islamic history based upon two agreements concluded between the clans of Medina and the Prophet Muhammad soon after the emigration to Medina in 622. The agreements established the early Muslims who followed Muhammad, known as the *Muhajirun,* on a par with the eight clans of Medina, called the *Ansar,* or helpers. Collectively, the nine clans, or tribes, to include the Muslims, formed the first Muslim community, or *ummah.* The agreements also regulated the relations of the Muslims with the Jews of Medina.

Misr al-Fatah, formally known as the Jam'iyat Misr al-Fatah in Arabic, meaning the Society of Young Egyptians, was founded in 1911 by one of the first Palestinian nationalists, Izzat Muhammad Darwaza (1888–1939). It was a secret Arab nationalist organization under the Ottoman Empire. Its aims were to gain independence and achieve unity for the Arab nations then under the Ottoman rule.

The name *Mongol* specifies one of several ethnic groups now mainly located in Mongolia, China, and Russia.

The *Mossad,* formally known as HaMossad leModi'in v'leTafkidim Meyuhadim, which means "Institute for Intelligence and Special Operations" in Hebrew, is the national intelligence agency of the State of Israel.

Mu'awiyah ibn Abu Sufyan (602 to 680) was a companion of Prophet Muhammad and later the Umayyad caliph in Damascus. He engaged in a civil war against Ali (Muhammad's son-in-law) and met with considerable military success, including the seizure of Egypt. He assumed the caliphate after Ali's assassination in 661 and reigned until 680.

Muhammad Abduh (born in 1849 in the Nile Delta, died 1905 in Alexandria, Egypt) was an Egyptian jurist, religious scholar, and liberal reformer. He is regarded as the founder of Islamic Modernism. Abduh studied logic, philosophy, and mysticism at the al-Azhar University in Cairo. He was a student of Jamal al-Din al-Afghani.

Muhammad Awad *bin Laden,* a poor, uneducated Yemenite, father of Usama bin Laden, emigrated to Saudi Arabia after World War I. He set up a construction company and came to Abdul–Aziz ibn Saud's attention through construction projects, later being awarded contracts for major renovations at Mecca. There he made his initial fortune from exclusive rights to all mosques and other religious building construction, not only in Saudi Arabia but as far as Ibn Saud's influence reached. Until his death Muhammad bin Laden had exclusive rights to restorations at the al-Aqsa mosque in Jerusalem until the Israelis captured Jerusalem during the 1967 Six-Day War. Soon the bin Laden corporate network extended far beyond construction sites. When Muhammad bin Laden died in 1967, his older son Salem bin Laden took over the family enterprises when he came of age, operating them until his own accidental death in 1988. Salem was one of at least fifty-four children Muhammad bin Laden had by various wives.

Muhammad Faraj al-Ghul is a member of the Palestinian Legislative council representing Gaza City and affiliated with Hamas.

Mullah Muhammad *Omar* (born 1959) is the reclusive leader of the Taliban of Afghanistan and was Afghanistan's de facto head of state from 1996 to 2001. Since 2001 he has been hiding and is wanted by U.S. authorities for harboring Usama bin Laden and his al-Qaida organization. He is believed to be hiding in Pakistan.

The *Muslim Brotherhood,* formally the Society of the Muslim Brothers, is a transnational Sunni movement and the largest political opposition organization in many Arab nations, particularly Egypt. The world's oldest and largest Islamist group was founded by the Sufi schoolteacher Hassan al-Banna in 1928. The Muslim Brotherhood has been described as both unjustly oppressed and dangerously violent.

Naqshbandi is one of the major Tasawwuf orders of Islam. It is the only Sufi order that claims to trace its spiritual lineage to Muhammad through Abu Bakr, the first caliph.

Naskh, a concept whereby newer verses revealed to Prophet Muhammad in the Qur'an supersede older verses. Militant Islamists perversely apply this concept to cancel out swaths of the Qur'an and marginalize verses not fitting with their worldview.

Gamal Abdel *Nasser* (1918–1970) was the second president of Egypt, from 1952 until his death in 1970. He jointly led, with General Muhammad Neguib (a figurehead) and a collection of disgruntled officers, including Anwar el Sadat, the Egyptian Revolution of 1952, which deposed King Farouk I. Nasser's charismatic style significantly advanced Arab nationalism, inspired pan-Arab revolutions in Algeria, Libya, Iraq, and Yemen, and played a major role in the founding of the Palestine Liberation Organization in 1964.

The *Negev* is a rocky desert region covering more than half of southern Israel. It forms an inverted triangle whose western side is contiguous with the desert of the Sinai Peninsula. The word "Negev" is derived from a Hebrew root meaning "dry."

The *Nicene Creed* (425), also known as the Nicean Creed or the Niceno-Constantinopolitan Creed, is a Christian statement of faith that is the only ecumenical creed, in that it is accepted as authoritative by the Roman Catholic, Eastern Orthodox, Anglican, and major Protestant churches.

Nigus, sometimes transliterated as Negus, means "king" or "emperor" in Amharic, the national language of Ethiopia. The Arabic, *Najashi,* refers to a Christian emperor of Abyssinia who offered religious asylum to Muslims escaping the Meccan genocide during the early phase of Muhammad's prophecy.

Omar ibn al-Khattab was born in Mecca, Arabia (now Saudi Arabia), in 586. From 634 until he died in Medina, Arabia, in 644, he was the second Muslim caliph, whose Arab armies conquered Mesopotamia and Syria and began the conquest of Iran and Egypt.

The *Palestine Liberation Organization* (*PLO*) is a political and paramilitary organization regarded by the Arab League since 1974 as the "sole legitimate representative of the Palestinian people." Founded by the Arab League in 1964, its original goal was the destruction of the State of Israel through armed struggle. It was initially controlled for the most part by the Egyptian government. In 1993, PLO chairman Yasser Arafat recognized the State of Israel in an official letter to its prime minister, Yitzhak Rabin. In response to Arafat's letter, Israel recognized the PLO as the legitimate representative of the Palestinian people. Arafat was the chairman of the PLO Executive Committee from 1969 until his death in 2004. He was succeeded by Mahmoud Abbas (also known as Abu Mazen).

Ramzi Ahmed *Yussef* or Ramzi Muhammad Yussef (birth name possibly Abdul Basit Mahmoud Abdul Karim, but he has been known by dozens of aliases) was born in Kuwait and is of Pakistani descent. He was one of the planners of the 1993 World Trade Center bombing. He was arrested at an al-Qaida safe house in Pakistan and extradited to the United States. In New York he was sentenced to life in prison without parole. Yussef's uncle is Khalid Sheikh Muhammad, a senior al-Qaida member also in U.S. custody.

Muhammad *Rashid Rida* (1865–1935) is said to have been "one of the most influential scholars and jurists of his generation" and the "most prominent disciple of Muhammad Abduh."

Sa'ad ibn Mu'ath, also transliterated as Sa'ad ibn Mu'adh, was the chief of the Banu Aus tribe in Medina, known then as Yathrib. Sa'ad adopted Islam in 622, when Muhammad arrived in Medina. He was among the leading figures among the *Ansar,* as Muhammad had dubbed the Medinese converts to Islam.

Muhammad Anwar el *Sadat* (1918–1981) was the third president of Egypt, serving from 1970 until his assassination in 1981. He was a senior member of the Free Officers group that overthrew the Muhammad Ali Dynasty in the Egyptian Revolution of 1952 and a close confidant of Gamal Abdel Nasser, whom he succeeded as president in 1970.

Sayyid Qutb (1906–1966) was an Egyptian author, Islamist, and the leading intellectual of the Egyptian Muslim Brotherhood in the 1950s and 1960s. Qutb was known for his intense dislike of the United States and is sometimes described as the man whose ideas would shape al-Qaida. Today, his supporters are often identified as Qutbists.

Selim III (1761–1808) was the sultan of the Ottoman Empire from 1789 to 1807. He was the son of Mustapha III (1757–1774) and succeeded his uncle Abdülhamid (1774–1789).

Shia Islam is the second-largest denomination of Islam. Shia Muslims believe that, like prophets, imams after Muhammad have also been chosen by God. According to Shias, Ali was chosen by Allah and thus appointed by Muhammad to be the direct successor and leader of the Muslim community. They regard him as the first Shia imam, which continued as a hereditary position through Fatimah and Ali's descendants.

Sufism is the inner, or mystical, dimension of Islam. A practitioner of this tradition is generally known as a Sufi, though some senior members of the tradition reserve this term for practitioners who have attained the goals of the Sufi tradition. Another common interpretation is the word "dervish." The traditional Sufi orders emphasize the role of Sufism within Islam. Therefore, the sharia (traditional Islamic law) and the *sunnah* (customs of the Prophet) are seen as crucial for any Sufi aspirant. Among the oldest and best known of the Sufi orders are the Naqshbandi, Qadiri, Chisti, Shadhili, Jerrahi, and Nimatullahi.

Sunni Muslims are members of the largest denomination of Islam. The word "Sunni" comes from the word *sunnah,* which means the teachings and actions or examples of Prophet Muhammad. Therefore, the Sunni are those who follow or maintain the *sunnah* of Muhammad. The Sunni believe that Muhammad died without appointing a successor to lead the Muslim community. The four schools of thought *(madhabs)* or religious jurisprudence *(fiqh)* within Sunni Islam are Hanafi, Shafi, Maliki, and Hanbali.

Leon *Trotsky* (1879–1940), born Lev Davidovich Bronstein, was a Russian revolutionary and Marxist theorist. He was one of the leaders of the Russian October Revolution but was later expelled from the country and assassinated in Mexico by a Soviet agent.

In post–World War I Egypt, the term *wafd* referred to a "delegation," more specifically one that had the direct goal of achieving the complete and total independence of Egypt. This delegation hoped to gain representation at the 1919 Paris Peace Conference, a request that was harshly denied by the British high commissioner. The *wafd* therefore brought their demands to the Egyptian populace. This led to the formation of the nationalist *Wafd Party*. The party rapidly became the dominant political organization in the country and was the governing party through most of the liberal period, which came to an end with the rise of Gamal Abdel Nasser. The party was dissolved in 1952, after the military coup of that year.

Wahhabism is the conservative eighteenth-century reformist movement of Sunni Islam, the origin of which is attributed to Muhammad ibn Abdul-Wahhab, an Islamic scholar from what is today Saudi Arabia, who became known for advocating a return to the practices of the first three generations of Islamic history. The term "Wahhabi" was first used by opponents of Ibn Abdul-Wahhab and is considered derogatory and rarely used by the people it is used to describe, who prefer to be called "Unitarians" *(Muwahiddun)*. The terms "Wahhabism" and "Salafism" are often used interchangeably, but Wahhabism has also been called "a particular orientation within Salafism," an orientation some consider ultraconservative.

Waraqa ibn Naufal was Khadija's (Prophet Muhammad's wife) cousin and a Monophysite Christian monk, who reassured Muhammad that the divine revelations from Angel Gabriel were not demonic possessions but that he was to prepare himself to become a Prophet and Messenger of God sent to the Arabs. He died a Christian, never having converted to Islam.

Western Sahara, a territory on the northwest coast of Africa bordered by Morocco, Mauritania, and Algeria, was administered by Spain until 1976. Both Morocco and Mauritania affirm their claim to the territory, a claim opposed by the Frente Popular para la Liberación de Saguia el-Hamra y de Río de Oro (Frente POLISARIO).

Yathrib is the original name for an ancient city in the Arabian Peninsula, later renamed Medinat al-Nabi, or "City of the Prophet," and then shortened to Medina, or just "the City."

Yazid ibn Mu'awiyah ibn Abu Sufyan, born in 645, was the second caliph of the Umayyad dynasty and ruled from 680 until his death in 683. His mother, Maysun, was Christian. He is notable as an object of animosity among Sunni Muslims and Shia Muslims, who reject his legitimacy and condemn his actions in the Battle of Karbala that resulted in the death of Hussein ibn Ali ibn Abi Talib.

Abu Musab al-*Zarqawi* (1966–2006), born Ahmad Fadeel al-Nazal al-Khalayleh, was a Jordanian militant Islamist who ran a training camp in Afghanistan. He was believed to have formed the group known later as al-Qaida in Iraq in the 1990s and led it until his death in a U.S. air strike in 2006.

Zayd ibn Thabit was thirteen years old when he asked permission to participate in the Battle of Badr. Since he was less than fifteen years old, however, Prophet Muhammad did not allow him to do so and sent him back home. He then decided to try to win favor with Muhammad by learning the Qur'an. Muhammad also asked him to learn the Hebrew and Syriac languages. Later he was appointed to write letters to non-Muslims and to collect and keep records of the Qur'anic verses.

INDEX

Iraq: American public support for efforts in, 175; Awakening Council leadership, 202; focus of al-Qaida, shift from, 211; governance of Islamic societies, 55–56; importance of to al-Qaida, 174; Islamic State of Iraq (ISI), 94–95, 101, 131–32, 198, 199; Karbala, 44, 45, 113, 178, 186; Najaf, 44, 184, 185, 186, 193; Qaida in Iraq, al- (AQI), 94–95, 101, 102–3, 131–32, 176, 190–91, 206, 211; Qom, 181, 184, 185, 186; Shiites, beheading of, 167–68, 174–75, 176; violence and voting in, 128

Iraqi Freedom, Operation, 181

Islam: books about, 213; Christians, importance of to, 10, 14–15, 108; colonizers of, 209; damage to by Militant Islamists, 9, 17–18, 64–65, 110, 111; definition of, 2; distinguishing between Militant Islamists and, xv–xvii, 1, 2–6, 98, 100–101, 207–8, 212; early Islamic period, 19; enemy label, 155; equality advocated by, 30–31; excess in religion, 75–77, 81; expansion of empire of, 37, 41–42, 217n5; experts in, 204; extremes of national security policy discourse, xvi–xvii, 6, 203–4; fragmentation and distortion of by Militant Islamists, xvi–xvii, 3, 6, 7–9, 32, 35, 83–84, 110–11, 132; freedom of thought and worship, 74–75, 100, 148; governance of Islamic societies, 30–31, 49–51, 53–54, 55–56, 57, 63–69, 186–87, 208; hijacking of by Militant Islamists, 12, 214; innovations (bid'aa), 79–80, 84, 110, 182, 200; Islamism, definition of, 4; judgement of intent by God, 60; misuse of by Militant Islamists, 115; modernization of, 62–63; number of wives allowed, 159; as state religion, 60; teaching about, 77–78

Islamic Group. See Gamaa al-Islamiyah (IG)

Islamic land, fringe of, 147

Islamic Party, 46, 102, 133

Islamic Salvation Front, 50, 52, 194

Islamist political groups, 3–4, 7–8

Islamists: classification of movement, 115; competition of ideas and methods

between Militant Islamists and, xvi, 4, 201–2; definition of, 2, 4; disagreement with al-Qaida, 18; disagreements and disputes between, 45–48, 132; distinguishing between Militant Islamists and, xv–xvii, 1, 2–6, 98, 100–101, 133, 207–8, 212; fluidity of focus of movements, 206–7; ideology of, 2, 4; military training of, 139

Israel: Arab-Israeli War, 117, 132, 135, 138–39; Hezbollah, war with, 46, 47, 193; peace negotiations with Palestine, 154

Jews, 10, 13–15, 36–37, 133, 138, 141. See also Israel

Jihad: altering prayer times during, 35, 148; appeal for fighters for Afghanistan and Palestine, 147–48; Azzam's view on, 139, 141; dawa and, 17–18, 99; definition of, 34, 209; elections and, 94; globalization of, 148, 150, 172–73; as higher significance of, 38; Muslim emir for, 149; narrow definition of, 32–33, 100; near and far enemies, 129, 200, 208; obligation of, 34, 35, 105, 136–37, 139, 141, 142, 143, 144–45, 146, 149, 150; permission for, 104, 137, 142, 143, 145, 146, 148–49, 150; perpetual conflict, 141; phases of, 99–100; as pillar of Islam, 80, 143; Qur'anic justification for, 25, 99–100; against Soviet Union, 135, 140, 141, 148–50; warfare aspects of, 142

Jihadists, 4, 5, 30, 67, 210

Jordan, 55–56, 118

juripridence (fiqh), 64, 65

Kenya, 106, 162, 163, 165, 171

Khalidi, Abdel-Fatah, 125, 126

Kharijites, 38, 44, 62, 66

Khomeini, Ayatollah Ruhollah, 135, 181, 185, 186–88, 208

knowledge (ilm), 10, 33, 85, 96, 137

Kuwait, 68, 118, 161, 170

Lebanon, 47, 131

Libyan Islamic Fighting Group (LIFG), 87, 101, 173

to al-Qaida by, 46; condition of being member of, 130; criticism of, 103, 131; election to parliament of members of, 3, 46, 47, 94; exile of members of, 118, 121, 126, 132, 140, 160; failure of, examination of, 118–19; fluidity of focus of, 206–7; founding of, 63, 70, 106, 116; Free Officers Movement and, 117 18, 126; governance of Islamic societies, 68; Hezbollah and, 4; ideology of, 3, 5, 47, 123, 127; influence of, 121; insurgency tactics of, 132; Islamic state goal, 117, 118; as Islamists, 2, 116; Jews, dispute with, 133; model for, 116; Nasser and, 117–19, 121, 126; political interests of, 116–17, 118; Qutbist theory and, 130–31, 132; Sadat and, 119–20; schism within, 130–31, 132; society interests of, 201

Muslims: civil wars, 41–45, 64, 108; contributions of during Dark Ages and Renaissance, 10, 79; decline of civilization of, 134; diversity in community of, xvi, 2, 4, 66–67, 73–74, 81–82, 209; freedom of thought and worship, 74–75, 100, 148; genocidal campaign against, 14, 16; isolation of, 79, 127, 129–30; killing of innocent Muslims, 86, 88–89, 93, 111, 147, 195, 209–10; murder of intellectuals, 52; number of worldwide, xvi, 2; observant Muslims, suspicions about, 77; outage over distortions of Islam, xvi–xvii; prayer of the dead, 142; questioning misuse of Islam, 8; reading and writing, teaching, 30

Nasser, Gamal Abdel, 117–19, 125, 126, 139, 158

National Democratic Party (NDP), 3, 116, 119, 201

National Islamic Front, 116, 164

national security: distinguishing between Islam, Islamists, and Militant Islamists, xv–xvii, 1, 2–6, 98, 100–101, 133, 207–8, 212; extremes of policy discourse, xvi–xvii, 6, 203–4; Militant Islamists, definition and threat from, xv–xvii, 2; military leaders, training of,

210; mindsets that interfer with ability to counter Militant Islamist Ideology, 204–11; objective in fighting Militant Islamists, 2; research to benefit, 210–11; strategy to counter Militant Islamist Ideology, xvii, 8

near and far enemies, 129, 200, 208

Nicene Creed, 13–15

9/11 attacks, 86, 87, 102, 129, 153, 172, 189, 196

Omar, Mullah, 30, 67, 87, 98, 102, 176, 195–96, 199

Pakistan, 97, 170, 173, 175, 207–8

Palestine and Palestinians: Afghan Jihad as model for, 141, 154; appeal for fighters for Jihad, 147–48; defenders of, 47–48, 133, 154; Jewish immigration, 138; Jihad in, 145; Muslim Brotherhood fighting in, 132; Muslims banding together in, 149; peace negotiations with Israel, 154; Soviet support for, 149–50. *See also* Hamas

Philippines, 162, 165, 173

prayers, 35, 142, 148

proselytize (dawa), 17–18, 47, 74, 77–78, 98, 99, 110

Qaida, al-: Arab scholars' perspective on, 169–70; blows to by Muslim Brotherhood, 46; books about, 168–69, 213; clerical support for, 87, 104; counterarguments to, 93–94, 205–6; creation of, 106, 137, 138; criticism and disagreements about ideology of, 18, 93, 94–95, 98, 101–5, 199, 221n6; criticism of, 209; criticism of Hamas and Muslim Brotherhood by, 103; damage to Islam by, 9, 45 46, 64–65, 110; dead-end ideology of, 200; decline of, 207; defensive stance of, 95; disagreements and disputes within, 5, 104, 199; divisions within, 103; failures of, 52, 93; focus of, shift from Iraq to Afghanista, 211; goals of, 109; groups and events inspired by, 206; heirarchical structure of, 30–31; history of Islam, use of by, 217n5; ideological challenges,

90–91; combined-arms approach to shadow-war techniques, 213; etiquette of, 34; proxies, use of, 206, 213; tactics and strategies of Muslim armies, 35–36; tactics and strategies to oppose Militant Islamist Ideology, 151, 210; women's role in, 34–35, 36
websites, 105, 199–200, 207
World Islamic Front for the Jihad against Crusaders and Jews, 176, 177

Yathrib. *See* Medina (Yathrib)
Yemen, 105, 119, 121, 158, 162, 163–64, 171, 211

Zarqawi, Abu Musab al-, 5, 101, 128, 167–68, 174–75, 176
Zawahiri, Ayman al-: advisory role of, 176–77; alienation of Militant Islamists, 177; Azzam and, 131, 138, 155; bin Laden and, 176–77, 196; clerical support for al-Qaida,

87–88, 104; Combating Terrorism Center and, 169, 200, 214; criticism of, 177, 221n6; criticism of Hamas and Muslim Brotherhood, 103, 131; criticism of Hezbollah, 133; culture clash objective, 162; damage to Islam by, 17; deconstruction of, 85–86; governance of Islamic societies, 68; ideological challenges, 86; ideology of, 94, 120, 132–33; insecurities of, 87–88, 105, 176, 200; Jihad globalization, 148; leadership and authority of, 175, 176–77; near and far enemies, 129; Palestinian-Israeli peace negotiations, 154; pseudo-intellectual outlook of, 90, 168; questions and answers, 86–88, 93; Qur'an, justifying actions through, 29; rebuttal to Dr. Fadl, 86, 95, 105; Talaa al-Fath, 170–71; terrorist architecture, 162; visionary aspirations, 133–34; Zarqawi, letter to, 167, 174–75
Zayat, Muntasser al-, 130–31, 177, 221n6

ABOUT THE AUTHOR

YOUSSEF H. ABOUL-ENEIN is a U.S. Navy Medical Service Corps officer and Middle East Foreign Area Officer. He has served in operational tours in Liberia, Bosnia, and the Persian Gulf; he currently attends the National Defense University's Industrial College of the Armed Forces. Commander Aboul-Enein's last assignment was as senior counterterrorism analyst, warning officer, and instructor on Militant Islamist Ideology at the Joint Intelligence Task Force for Combating Terrorism in Washington, D.C. His analysis and assessments on al-Qaida were featured in the presidential daily brief; he wrote ten courses on the nuances of Militant Islamist Ideology for the Defense Intelligence Agency. From 2002 to 2006 Commander Aboul-Enein was country director for North Africa and Egypt, assistant country director for the Arabian Gulf, and special adviser on Islamist militancy at the Office of the Secretary of Defense for International Security Affairs. He has participated in negotiations on Libyan disarmament and Saudi energy infrastructure security, has engaged in bilateral talks with Algeria, and was part of an interagency team that arranged the freedom of 407 Moroccan prisoners of war held by the POLISARIO Front.

Commander Aboul-Enein has published articles on Islamist militancy, Arab affairs, and Middle East military tactics for *Military Review, Infantry Journal, Armor, Marine Corps Gazette,* the *Foreign Area Officer Journal,* and the Naval Postgraduate School's online journal, *Strategic Insights.* He has published a multipart series on Usama bin Laden's Arabic street literature and the memoirs of a Hamas operative, and he has served as consultant in an episode of the BBC/Discovery Channel documentary *20th Century Battlefields* on the 1973 Arab-Israeli War.

He holds an MS in strategic intelligence from the National Defense Intelligence College and is a graduate of the Naval War College's Command and Staff College and of the Army War College's Defense Strategy Course. Commander Aboul-Enein has lectured at the U.S. Army War College, the Joint Forces Staff College, the Joint Advanced Warfare School, and the Naval War College. His personal awards include the Defense Meritorious Service Medal, awarded by the secretary of defense.